The GOSPELS

In Their Original Meaning

By
Lawrence R. Michaels

Bovee Productions, San Diego, California

I have concluded that the materials presented in this work are free of doctrinal or moral errors.

Bernadeane Carr, STL
Censor Librorum
28 November 2001

In accord with 1983 CIC 827 § 3, permission to publish this work is hereby granted.

+ Robert H. Brom
Bishop of San Diego
30 November 2001

Most Scripture texts in this work are taken from *The Jerusalem Bible*, © 1966, 1967 and 1968 by Doubleday & Company, Inc.

Cover design by Barbara A. Bovee
Published by Bovee Productions
San Diego California USA
Printed in the United States
ISBN 0-9705295-1-1

TABLE OF CONTENTS

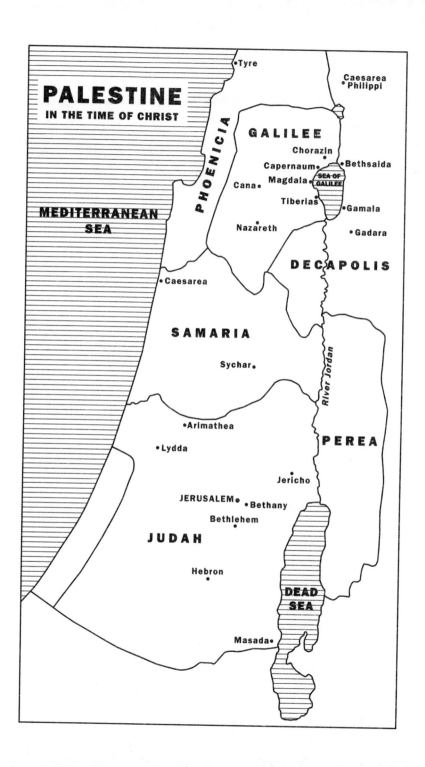

PREFACE

The stories of Jesus that are found in the Gospels are by far the most widely known section of the Bible by Christians. Even Christians without a Bible background could read through the four Gospel accounts and find little that was not familiar. Many of the stories would be recognized by people who have no practiced religious interest or background. Yet, the reality is that only a relatively few Christians actually read the four Gospels for the purpose that caused their individual composition. For most, the Gospels are merely a collection of stories and teachings from Jesus with no other purpose than being a written source of such material.

The Gospels, when read as individual books of the Bible or used as a series of Sunday readings, are often thought of as a biography of Jesus' public life. An interpretation in a homily nearly always reflects the context of Jesus speaking to the Jewish people of that time. Surely that is how the stories were originally used, immediately after the Resurrection, to teach or explain the Christian message. In a relatively short time the passion and death narrative must have been written down to explain to Jews that Jesus was above the Jewish Law, and so was his message. Likewise, the stories about Jesus' works and teachings would have been put into writing quite early, collected together and copied as a standard collection for distribution to other Church communities. There is some evidence to support such a conclusion, and unless we were told otherwise, we would assume such a conclusion. However, the collections would have been most useable for instructions if the accounts were segregated into different groupings, such as miracle events, teachings and, perhaps, short sayings. They must not have been put into a biographical form or they could not have been used so freely in composing the different Gospel accounts.

The four written Gospels are almost always seen by scholars as later writings which may have been composed by using the early collections as sources. The most widely accepted dating for these writings is between forty and sixty years after the Resurrection. Perhaps the most extreme range could be from a starting point about twenty-five years after the Resurrection to about the end of the first century. Yet, many Christian communities, and perhaps a majority of individual Christians, make no real attempt to relate that late dating to an interpretation of the text.

Theories exist, and are widely accepted by Scripture scholars, that the Gospels were written for very specific purposes. A relationship between Mark, the first written Gospel, and questions that arose about the suffering that Christians experienced during Nero's persecution is supported by very early traditions. When this relationship is used in interpreting the Gospel text, it provides advice to the Christians of Rome that seems sufficiently clear that it couldn't have come by accident. Similar results can be obtained from Matthew and Luke, even though traditions don't provide such direct knowledge of the contexts for those two Gospels. John's Gospel is usually interpreted almost entirely from an internal analysis pointing to the obvious argument that Jesus is Divine.

The result of this situation is that most use of the stories from the Gospels is related to the teachings and events of Jesus' public life in revealing a message to Jewish people in Palestine. This would be the same as how the stories from the early collections must have been used because it follows the use of the Old Testament readings in the synagogues. The present day interpretation of the stories as information from Jesus' public life would seem to have been the intent of those producing the early collections.

However, the four Gospel writings, which the Church has treasured, are compositions that use the early stories from those collections at a later time to answer questions arising at that later time, among Christians primarily living outside of Palestine. Clearly the intent of the Evangelists who composed the written Gospels, and the Church that accepted these four writings, must have been to respond to later problems. The Evangelists responded to major problems by using Jesus' own teachings for situations not faced by Jesus in his public life.

Both interpretations, as biographical stories of Jesus' public life and as Gospel accounts addressed to later situations, would be true since the individual teachings of Jesus came from his public life. However, it is the later reuse of the same teachings in Gospel accounts that are accepted as writings inspired by God and have been preserved in history. No one would object to a preacher using part of the later composition in an interpretation based on the earlier context from Jesus' public life. However, the later Gospel writings can be interpreted in the later context that caused the actual composition. We can and should read the Gospels to see the interpretation which caused the compositions that together are the centerpiece of the New Testament and, for Christians, of the whole Bible.

This commentary is directed almost entirely to the Gospels as individual writings responding to the context that caused the writings. The interpretations given in the commentary result from how the writings answer questions or address problems of the Church in the period from about 70 to 90 AD. This view of the Gospels themselves is not as actual biographies of Jesus, even though all the events and teachings come very literally from Jesus during his public life. The selection and arrangement of the stories was not intended to provide information about the daily events of Jesus in biographical order. Rather, the composition was to provide answers to later Church questions using Jesus' own words and acts.

These Church questions are what caused the writings to be prepared long after the Resurrection and were the original meaning of the individual writings. This commentary will reflect a view which is as old as the writings themselves. The change in understanding is not intended to oppose the traditional interpretation of these events and teachings that the

stories originally came from Jesus' own public life. Interpretation of the stories in the public life context is obviously valid
since that is where the events and teachings first occurred.

For most readers, this commentary will present meanings that the reader has never seen or heard before. However,
there will be no changes in the stories, nor will there be any
rearrangement of the text. To make any changes would be an
admission that the interpretation was not the view of the
Evangelist. This is an examination of these complete writings and the meaning that was generated when they were
composed. It is a study of the written Gospels to the
Christian Church more directly than teachings and events in
Jesus' public life in Palestine. It is an interpretation of the
actual writing in its original meaning.

I wish to express my sincere appreciation to many others
who have played important roles in the production of this
work. First, of course, to the Lord Jesus Christ who provided
the very words reviewed in this book and, especially, for calling me to take a great interest in the Gospels. Likewise, a
special thank you to my wife, Jean, who has given so much of
herself that this work and the ministry behind it are joint
efforts from beginning to end. To Barbara and Michael
Bovee, who take a draft copy and return a professionally produced book, my deepest appreciation for completing the
dream. To Bernadeane Carr, who with her comments and
questions refines the entire project as no one else can, a special thank you. Finally, to Richard Bohen, both dear friend
and valuable mentor, this book is dedicated. He was the one
I turned to when the idea of publishing first arose and he has
provided the support and advice to make it happen.

INTRODUCTION

Gospel, or Good Message, exists in its most complete form in the life of Jesus - a living in the closest possible relationship with God. Since Jesus is Divine, there can be no more complete relationship than his own. Everyone is offered such a sharing of life in this world, and if it is accepted and lived here on earth, it becomes ours for an eternity in heaven. Jesus' human Incarnation is God's view of how that life should be lived. Copying Jesus' life would constitute our acceptance of the gift we call grace and making it our own.

It is the Church's mission to bring this relationship, as a gift from God, to all peoples. It is, then, a Church message which must be made clear to the world, in a way that surpasses all difficulties of language, culture and merely human understanding. To do that requires a living organization that continues through history, an organization which we know as Church. The Church always ties Gospel teachings back to Jesus' words directly and, yet, there is always the appearance of development as the Gospel is applied to different times and situations. Therefore, the Gospel is living in that, over time, it always relates to life on earth.

The teachings of Jesus were heard by disciples who also were witnesses to the events of his public life. Descriptions of events of Jesus' life and his teachings were repeated by such disciples to others, both from Palestine and pilgrims who came from other countries. That retelling occurred first to Jewish people in synagogues both in Palestine and in other lands. Later the teachings must have become known to God-fearing Gentiles within synagogues. God-fearers is a term applied to Gentiles who had some acceptance of Judaism and a partial living of Jewish Law, yet didn't actually become Jews. In time the accounts were written down, collected by early Church communities and circulated both as small local collections and then in larger standardized collections.

The evidence for this process is not very great, but it is obvious that such a process would be followed, as it had been with later Jewish writings from before the Christian era. These later writings remained as part of Christian Scripture and were listed as part of the official Christian Canon of the Old Testament in 393 AD at the Council of Hippo, even though Judaism did not include all of them in its own canon of Scripture. It is reasonable to assume that since Christians collected late Old Testament writings and preserved them, they would write, copy, collect and distribute accounts of the events and teachings of Jesus' life, unless we were told explicitly that it was not done. Such writings included the meaning of their own beliefs. The evidence then for such written records does not need to be either great, or direct, to be accepted, since even without evidence, it is almost certain to have been done.

The early Church in the first four decades after the Resurrection must have produced a rather complete body of stories, and they must have become familiar to all Christians. That material would have been used as part of the process of bringing new converts into Christianity. It would have been used as well to respond to questions that arose as the Church expanded outside of Palestine. Later, as very serious problems arose in the early Church, problems that called into question the Church message, the same process would have been followed.

The Church's response, through the four authors of the Gospels, was to collect and arrange a portion of the material known to the Church, to show from Christ's own acts and words how the Gospel meaning was fulfilled in what appeared to be great problems. This is no different from the first Gospel writing of the passion and death narratives to Judaism that probably occurred in the first decade after the Resurrection. Dying on the cross according to Jewish Law (Dt 21:22-23) meant that such a person was cursed by God, yet the Resurrection said the opposite. What should have happened to Jesus due to the Law, did not happen. While the crucifixion was a problem for Judaism, it showed Jesus was above the Law. Therefore, Judaism had a greater obligation to accept the message, rather than to refuse to accept something at odds with an interpretation of an old section of the Law.

The four Gospel texts show the application of events and teaching from Jesus' life to problems that called into question the understandings of Christianity. In the order they were written, these would be the problems:

1. In Mark, the suffering experienced in the persecution of Nero
2. In Matthew, the decision required of Christians as Christianity was forced out of Judaism
3. In Luke, the meaning of living the life of Christ in a kingdom not in Palestine and not only for Jews as originally thought
4. In John, the coming to know Jesus not in the title Son of God, which designated David as king, but as God taking on a human nature and living as a union of human and divine life among humanity. That Incarnation would show not only the union, but that it was a gift, which was ours, if we accepted and lived it.

The Gospel message of the Church is seen most completely in these major writings, rather than in only individual stories not connected to such major situations. The four Gospels then became the documents that were treasured, copied, and made known and understandable in preaching down through history. The original standardized collections of stories, used as sources for creating the four Gospels, were not recopied and kept, but had been superseded. It is likely, and there is some evidence to justify such a conclusion, that not all of the stories in those earlier collections were used in these four Gospels and some may have been lost. It isn't more stories or more details that are important to the Church mission, but that the Gospel message be seen more completely and lived that way by all who accept Christ. The written Gospel became the great instrument for teaching the meaning of being part of the Body of Christ.

The Gospels often are assumed to be just a collection of stories and, to some, are used as a biography of Jesus' life. Such a description can be seen as not reflecting the Gospel very well even by a simple reading of the texts. Would there be four biographies published separately with such significant differences on one hand and with so much direct duplication on the other? Surely, the early Church would have consolidated the four into a single text if the individual Gospels had no independent meaning. Such consolidated narratives were prepared in the early Church and one of them, the Diatessaron, was the official Gospel writing of the Syrian Church until the fifth century. However, it was the four separated Gospels that were included in the official canon of the New Testament declared at the Council of Hippo in 393 AD. The Four Gospels were shown in the Syrian Canon by the end of the fourth century and all the copies of the Diatessaron were collected and destroyed.[1] The message of each independent Gospel would have been lost in a consolidated narrative. Yet, it was the independent message that was designated as the inspired word of God, even though the collection of stories used as sources to produce the Gospels came directly from the remembered words and events of Jesus' life. The independent Gospel message goes far beyond just the collection of material.

The four canonical Gospels were written to communities that already knew all the stories about Jesus. However, they provided a fuller understanding of the Gospel message as it applied to special situations. The Gospel is always more than just stories. Therefore, the keeping of the original four Gospels, rather than just a collection of stories, provided an application of the Good News to four problems facing the early Church. This commentary is simply an application of the Church's intent in keeping the four as separate texts. To examine these four in their original meaning is a complete examination of Gospel.

In using the Gospel teachings in the Church today, the stories are used individually each week, perhaps in a way not much different from how the collected material was used in the very early Church. They are introduced as part of one of the four Gospels, rather than as "another story about Jesus." The readings are always as part of a written Gospel. So in finding the meaning for ourselves by reading the Gospels, we should keep in mind that the whole Gospel account was declared to be an inspired writing and the individual story gains its designation as inspired by being part of the inspired whole Gospel. Naturally, a whole Gospel itself cannot be used in each weekly Eucharistic service, but is broken down into a series of weekly readings. The four Gospels provide sufficient weekly readings to cover a three-year period of Sunday readings. Each reading must be examined in detail if we are going to live out the full message, yet, the full Gospel should always be seen as the complete text.

In each Sunday's Gospel read, the focus is on part of Christ's life not only in hearing it read but also in a special homily to show how it fits into our everyday lives. However, the homilist must look at the entire meaning of that particular Gospel to interpret an individual account as the Church requires for interpretation of Scripture in the Church.[2] Therefore, it is reasonable that every disciple examine that larger meaning to gain their own understanding of it and allow reflection on the individual account and its homily for a personal meaning.

Dates that are used in the remainder of this commentary are AD unless noted. All Scripture references without a book name, but only a chapter and verse designation, are taken from the writing being examined. Introductory material generally is placed in the introduction chapter since it often relates to the understanding of all the writings. This practice eliminates duplication of the same material when it relates directly to more than one Gospel. It may be a reasonable idea to reread the context section for each Gospel before studying the commentary section for that writing. Keeping the context in mind is essential to understanding the commentary since the interpretation relates to that context.

THE CONTEXT OF
THE GOSPELS

BASIS FOR THE CONTEXTS

The Gospels of the New Testament are a unique form of writing. They are composed of material from the life of Jesus, the Messiah, and are a chronicle of some events and teachings from his lifetime. The Christian belief that Jesus has both a divine nature and a human nature causes them to be accepted as the Word of God in a most direct fashion. Yet, their composition was in response to conditions which faced the early Church forty to sixty years after the end of Jesus' public life. Therefore, they represent two distinct contexts: First, the original stories are from a Jewish situation and a Palestinian area with Jesus speaking to Jewish people. Second, the selection and arrangement of the stories are from Jewish and Gentile situations in non-Palestinian areas throughout the Roman Empire, as the stories are used by the Church to address later problems.

The context of a writing is a very important factor in understanding its message. That is especially true of the Gospels. The basic stories arise from the first context, yet are used to address exceedingly different situations of the second context. The actual words, teachings and events do not change except in being translated into Greek. Their interpretation in a different context, however, requires the reader to recognize the changed context to understand the meaning of the actual composition of the Gospels.

Commentaries on the Gospels nearly always recognize the importance of context and include some background on the Evangelists and traditions from the places of composition. However, once the commentator begins to analyze a passage of the text, technically called a pericope, it is often done in the context of Jesus' public life. The context of the Evangelist, when the stories were selected and arranged to form the Gospel account, receives much less attention. The context of the original setting with Jesus is only generally known as the Jewish situation of the first century Palestine prior to the destruction of the Temple. Hints of place and time may be included in the text for some pericopes, but not always completely and, in some cases, perhaps not very accurately. However, the context of the whole composition of a Gospel, and the reason for the selection and arrangement of the pericopes into a longer narrative, certainly belongs to the place and time of the Evangelist. Therefore, the meaning for the Church at the time of the composition was in the actual context of the Evangelist. That context may be separate from both Judaism and Palestine and, yet, should be very important in interpreting the individual Gospel message.

Another factor to consider is the actual source of material used for the writing, since only the Fourth Gospel is thought to have an actual eyewitness as the Evangelist. The transfer of information from the time of Jesus to that of the Evangelist is normally considered to be in an oral tradition resulting from the preaching of the early Church. Often this factor is passed over quite simply by the commentator without fully examining the consequences of that assumption. Surely the use of traditional material in composing the Gospels is essential to Church acceptance of the final compositions by the Evangelists. Otherwise there would be questions raised if some new material suddenly became available in a published Gospel, without an eyewitness source, and after the lifetime of nearly all of the eyewitnesses. To accept the work of an Evangelist, the people would have to recognize nearly all of the teachings, sayings, and events included in the Gospel account, especially if the reason for producing the Gospel account involved an important question of the community.

The belief that the transfer period was primarily one of oral tradition is not borne out completely in some of the assumptions made about the Gospels. Normally, it is accepted that the passion, death, and empty tomb accounts were committed to writing quite early. Even though the four Gospels come from widely separated areas of the Mediterranean world, and in John from what seems to be quite a separate community, the passion narratives are remarkably similar. Each account has some unique details which have been added, but the basic account appears to be the same continuous, integrated narrative in each Gospel. That similarity suggests a relatively early written source.

The passion narrative provides the basic argument that Jesus was above the Law since the Law states that a criminal who dies by being hung on a tree is cursed by God (Dt 21:22-23). However, the Resurrection would indicate to Jewish people that Jesus was blessed in the most complete way by God. That conclusion could be seen as one of the earliest Christian arguments to Judaism that Jesus was the Messiah who brought a revelation beyond what was accepted by Judaism. Development of that argument would cause a written record of the passion and death narrative to be produced. The similarity of the four Gospel accounts suggests such a written record.

Likewise, attempts to understand the sources for the additions made by Matthew and Luke to Mark's original Gospel account rely on what appears to be a written collection of Jesus' teachings. Both Evangelists responsible for Matthew and Luke use some material which is almost identical, pointing toward a written source. Also, there are some cases in which each Evangelist has included material in the same order which points to a common written source. It does not appear that one of the two Evangelists used the final Gospel account of the other, because of the way the material was used or not included. Therefore, a written source is proposed which is known as "Q" (from the German word for source which is Quelle). The existence of such a written source can be substantiated only for the common material added by both of the Evangelists responsible for the Gospels of Matthew and Luke. However, once the existence of such a written source seems likely, there is no reason to believe that it started and stopped with the common material.

The written source could have been a much more extensive collection of teachings, sayings and events, which also might have included much of the material used by Mark and the separate material added to either Matthew's or Luke's Gospels. In seeing Mark's Gospel, the Evangelists behind Matthew and Luke would have immediately recognized how it had been created from material that was widely known or from a written source more extensive then Q. They would have been comfortable in adding material from similar written sources to produce their own versions. Matthew and Luke would both come to use an expansion of Mark's Gospel without knowing about the other's use of that technique. It also would explain why the Church would generally accept the revised Gospel accounts of Matthew and Luke, after Mark's version had gained acceptance, and even why John's Gospel, with its different composition and message, was accepted.

The structure and description of events for the Gospels of Matthew and Luke are almost the same as in Mark, while the additions by Matthew and Luke are primarily teachings of Jesus. Commentators often propose that the written source Q was almost entirely a list of sayings and teachings with only a small amount of narrative material on events. However, the common material used in Matthew and Luke is only a proof that a written source exists; it is not proof that the written source was limited to the common material. There are no manuscripts of such a source, even in a fragment form. However, since such a source would not be copied and retained after most of the information had been included in Gospel narratives, such an absence is not unexpected.

The theory based on the use of only Mark and Q for developing Gospels by Matthew and Luke is called the Two Source hypothesis. It does not prove that either Matthew or Luke used all of the material available in the Q source and, except by definition, it does not rule out that some of the

Markan material was present in Q. That theory is shown in the following diagram.

Two Source Theory

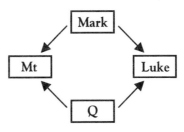

Since a significant amount of material in Matthew and Luke is particular to each Gospel without parallels in the other or in Mark, the two-source hypothesis has often been questioned as an inadequate explanation of all the sources for composition of those two Gospels. Therefore, another hypothesis has been promoted which assumes that in addition to Mark and Q, the writers of Matthew and Luke also had individual sources. Those sources most likely came from their communities, rather than from private sources, and were used to develop the unique portions of their Gospels. This approach, with written sources designated as Mark's Gospel, Q, M (for Matthew's private source), and L (for Luke's) is appropriately called the Four Documents or Four Source hypothesis, as shown below.

Four Documents Theory

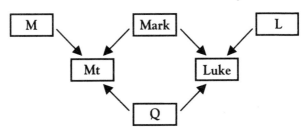

Again, there is no manuscript evidence for written M or L sources. Regardless of the number of sources, the conclusion from both proposals is that most of the information used in composing the Gospels was in a widely known and probably a written form, not composed as new stories by the Evangelists.

One last comment on sources concerns the Old Testament quotations added by Matthew which are described as fulfilled in the life of Jesus. That source includes quotations from a number of different Greek versions of the Old Testament, which would not have been used to any extent in Jerusalem. Therefore, it is unlikely that the collection was made by one author. The fulfillment texts are a very Jewish approach to identifying the Messiah and originally the process could have started in Jerusalem. Sometimes it is suggested that such a source could be a result of the so-called Aramaic Gospel of Matthew. However, the use of different Greek versions of the Old Testament as sources for the fulfillment texts argues for a collection process in areas outside of Palestine and, perhaps, by a number of Jewish Christian scholars. Matthew probably made particular use of those texts because of his reason for writing the Gospel rather than because he was the collector. Since fulfillment texts are not sayings of Jesus, they would not be Gospel writings, but it does show how written information would be developed.

These theories provide answers to the question of why the Gospels of Mark, Matthew and Luke, known collectively as the Synoptic Gospels, resemble each other. They all use Mark's Gospel as the record of events in Jesus' public life. Then Matthew and Luke add some common teachings of Jesus to give another layer of material. In the past, the common resemblance of the three was accepted by some non-Catholic commentators as a proof that the Synoptic Gospels represented the authentic account of Jesus' public life. Such commentators suggested that John's Gospel, with its very different format, must not be authentic and, perhaps, came from sources separate from Palestine. However, once it was realized that the common appearance is a result of how the texts were composed from common sources, all four Gospels were accepted by everyone as an authentic use of sources that originated from Jesus' public life.

The period between the Resurrection and the composition of the Gospels was surely dominated by oral teaching. However, it also would have been a period when the basic stories and teachings of Jesus were slowly recorded, collected, and circulated in the form of well-developed sources of material used for catechetical purposes.

The traditions of one local church community may have differed somewhat from the written versions of certain stories that were circulated in published collections. An Evangelist, such as Matthew or Luke, using the tradition of a local community for whom he was writing, could substitute a slightly different version of a pericope into Mark's Gospel material, when preparing an expanded Gospel for that community. Such changes would appear to be a rewriting of that particular story, yet the second Evangelist may have been making a simple substitution of a local tradition for what Mark had used from the Roman Church. In cases where the change is an addition or further meaning (e.g. Mt 16:16-20) that additional meaning should be obvious.

When the period of oral preaching covered more than forty years and the Christian message became known throughout the Mediterranean world, a conclusion that remembrances would be put into a written form is justified, unless there is some reason to doubt it. That Paul not only wrote messages to many communities but suggested circulating his instructions from one community to another (Col 4:15-17) supports this conclusion.

EXPANSION OF THE EARLY CHURCH

A picture of the early Church drawn from the New Testament could be more complex than that of a tradition of the Apostles moving out of Palestine shortly after the

Resurrection and preaching the revelation of Jesus Christ to everyone. Perhaps the earliest statement about the meaning of the passion events comes from the account of two people returning to Emmaus after the Sabbath at that fateful Passover (Lk 24:13-35). After meeting, but not recognizing, the risen Christ who had joined them, one states that Jesus "must be the only person staying in Jerusalem who does not know about the things that have been happening there these last few days." Naturally there may be a slight exaggeration in the statement that everyone knew and understood all that happened. However, it also seems very likely that Jewish pilgrims, from many different parts of the Mediterranean world and the Middle East, would have been in Jerusalem at that time and would have heard about Jesus. As someone thought to be the Messiah and given a great display of support on Palm Sunday (Mt 21:8-11), Jesus would have been a major topic of conversations. When all those pilgrims returned to their own homes, it could be expected that some mention would be made of the event.

It may be assumed that most Jews from Judea and, perhaps, many from Galilee would try to come to Jerusalem for the three pilgrimage feasts: Passover, Pentecost and Tabernacles. However, not all Jews, even from those two areas, would actually come to Jerusalem for all three feasts each year. Those Jews from more distant synagogues would rarely attempt to come for all three feasts, but some would come for Passover and, perhaps, Pentecost. The numbers would be significant from places such as Antioch and Alexandria, and fewer from more distant synagogues. Those coming would not be the same people each year, but the numbers from each synagogue might be similar. It also may be assumed that all Jews throughout the world might dream of visiting Jerusalem at least once in their lifetime.

Just before the birth of Christ, there were changes that made travel to Jerusalem more desirable and safer. The rebuilding of the Temple by Herod the Great and the safety of sea travel instituted by expansion of the Roman Empire encouraged pilgrims to an extent not possible earlier. For a synagogue of 100 families, an average of about two families would have to make the trip each year to accomplish the life-time goals for such visits. Therefore, a case could be made that at the Passover where Jesus was crucified, there might have been at least one representative from nearly every synagogue in every country. That case would improve if representation was considered at Passover and/or Pentecost in the first few years after the Resurrection. This would be the time when Christian preaching about the Messiah would seem to have been prevalent on the Temple Mount.

Therefore, the initial circulation of information about Jesus being the Messiah would not be through the Apostles moving out of Jerusalem and preaching, perhaps years after the Resurrection, but within Judaism in the first weeks and months after the Resurrection. Such Jewish pilgrims would understand the significance of the Messiah and have a great interest in telling of their experience. The acceptance of Jesus as the Messiah was witnessed by the crowds cheering his entrance into Jerusalem on Palm Sunday and is indicated by the response of Jewish officials to that demonstration (Jn 12:12-19). Those pilgrims, upon returning home, would be anxious to tell others in their own synagogue communities about what seemed to be the story known by everyone "staying in Jerusalem these last few days."

At Pentecost, some fifty days later, Peter gave a public speech to pilgrims who had come to Jerusalem for that feast from all over the world (Acts 2:14-36). The speech is directed to Jewish people and includes the phrase "this man...you took and had crucified...God has raised him to life." It reflects the conclusion mentioned earlier that in the Resurrection, Jesus, who would have been cursed under the Law (Dt 21:22-23), was in fact blessed by God beyond any expectation by being raised from the dead. The result of the speech was that three thousand became Christians (Acts 2:37-41). If those hearing the speech and responding to baptism included a representation of those who are listed as coming from other countries (Acts 2:7-11), the result means that some primitive Christians would be present in the synagogues of quite a number of countries as soon as they returned home. If the earlier pilgrims who had been at the Passover of the crucifixion heard about those conversions, they also might take an interest in Christianity which at that time was a movement within Judaism.

A short summary following that initial conversion experience (Acts 2:43-47) indicates the Christian community within Jerusalem continued to grow. They regularly celebrated the Eucharist, and they went as a body to the Temple every day presumably to proclaim the message of Christ. It is a statement which indicates that while Christianity was entirely within Judaism, it had started to gain its own identity as a special Jewish sect.

Peter is shown as repeating the message to Judaism in similar speeches in chapters three, four, five, and ten of Acts. The preaching is directed toward Jewish listeners except in chapter ten. It does not take much of an assumption to recognize that it would be directed at pilgrims at each of the three major feasts, Passover, Pentecost and Tabernacles, when the greatest number of non-Palestinian Jews might be present. Certainly, there would be some interest by those who had accepted Christ at that first Pentecost after the Resurrection or by those present at the Passover of the crucifixion even if they had not become Christians.

There is no indication of how Christianity started in nearby Damascus, but within a few years Paul had authorization to arrest and bring to Jerusalem any Christians he could find in the synagogues of that city (Acts 9:1-25). There is no record that one of the Twelve went to Damascus and started a church or that it started because many Jews from Damascus would make the trip to Jerusalem for the major feast days and a significant number accepted the new teaching. Yet, the second approach is more logical if the text does not say otherwise.

The disciples who escaped Jerusalem after Stephen was killed (Acts 7:55-60) went to Samaria, and also to Phoenicia,

Cypress and Antioch, proclaiming the message to Jews. However, in Antioch the message also was presented to some Greeks (Acts 11:19-21) who may have been present in the synagogues as God-fearers. It would be difficult to assume that those synagogue members had never heard of Jesus in the fifteen or more years since the Resurrection. Surely a great number of members of those relatively nearby synagogues would have made the trip to Jerusalem during those years and would have some familiarity with Christianity.

Paul visited Corinth for 18 months, perhaps 20 years or so after the Resurrection, and seems to be given credit for founding the Church there. However, when writing to Corinth a few years later he says, "I never baptized any of you except Crispus and Gaius" and then adds the family of Stephanas (1 Cor 1:14-16).[3] It is reasonable to conclude that some of that Church had been baptized earlier than Paul's arrival. Suetonius, a Roman writer of the century, describes the event that brought Priscilla and Aquila from Rome as "disturbances at the instigation of Chrestus," which is often seen as a reference to Christians. Some scholars assume that Priscilla and Aquila could have been Christians before joining Paul even though they are designated as Jews (Acts 18:1-11).[4]

A short section in Acts about the Church in Ephesus tells of a Jew named Apollos preaching about Christianity even though not to the satisfaction of Priscilla and Aquila (Acts 18:24-28). That description seems to indicate that a knowledge of Christianity had spread widely from Palestine, although entirely within Judaism, and at least partly without the direct involvement of Apostles. Likewise, there is a description of some "disciples" of Christianity in Ephesus who only had experienced the baptism from John the Baptist and were rebaptized, at that time in the name of the Lord Jesus, by Paul (Acts 19:1-7). Paul seems to be correcting some understandings and practices among Christians in addition to justifying Christian teachings to Jews who have not yet accepted the new teachings.

In summary, the picture of the early Church from Acts and the early writings of Paul indicate that the earliest knowledge of Christ was spread within Judaism by pilgrims who had contact with Christian teaching while in Jerusalem. Surely any pilgrim at the Passover of the crucifixion would have reported the event to their own synagogues elsewhere in the Roman Empire and beyond it to the east. Some initial spreading of the story of Jesus as an expected Messiah and his crucifixion and proclaimed Resurrection would be told within a few weeks or months in every synagogue represented at that Passover. The initial message would be expanded by pilgrims at later feasts if they heard the Apostles preaching on the Temple Mount.

This knowledge of Jesus Christ by itself does not constitute the establishment of a Christian church or even a Christian sect within one of those distant synagogues. Even if some of those pilgrims were baptized, as may have occurred at Pentecost, perhaps a very small percentage of the 3,000 (Acts 2:41), they would not constitute a functioning Christian community.

The early expectation of Christians seems to be that baptism was the accepting of Jesus as Messiah prior to his early return to establish a kingdom. Apollos is described as a Jew who had been baptized only by John the Baptist, yet he functioned as a successful preacher with an accurate knowledge about Jesus. Likewise, Paul meets some disciples of John the Baptist at Ephesus and rebaptizes them, but is told they had never heard of the Holy Spirit.

This situation, more than 20 years after the Resurrection, indicates that knowledge of Jesus and some acceptance of his kingdom existed among Jews without functioning Christian communities. There is little reason to believe that the same situation would not have existed among some early pilgrims who had been baptized by the Apostles as they were preaching in Jerusalem (Acts 4:33).

The critical element in the spread of Christianity as functioning churches, even when Christianity was still within

Judaism, would go beyond only the knowledge of Jesus the Messiah by Jews. Work by Paul and the Twelve would be necessary to follow up the early contacts, build on them, and actually create Christian sub-communities within Judaism. In Acts, Luke presents a consistent picture of Paul going on missionary journeys in which he went first to the synagogues in every city. Peter's role in such work is not well chronicled in Acts, but the Church celebrates the feast of Peter's Chair in Antioch and has a tradition that he ruled there for seven years. Paul's conflict with Peter (Gal 1:11-14) in Antioch makes sense if Peter is the head of that Church and Paul wants to register a complaint.

Acts was written for a different purpose of Luke to show that, especially in Paul's work, the message went beyond Judaism. First it went to God-fearers who, even though Gentiles, took part in the synagogue services, and then, in some instances, to Gentiles who were pagan with no Jewish connections. This move beyond Judaism to Gentiles is chronicled in Acts and is one of its themes. Likewise, Paul's letters to the Corinthians addressed problems that seemed to result when Gentiles, in accepting Christianity, got involved in the Jewish community where Christianity resided. Gentiles without an appreciation for Jewish customs and food laws caused difficulties that did not exist when all Christians were Jewish.

If this is a reasonable understanding of what occurred in the first decade or two after the Resurrection, it describes a context for Christianity not often stated clearly but which sets the background for the later composition of the Gospels. As mentioned earlier, the pilgrims returning from Jerusalem would be the initial bearers of information on Jesus as the Messiah and, most likely, the initial source of recorded stories. Each year as those associated with Christianity, or fellow synagogue members, made the trip to Jerusalem, they also would hear Peter and other disciples preach about Jesus and would bring those descriptions back to their own countries. Synagogues close to Jerusalem would have many members go each year and even the most distant may have had at least a single member in Jerusalem each year. Once the interest in the Christian message had started outward, it would be expanded by new Jewish pilgrims each year.

There is no manuscript evidence of any such accounts separately or in collections. There are no manuscripts that date to the first century and only a single small fragment of John from the second century. Any such collections that would have been available before the Gospels were written would not have been copied extensively after the same information was used in a Gospel. So the lack of manuscripts is not a very valid argument against such early records. The only direct information that such written records had existed prior to a Gospel is the prologue of Luke saying that "many undertook to draw up a narrative of the events that have taken place among us just as the original eyewitnesses and ministers of the word passed them on to me." That is interpreted by scholars[5] to be a series of written sources of which we could say that one account was Mark's Gospel. An indirect source of early writing would be the recognized Q material used by both Matthew and Luke to add to the material they used from Mark's Gospel in producing their own Gospels. The Q material sometimes is used in the same order by Matthew and Luke in a way that suggests a standardized collection of early material.

If Peter and the other disciples in Jerusalem preached in Aramaic, as is normally believed, the message might be retold in Greek or another local language as the pilgrims returned to their native lands. Such retelling in a different language would result in better and more correct Greek, as is shown in the Gospel stories, than would be found in a translation to Greek from an Aramaic writing. If Peter or the other disciples told the stories in Greek, they could have been written down wherever the preaching was done and not show the effects of an Aramaic original writing.

A logical place for producing a large collection might be Antioch, a large city with a significant Jewish-Christian community and a place connected to Peter's ministry. Like-wise, the accounts of teachings and events could be told by different disciples in Jerusalem in slightly different versions just as Jesus may have used the same themes from time to time, but with some variations. The retelling by the pilgrims in a different language after returning to their synagogues would magnify the differences somewhat. The main points of the teachings might be the same even if some retelling was in longer or shorter versions. In the nearly forty years before Mark composed his Gospel, there certainly would be some recording of the teachings and, most likely, the development of collections of the stories and teachings. The ones recount-ed often in a community would become known in the format of how they had been written down.

Larger communities, such as Antioch, Alexandria, or Ephesus, might well produce standardized Greek-language collections of the teachings and descriptions of events in Jesus' public life. Each of the synagogue-oriented Christian groups in those cities would have the standardized versions which might be copied for synagogues elsewhere that wanted a complete collection. However, even where a standardized version was obtained by a community, some different versions of particular pericopes might be retained if that community already had knowledge of such versions. In some cases, the community would not know if a different version of a story was simply that or if it reflected a similar but quite different event.

The source material that may have been available to a community where a Gospel account was produced might be a rather substantial body of information about the teachings of Jesus and the events of his life. The Evangelist is normally considered to be a writer, yet most of what he could say to a major community would already be known. A Gospel mes-sage that carried real meaning and was likely to be accepted would be one faithful to what the community knew about Jesus, not one introducing a number of new and unverifiable stories at a very late date.

The availability of written material and its use in producing a Gospel would have no effect on the historical teaching that the revelation is produced by the original Apostles in some fashion. It is accepted that the four Evangelists would have perhaps the most complete knowledge of original stories derived from Jesus' public life. Mark, as the starting Evangelist to produce a Gospel, had a long and close association with Peter, to the point of being called his son (1 Pet 5:13). He could have easily produced the Gospel without the use of existing written material and, in spite of the theory expressed here, may have done so.

A reason for suggesting that Mark used written material is that Mark's Gospel is usually characterized as having more "Latinisms" than the other Gospels.[6] Latinisms are words originally from Latin that were incorporated into the Greek language. With Rome ruling the Mediterranean area, Latin would show up to some extent everywhere, but to a greater extent at Rome. The Latinisms suggest that Mark used written material from the Roman Church rather than adjusting his own knowledge of Greek to produce such an effect. The other side of this whole point is that acceptance of the Gospel might be greater if the Roman Church was familiar with every account used by the Evangelist without any changes. Since the purpose of Gospel was to answer questions that arose from Nero's persecution which was a life or death event for Roman Christians, such acceptance was vital.

CONTEXT OF MARK

The need for a longer written Gospel occurred when a situation arose that could not be explained by a simple appeal to accounts of some event, story, or teaching by Jesus in his public life. This need resulted in a change of context from the individual accounts, related to the public life of Jesus, to the context of the later situation. It would be the local situation or problem that would be addressed in a selection and special arrangement of such accounts to produce one of the

Gospel writings. The first such Gospel account probably occurred as a result of the persecution of Roman Christians by Nero in 64-68.

In 64 a fire broke out in Rome and destroyed about half of the city. One of the areas destroyed was the intended site of a great government and public center. Rumors spread that Nero had some complicity in starting the fire or allowing it to burn through the desired area. Nero's intent seemed to have been the construction of the center on what had been private land which, after the fire, could be taken with little payment to the original owners. Nero's response was to indicate that the Roman gods were displeased at something and had withheld divine protection from the city. Therefore, he offered sacrifices to the gods to pacify them and urged Roman citizens to do the same. Jews, under an exemption from Julius Caesar, were exempt from offering sacrifices in pagan temples in Rome.

By that time Jewish Christians in Rome were sufficiently separated from Judaism that they may not have been able to claim the Jewish exemption. Certainly, Gentile Christians could not be considered exempt. Since the two groups would not offer pagan sacrifices, they could be blamed for the disaster. There would be no need to provide evidence that Christians started the fire, only that they had not been loyal to the Roman gods as would be shown by their lack of sacrifice.

The normal mission of Christians would be to witness to their Christian faith, so identification of Christians may have been quite easy and no other proof was necessary for execution. Many Christians died cruel deaths by being wrapped in pitch-soaked cloth, tied to poles, and burned as torches. There is no evidence that the persecution was directed at Jewish people or other groups.

The Christian question that arose from the persecution could easily have been why Christians were persecuted when the reason for becoming Christian was to be part of the great reward of the Second Coming. It is not hard to imagine Christians questioning why such suffering had occurred, why

Christians were singled out, and why the teachings of Jesus hardly indicated such suffering was in store for them. Certainly, they would have become very reluctant to witness to their Christian identification and beliefs during the persecution and afterward.

The early belief of Christians seemed to be centered on an early Second Coming of Christ. Jesus as the Messiah would have been seen within a Jewish structure as someone selected by God to rule on earth as a king, not unlike King David. The meaning of the original coming was always expressed in the concept of "kingdom" both in Judaism and by Jesus. The Resurrection was followed by an Ascension into heaven which may have appeared to be an interlude before the actual crowning of Jesus as king. A reverse result of the expected "curse" of someone who died as a crucified criminal (Dt 21:22-23) had occurred when Jesus was "blessed" with a return to life. It showed Jesus as "above the Law" and clearly superior to King David. The Ascension into heaven simply confirmed that Jesus would have a relationship with God also greater than King David, even though a human being equal to God could not be mentioned within Judaism.

Paul tried to explain in his earliest writings that the delay in the Second Coming would not change anyone's reward (1 Thes 4:13-18). He also explained that the change would be in an instant, presumably requiring a decision about accepting the kingdom prior to the Second Coming event, and that the glory of the kingdom would be everlasting (1 Cor 15:50-58). This type of teaching confirmed the decision Christians had made, and Jesus' words indicated there would be some persecutions at the time of the Second Coming.

Disciples of the Church in Rome would have been shocked at the onset of the persecution and would become very careful about proclaiming their Christian identity. Yet, they also recognized that even with such suffering it was most likely the time of the Second Coming and they held to their faith in spite of the suffering. Then when Nero died in 68, the edict of persecution disappeared and the suffering ended.

No Second Coming had occurred in the way they expected so there was no apparent reason for the persecution, yet, they as a group had been singled out during it. This was hardly the reason they had become Christians, and it was reasonable that questions would be raised.

Someone like Mark, who had been with Peter, the earlier doubter, and had an extensive background and familiarity with the teachings of Jesus, would have recognized that on a larger scale these teachings could address the questions of the Roman Christians. There were no specific teachings that addressed the question of suffering by the Roman Christians. However, looking at a broader view of all the teachings, rather than searching for a particular teaching, would respond to the doubts arising from persecution.

Mark may have started with the passion and death narrative, already in a written form, which formed the basic idea of suffering connected with Christianity. He then would have selected stories and teachings which must have been known to the Roman Church and attached them together as a long introduction to the passion account as shown below.

Mark

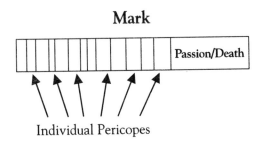

Individual Pericopes

There can be no overwhelming proof for this procedure and, perhaps, none against it. The concept has been used by some Scripture scholars.[7] Perhaps the best argument for it will come as the reader sees a new meaning from groups of pericopes against what comes from the separate pericopes. This longer Gospel of selected teachings in a special arrangement gave an understanding that did not seem to be present in the individual pericopes. It was a story of very rapid acceptance of Jesus as Messiah by the Apostles, but without any real understanding of what type of messiahship had come among them. Even with warnings about suffering and death, the disciples came to Jerusalem without understanding what was to occur and almost were in denial of the warnings given by Jesus.

Union with Jesus in a new covenant was accepted by the disciples at a Passover-like meal on Holy Thursday. However, when suffering and death actually came the following day, the disciples were unprepared, frightened, and in disbelief, and they fled from that definition of kingdom and discipleship. After the Resurrection, these same disciples would reaccept their union with the Lord, proclaim it widely and, seemingly, never be afraid again. However, their acceptance of union with Christ meant they too would have to face suffering and even death at some point in their journey. In continuing their discipleship, they showed that, like Jesus, such a threat did not deter them in the least.

The Roman Christians would see the description by Mark as a mirror image of their own experience. They may have accepted baptism as a simple rite in which they witnessed to their acceptance of Jesus as the expected Messiah. Their decision was to become part of the kingdom when it was formed by the Messiah. Other than that acceptance, Jewish Christians would live life as faithful Jews until the kingdom was formed. The decision was so straightforward and easy that it may not have been questioned by anyone who accepted Jesus as the Messiah. Gentile Christians who originally became Jews before becoming Christian would have the same easy decision. Those baptized after the Council of Jerusalem in about 48 (Acts 15) could be baptized without becoming Jews with a less determined result than if the kingdom were seen as being on earth.

The Second Coming was expected very soon after the Ascension, yet years and decades passed with no Second Coming. The delay or its effect on their decision to become Christian was not questioned. Then when they were faced with suffering and death in persecution, they had no understanding. Yet, their experience as disciples was the same as the original disciples who were surprised by the crucifixion on Good Friday. After the Resurrection, those first disciples had responded with faith-filled lives of discipleship even when they faced death in persecution as had Peter and Paul in Rome. The Roman Christians were expected to witness in the same way when they faced persecution. The message could be seen in a compilation and arrangement by Mark of the same stories about Jesus with which they were so familiar.

Factors that should be considered in understanding the Gospel message of Mark are as follows:

1. The stories used in the Gospel account were probably all known to the Church of Rome. A sudden influx of new, unheard-of information almost 40 years after the public life of Jesus would be far less credible than the use of information already familiar to the Romans. The selection and arrangement of the stories effectively produced a greater meaning than could be found in the stories themselves. In some cases, several stories are grouped together and must be read as a group to gain Mark's special meaning.

2. There is no reason to believe that every story known by the Romans was actually used. If the Gospel account was intended to express a particular message, information not part of that message would only dilute it. This is clear to those who recognize that the writing of Mark is included in the Gospels of Matthew and Luke. Mark's message does not project itself so clearly there because it is mixed with other information added for a different purpose. Such information about Jesus from the early collections probably had been used in the pre-Gospel period in precisely that way. Stories about Jesus either were used independently, or perhaps several together, to

address particular questions. The use of a longer sequence preceding the developed narrative of the passion and death would have been a logical step for the early Church when addressing a great problem. It only seems novel in retrospect, because the earlier collections of stories were not copied and preserved once the longer Gospels were written. So we see only an end product with no written record of its development.

3. Mark's primary writing would have been the short connectors between the pericopes which had been set in a specific arrangement. The connectors give the impression of a continuous narrative even though the added material often is only a few words long and in no way changes the individual pericopes. In some cases, where a point could not be made only from adding a single pericope, Mark interjects one story into another (5:21-43) or sets one story between two related stories (11:12-25) to produce a single understanding that can only come from two or more pieces of information seen as a unit.

4. Mark shows that the very difficulties of the post-persecution Roman Church in misunderstanding the Second Coming, the need for witnessing, and accepting suffering were not new conditions. They existed even with the original disciples during the public life of Jesus.

The resulting Gospel of Mark is a use of the teachings and events of Jesus, given in a Palestinian setting, for understanding a very different problem in a very different setting some decades after the Resurrection. We can assume that such an approach had been used in the past on a smaller scale. The Church must have seen its historical preaching mission as making those teachings and events meaningful to each generation and culture. The Gospel writing is much longer than such earlier attempts because of the magnitude of the problem.

The attribution of this Gospel to Mark, like the use of names on the other three, is a later addition to the Gospel text. It is an early recording of the name of a traditional author, not a name found on the originals. The basic source for the naming of the Gospels is Papias, Bishop of Hierapolis, who probably lived from 65 to about 140. His writings have been lost but he is quoted by Eusebius, a later historian. There also are statements by later Church Fathers, such as Irenaeus and Jerome, but their source is probably the same Papias even though some of their comments seem to conflict with each other.

Mark was probably a disciple with Peter in Rome at the time of Peter's death. He is likely to be the same Mark as mentioned in 1 Peter 5:13, but not necessarily the same as four other Marks mentioned in the New Testament. Mark was the most common name in the Roman Empire, so there is little to use for identification. However, there is no reason to doubt that this Gospel was written from Rome, after Nero's persecution, by a disciple of Peter, who was very familiar with the accounts of Jesus' public life. However, he was not an eyewitness to the public life, according to the historian Papias.[8] Certainly, the Gospel contains questions about suffering which the disciples with Jesus did not accept. It also includes statements about the need to witness to everyone even those who might not seem destined for salvation, a condition which fits the persecution situation. That is the tradition behind the Gospel and since it seems to show through in the Gospel writing, it is the understanding upon which this commentary is based.

CONTEXT OF MATTHEW

The Gospels of Matthew and Luke build on the narrative of Mark to address conditions in their own situations. If Mark was not an eyewitness to the public life of Jesus, it would seem that the other two Evangelists also were not eyewitnesses. They make no effort to correct the order of events in the narrative, but for the most part use Mark as the basic outline for their own work. If Matthew was actually the tax collector called Levi by Mark (Mk 2:14) as is assumed, why would he use Mark's account of the calling with no other change than the name of the tax collector (Mt 9:9)? Why wouldn't the structure of Jesus' public life reflect the additional journeys to Jerusalem found in John's Gospel, who does seem to be an eyewitness? Instead, both Matthew and Luke are content to add primarily teachings and stories to Mark's account with little change in the basic format.

The best understanding of Matthew would occur if the place of its composition is Antioch in Syria in the decade between 75 and 85. Historical evidence points toward such an understanding. Matthew's Gospel seems to be written to a church with a strong Jewish Christian membership at a time when Jewish reforms were forcing Christians out of the synagogues. The Jewish leaders had established an academy or council at the city of Jamnia (present day Yavne) after the destruction of the Temple in 70. There they started the revision of Judaism from a temple religion to a synagogue religion. As part of those reforms, Christians were expelled from the synagogues starting in Palestine and then spreading throughout the Mediterranean world. Pressure was put on Christians to refrain from any witnessing to Christ, and there was the introduction of a synagogue prayer condemning Christian beliefs. The result for Christians was a choice of remaining within Judaism and abandoning any witness to Jesus as Messiah or remaining Christian in a church that has severed all ties to the Jewish community.

Jewish Christians would be pulled very strongly to retain their Jewish ties since that was their culture and family relationship. Gentile Christians would tend to emphasize the choice of remaining Christian since their introduction into Christianity was their strongest and perhaps, in some cases, their only connection to Judaism. However, the split is not so simply defined and Raymond E. Brown, the prominent

American Scripture scholar, identified four different groups of the early Church shown in New Testament writings.[9] He concluded that all four groups would be present in the problems addressed by Matthew's Gospel. The four groups could be summarized as follows:

Four Groups of the Early Church

Group 1
Jewish Christians and Gentile converts who insisted on full observation of the Mosaic Law, meaning that only one who was or had become Jewish could become Christian. The converts would have been converts to Judaism as well as to Christianity.

Group 2
Jewish Christians and Gentile converts who did not insist on circumcision but required Gentiles who were converts only to Christianity to keep some Jewish observances, in particular those that would be necessary to become united with Jewish members in a common Christian community.

Group 3
Jewish Christians and Gentile converts who did not insist on circumcision or Jewish observances, but would be expected to respect the Jewish observances of Jewish members of the Christian community to avoid scandal.

Group 4
Jewish Christians and Gentile converts who saw no particular significance to circumcision or Jewish observances, but would keep the moral code included in the Old Testament revelation.

All four groups would include both Jewish Christians and Gentile converts, even though those of Gentile origin would be less plentiful in group one and would have been

converts also to Judaism. Most Gentile Christians would
have found movement to group four to be easier than would
Jewish Christians. This view of divisions within the early
Church is far more consistent with the New Testament text
than a simple division into Christians of either Jewish or
Gentile origins. Matthew's Gospel might be composed by
someone representing group three or, if they existed, group
four to induce the other groups to remain Christian as separation occurred from Judaism.

It should be noted that these were not only groups that
formed in the first century Church, but that they also reflected the progression of beliefs of the Apostolic Church during
that period. The Apostolic Church must have resembled
group one immediately after the Resurrection and, to a great
extent, for nearly the next two decades afterward. The
Apostolic Church adopted the group two view at the Council
of Jerusalem (Acts 15) in 48, however, some members
remained at the group one position. Such group one members were known as Judaizers since they attempted to reestablish the group one position for all Christians. Group three is
distinguished from group two by the advice of Paul to the
Corinthians which allows a Gentile Christian to participate
in a meal with non-kosher meat originating from a pagan sacrifice (1 Cor 10:23-33). However, Paul included the caution
that eating such food is not acceptable if it is offensive to
others of the community. This position may have been the
real but unstated intent of requiring the keeping of some
Jewish observances at the Council of Jerusalem (Acts
15:19-21) and, therefore, was the Apostolic Church view as
Christianity started to separate from Judaism after 70. Group
four is most clearly shown in the rejection of Judaism in the
Gospel of John, especially in moving so far beyond Judaism in
the obvious acceptance of the Divinity of Jesus. However,
the rejection already is evident in the anti-temple speech of
Stephen (Acts 7:1-60) and his resultant martyrdom.
Therefore, group four probably developed in a community
separated from Judaism. If so, then group four became the

epted condition of Christianity as all of Christianity became separated from Judaism later in the first century.

Some of the Gentile Christians had become converts to Judaism either because they became Christian before the Council of Jerusalem or by embracing Judaism after becoming Christian as a result of pressure from Judaizers within Christianity. That condition would be seen in Paul's letter to the Galatians where Gentile Christians yielded to pressure from such a group of Judaizers just as the opening of Christianity to Gentiles was starting to spread in the mid-50s. Later, at the time of the Council of Jamnia, such converts might seriously consider remaining within their adopted Jewish cultural situation. An opposite situation would have resulted from some Jewish Christians who may have had some anti-temple inclinations even as Jews before their Christian decisions. Jews associated with Essene teachings could have had such a background, and it is that type of understanding which seems present in the speech of Stephen, the Hellenist Jewish worker in chapter seven of Acts.

The conclusion of Raymond E. Brown is that Jewish Christians and Gentile Christians would be present in all four groups identified in the early Church. That could still be consistent with the crisis addressed by Matthew's Gospel, that those choosing to remain Jewish would tend to be Jewish Christians, while Gentiles would be more likely to remain Christian. However, all Jewish Christians had made a commitment to Christ as Messiah and probably the great majority remained Christian. That would produce a successful conclusion from Matthew's writing and may even be a reason for its historical prominence.

The very fact that Matthew's Gospel addressed a crisis occurring about fifty years after the Resurrection, and nearly that long after Christian groups may have been identified in Antioch synagogues, means that, for many, the choice was a second generation question. A large number of Christians in Antioch could have been children of the original Jewish-Christians or Gentile converts who made a decision on

Jesus as Messiah. For them, the choice was not a simple decision of moving back to some earlier condition, but of giving
up a significant part of life either way the decision was made.

Matthew's Gospel message would come from the group
which had already made the decision to remain Christian. It
is addressed to those who would see the loss of Jewish heritage
and culture as a very difficult choice to accept. The basis for
the Gospel message is that the whole meaning of Judaism is
fulfilled in the coming of a Messiah who introduced a new
relationship with God. Just as Moses had brought a message
of a new relationship with God and forced a change in the
mind of the Israelites, Jesus Christ repeated that process on a
grander scale. To remain Jewish would be the equivalent of
Israelites remaining in slavery in Egypt rather than accepting
the promise of a new kingdom. It was not an easy choice for
Israelite slaves to walk away from Egypt, as the richest and
most powerful land in the world, and move into a desert
where their survival would be in doubt. However, all Jews are
descendants of those who made that choice. In Passover celebrations all Jews of every age make that same decision to
accept the promise, regardless of difficulties or of what must
be left behind. Matthew's Gospel is based on showing first
century Christians that the decision to accept Jesus as the
Messiah parallels their Passover situation.

To produce this understanding, Matthew took the
Gospel of Mark, split it apart in several places, and added
additional teachings of Jesus and Old Testament quotations.

Mark

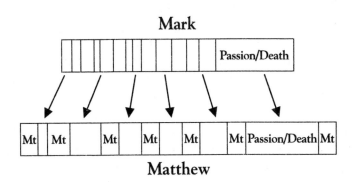

Matthew

The additions show that in the coming of the Messiah the real meaning of Judaism is fulfilled. Events are included in a birth narrative to introduce that meaning. The major step in the revelation process was to move from a relationship with a small kingdom of people in the Middle East to one with all people of creation. This is done in the command of the Risen Christ at the Gospel's end. To the readers, the conclusion of the message is that Christians were not giving up the real Judaism in accepting Jesus as Messiah but of embracing it fully. The choice for following Moses was not an abandonment of Abraham, nor was the loss of the independent physical kingdom of David the loss of the promise made to the Israelites. Both were steps in a development which leads to the true kingdom of God established in the hearts of everyone. The final stage of that development is entered in the relationship with Christ and in that is the fulfillment of the entire journey.

The ties of this Gospel to a disciple named Matthew who was one of the Twelve are very slim. Papias tells us that "Matthew composed his (Christ's) discourse (or sayings) in the Hebrew dialect (meaning Aramaic) and everyone interpreted (or translated) them to the best of his ability."[10] The version of Matthew's Gospel included in the New Testament was written in Greek. It is based on Mark's writing in Greek and some common lists of sayings and teachings which also were in Greek. Only in Luke's version do some of the sayings seem closer to an Aramaic source. So whatever the Apostle Matthew wrote in Aramaic may have become a starting point for collections of sayings. Perhaps, at some later date they reached Antioch and carried the Matthew attribution even after they were translated, expanded, and finally folded into Mark's Gospel. However, there is no evidence for such a scenario.

A second tie is the use of the name Matthew for the tax collector and disciple (Mt 10:3) who is called Levi in Mark (Mk 3:18) and Luke (Lk 6:15). Each of the Synoptics and Acts (Acts 1:13) have a list of the Twelve which includes a

Matthew while none include the name Levi. Only in Matthew is the Matthew disciple listed as a tax collector. The Matthew list and the calling of Matthew account are taken quite directly from Mark except in the change of the name from Levi. One proposal to explain this situation is that Matthew's name was in fact Matthew the Levite and, at some point, it was mistranslated as Levi.[11] That would tend to explain why a tax collector would have a scriptural background and start collecting the "discourses" of Jesus in writing. A Levite who became a tax collector would have been a disgraceful change of profession in Judaism.

CONTEXT OF LUKE AND ACTS

The Gospel of Luke, written independently of Matthew, appears to be addressed to a less definitive situation than either Mark or Matthew. Perhaps the best understanding would come from seeing the community of Luke as being more Gentile in background, probably a result of small Jewish communities originally. The dating would be after the separation from Judaism had already occurred and so Luke would follow Matthew. Macedonia, Greece, or even some parts of modern Turkey would fit as a likely place for the writing and be supported by internal clues. A weak tradition that Luke was a bishop in central Greece gives some added support for Greece as the place for the writing.

Questions must have risen in the early Christian communities, as the separation from Judaism occurred, regarding the success and future meaning of Christianity. First, the expectation of a quick Second Coming had not occurred. That could easily have been considered a failure, since nearly everyone who was a witness to the teachings of Jesus, which produced the prediction, had died. Second, the official Jewish rejection of Jesus as the Messiah also had the appearance of a failure. The message was intended for Judaism and given in Palestine. Yet, official Judaism rejected the message, and

Christianity had disappeared from most of Palestine during the Jewish revolt starting in 66. The primary people and area that were to be in the kingdom were not part of it and had rejected the whole concept. Finally, a question could be raised about Jesus' intentions for having the message spread beyond Palestine or Judaism. In short, the actual development of Christianity in their time seemed so different from the original expectation that it might be considered a failure. It again was a calling into question the whole concept of a Christianity separate from Judaism.

Luke's response is a picture of a kingdom that is intended to embrace the whole world. There are no special people in the kingdom; it is open to the most disadvantaged. Sometimes it is almost interpreted as intended for the disadvantaged even though Jesus clearly means it for everyone. Judaism understood disadvantages as resulting from a life lacking in holiness. Jesus used examples of disadvantaged people being part of the kingdom to change that understanding, rather than to indicate that the kingdom was intended only for the disadvantaged.

The kingdom was always greater than a geographical area; it exists where anyone accepts the reign of God in their hearts. The kingdom is created by disciples here on earth more as preparation for the Second Coming rather than as a result of it. The message emphasizes how discipleship should be lived in a kingdom being developed rather than by a people waiting for one to be formed. If the kingdom is defined as those who live as the Body of Christ, as Paul taught, Luke's Gospel emphasizes how that life is to be lived before the world.

Luke's changes to Mark's Gospel are done in a cleaner and more simplified way than Matthew's changes. He also adds a birth narrative that introduces Jesus in a Jewish context, but emphasizes an openness to outsiders. Then he opens up Mark's script in two places and adds material that shows the problems of his place and time in the Gospel account, as shown on the next page.

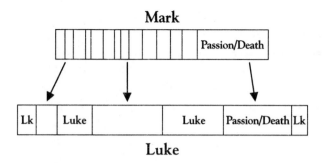

Mark

Luke

The first addition (6:20-8:3) opens the message beyond Judaism and to the world, and introduces discipleship to a greater degree than Mark. It points out that even those who should have recognized the Messiah did not fully understand why the meaning of his coming had changed. Unlike Matthew, Luke eliminates some material from chapters six to eight of Mark's Gospel. The second and greater interpolation occurs in the journey to Jerusalem (9:51-19:27). So much is added that the Jerusalem goal and its warnings of trouble in Mark's account are nearly lost. It becomes the journey of disciples with the Lord or on "the Way" as the early Church named it. Throughout his Gospel, Luke seems to have edited out comments more meaningful to a Jewish Christian church and, at the end, added a Resurrection account that also points outward beyond Judaism.

Gospel response for Luke is a discipleship that reflects the teachings of Christ in the situations of the world and is understandable in a world beyond Judaism. It is a picture of disciples living in a developing kingdom for the long period necessary to make it worldwide and making the life of Christ present there. To make that conclusion clear, a second account called Acts is added to show that such a mission was undertaken by the original disciples and that it was successful. The Spirit, in this second "Gospel" account, directs disciples to continue spreading worldwide what the Lord started in Palestine. Acts is composed of pericopes just like the Gospel even though some of the narratives are longer. It is reasonable to assume that the initial readers were familiar with the material and accepted Luke's argument because it describes so obviously the means in which the Gospel came to them. The Gospel answers the questions concerning the original intent of the Messiah. Acts explains how the Holy Spirit caused the kingdom to come to Gentiles in Greece.

Acts contains two expansion themes. The first expansion is geographical, easily seen in the writing, and the second is a theological expansion, also clear but often not recognized. The geographical expansion is stated at the beginning of Acts (1:8) where the disciples were told to spread the message beyond Judea by stages to the ends of the world. That actually is concluded in Rome, representing the capital of an empire that goes beyond the Mediterranean world. The theological expansion is a movement beyond Judaism to become a worldwide religion for all people. That change is the most difficult for early Christianity since Jewish Christians were more clearly defined by Judaism than by people living in a specific country. These two themes are shown to be the work of the Holy Spirit in the Church, rather than the understood mission of the disciples after the Ascension. The Gospel of Jesus is the bringing of salvation into the human arena anticipated to some extent in Judaism. The Gospel of the Spirit is the unexpected result not seen in Judaism and the answer to the questions raised by Luke's community. Luke's response is that the changes that occurred were God's plan from the beginning.

The only real agreement on the identification of the author of the Gospel of Luke is that it is the same person as the author of Acts. He was not an eyewitness to the public life of Jesus, not likely to have been from Palestine, but was a well-educated Greek writer. Tradition calls him the Luke who was a physician and a companion of Paul.[12] He may have been "the brother whose fame in preaching the Gospel is known throughout all the churches" (2 Cor 8:18). Irenaeus provides the first identification of Luke as the Evangelist, but he presents nothing except what could be deduced from Acts.[13] A prologue to a late second century manuscript of the Gospel describes him as Luke from Antioch.[14] Since Luke was not an apostle, there is less reason for anyone to place his name on a Gospel written by someone else. It certainly appears to be written to the larger Gentile Mediterranean world in a time when separation from Judaism had occurred at least in his region. This will be the basis for this commentary.

CONTEXT OF JOHN

The Gospel of John is a dramatic writing which seems to come from a different mold than the Synoptic Gospels. The emphasis is on the Divinity of Jesus with almost no mention of the kingdom. While the Synoptics could be said to be open to the Divinity of Jesus, John says Divine repeatedly and in every way possible. It is such an overwhelming statement that Christians read it back into the other books of the New Testament, since it is the obvious definition of Jesus.

Historically, the authorship of the Fourth Gospel has been attributed to John the Apostle, identified as a son of Zebedee and a brother of James, both counted among the Twelve. Traditions suggest that the Gospel was written by John at Ephesus near the end of the first century. Such traditions start with Irenaeus near the end of the second century, who indicates that his own teacher Polycarp knew John. This is not confirmed by an earlier historian, Papias, who may link Ephesus with a different John, who was called the "Elder."

This traditional authorship was challenged in the nineteenth century and the first part of the twentieth century by critics who thought the Fourth Gospel was the product of Greek thought with no connection to Palestinian Judaism. A dating for the composition at the end of the second century was proposed along with a rejection of anything in the writing as being related to the historical Jesus. Such proposals were first damaged by the finding of Papyrus P-52, a small fragment from John's Gospel including parts of five verses, in the early part of the twentieth century. It has been dated to about 130 and was found in Egypt.[15] The proposals also were affected by archeological evidence in Palestine in the 1920s that confirmed a description of the sheep pool in Jerusalem which is included in the Gospel (Jn 5:2) but unknown from any other source. This evidence strongly suggested a first century date for the writing and an eyewitness connection to Palestine as a source of the narrative. The final blow to the late date theories came with the finding of the Dead Sea Scrolls, which used the same supposed-Greek concepts as dualism found in John's Gospel. The scrolls have more affinities with John than with any other New Testament writing and tend to exclude anything but a Palestinian origin for the Gospel.

Internal evidence points directly to the person described as the Beloved Disciple as the source of information and the author (Jn 21:24). Historically, this disciple has been equated with John the son of Zebedee to maintain John as the author. That connection has some difficulties for many modern critics, including Raymond E. Brown who has done exhaustive work on the Fourth Gospel.[16] A primary difficulty with John the son of Zebedee being its author is that the Gospel is almost entirely about a ministry in Jerusalem and it is a much longer ministry than the year or less described in the Synoptics. The ministry in John is two or three years in which Jesus visits Galilee three times and those visits account for a total of about two chapters. The question that is difficult to address is how a disciple from Galilee seems to know primarily about a Jerusalem ministry and can only be identified at Galilee in the appendix of the Gospel in chapter 21.

A second problem arises when a connection is made between the Beloved Disciple and an unnamed "other" disciple (Jn 18:15) who assists Peter in entering the high priest's palace. That unnamed disciple is more clearly identified as "the one known to the high priest." The Beloved Disciple also is referred to as "the other disciple" later in the Gospel where he is more fully identified as "the one Jesus loved" (Jn 20:2). It would be difficult to accept a connection between John who in the Synoptics is a Galilean fisherman and someone who is known to the household of the high priest in Jerusalem. It is doubly difficult when the woman at the door, whom the "other disciple" addresses to gain Peter's entry, is the one who accuses Peter of being a disciple of Jesus. She could be seen as drawing a strong distinction between the two. Although this can be explained by the fact that the unnamed disciple in the high priest's palace is not identified as the Beloved Disciple, even the picture of a writing with a Jerusalem cast is not easily attributed by experts to a Galilean fisherman.

Offsetting this concern is the picture of a close, but competitive, relationship between the Beloved Disciple and Peter in the Passion and Resurrection events which is mirrored to some extent in the Synoptics and in Acts. In Acts Peter and John are together preaching in the Temple courtyard (Acts 3:11), are brought before the Sanhedrin (Acts 4:5), and bring the Holy Spirit to Philip's converts in Samaria (Acts 8:14). Philip's converts were Samaritans and his martyred fellow disciple, Stephen, is quoted (Acts 7) as giving an anti-temple speech with a conclusion that relates Jesus to divine power. Therefore, it would not be difficult to conclude that John would have had at least some contact with a group in the Church hostile to Judaism and more open to a concept of a Divine Messiah. Moreover, in such a scenario, John could be shown to have been connected with a church that had Jerusalem traditions about Jesus rather than Galilean traditions even if that connection occurred entirely after the Resurrection. Such a conclusion is not supported by Scripture scholars to any extent, but it does result in relating the Fourth Gospel to the person whose name has been on it in tradition.

The Gospel text has a fulfillment theme which, unlike Matthew, does not tie to Scripture passages, but is based on a replacement of Jewish feasts.[17] The replacements include the Sabbath (5:1-47), Passover (6:1-71), Tabernacles (7:1-8:59), and the Dedication (10:22-37). As this sequence replaces the Jewish feasts with Jesus, it eliminates the need for the Temple and Judaism. Such a replacement process may be reflected in the statement about building a new temple in three days, from the Synoptics (Mk 14:58), but it is never so clear or complete as in the replacement theme in John. This type of argument could have been a basic starting point for the Gospel writing and could have started very early, even in the decade of the 40s for a group with an anti-temple outlook.

The basic division of the Gospel text is into the Book of Signs in chapters one through twelve and the Book of Glory in chapters thirteen through twenty.[18] The prologue (1:1-18) and epilogue (chapter 21) are considered to be additions, perhaps by a redactor at the time the writing was finished. A progression of signs is included in the first half of the Gospel and is somewhat more than just another list of signs.[19] Just as Mark arranged the signs into a narrative to address something different from a proof of Jesus as Messiah, so John's progression carries a theme as well.

The seven signs start with a simple physical miracle at Cana (Jn 2:1-11). The change of water to wine is an adjustment in color, taste and an alcoholic character which might be seen as a typical magic act by Jews at that time. The next two signs are acts of restoring people to health. The cure of the nobleman's son (4:46-54) is the cure of a fever which could be explained in how fevers "break" quite rapidly sometimes, especially with children. However, the cure of the man who had an illness for 38 years (5:1-15), which appeared to leave him somewhat paralyzed, is more difficult to explain away. Such a condition would be so debilitating that restoring muscular functions sufficient to walk is more of a miracle itself than getting rid of the disease.

The next two signs are physical miracles but of a magnitude that they would be outside of the realm of magic. The enlargement in volume of bread (6:1-15) is beyond anyone's understanding and is witnessed by so many people that it is difficult to explain away. The walking on the sea (6:16-21) is a power over water in a way that, in Jewish terms, could only be attributed to Yahweh by the Jews of that time.

The cure of a man born blind (9:1-41) is a giving of something rather than a restoration. In Jewish understanding it is the giving of sight that Yahweh had not given to the man at birth and, therefore, is a redoing of the creation of the person. The last sign is the giving back of life to Lazarus (11:1-44) after a time when the body would have experienced the start of decomposition. For life to be restored to a body that is already decomposing, the body would have to be recreated and that would be an act of God in any understanding. Each sign in the progression points more directly to the power of God acting through Jesus. These signs increase in importance as the claim of Jesus to be Divine is made more specific and thereby act as proofs supporting the claim.

The Gospel is an interweaving of these two progression themes, with some specific instruction on the realized meaning of the sacraments of Baptism (3:1-21 and 4:1-42) and Eucharist (6:26-66). The themes are then connected to the common passion and death narrative in a way similar to Mark's own production. The connection point is a long discourse after the Last Supper (13:33-17:26) which, with earlier discourses, summarizes the meaning of the relationship between God and humanity. It has an emphasis on a coming of the Holy Spirit after the Resurrection or a continuation of a divine presence with humanity. Precisely how that integration occurred is unknown. However, the two progressions could have been developed early and led to an early understanding of a closeness of Jesus with divinity, at least to an extent that would not have been acceptable within Judaism. This would have been sufficient to cause a rupture between this community and Judaism, but also a practical separation from the Jewish Christian Apostolic community. With those separations, John's community would be open to anti-temple Jews such as Essenes, converts on the fringes of Judaism such as Samaritans, some followers of John the Baptist, and finally Gentiles. The beheading of James of Zebedee in about 42 (Acts 12:2) may be a reflection of something more severe than an anti-Christian act. Perhaps James was connected to

John's Samaritan ministry, since the act did not affect the Jerusalem Church as a whole.[20]

The community of John would have left Palestine at the start of the Jewish revolt in 66 when all Christians moved out of Jewish controlled areas. However, they could have left at a much earlier time if subjected to a persecution by Jewish authorities. The death of James happened during the three year period in 41-44 when Samaria and Judea were transferred from Roman rule to the rule of Herod Agrippa I. John's community may have been located in Samaria and affected by the loss of protection of Roman rule. Their movement to Antioch would have been likely since it was the refuge place for some of Stephen's associates. A later move to Ephesus would have been a reasonable step as a Gentile Christian church had developed there, if in fact there is a connection between John's Gospel and that area.

When the community came in contact with the Gospel of Mark, the arrangement of their own teachings into a similar format would be understandable, especially if their message was formalized for acceptance by the Apostolic Church. The late dating of the Gospel and its connection with Ephesus could be more a result of the date of reconnection with the Apostolic Church than the starting point for its initial writing or even the time in which the writings first were placed in a Gospel format.

USING THE COMMENTARY

This commentary is meant to be read with a constant reference to Scripture so that both the Gospel pericopes and their explanations are before the reader at the same time. However, it is intended that the emphasis in the commentary be on each entire Gospel writing rather than only on the individual pericopes. Therefore, it is necessary that the full view of each Gospel be in the mind of the reader during the review. It is this larger view that is at the heart of the meaning established by the Evangelist, seen in the selection and arrangements of pericopes from Jesus' public life, and applied to the later problems that caused each Gospel to be composed.

Therefore, a reading of each Gospel by itself should precede the review of commentary and Scripture together. In the case of Mark's Gospel, the initial reading of the Gospel alone should be done at one uninterrupted sitting, if possible, and immediately before reading the commentary review. Many of the important aspects of the composition will be seen as a unit in that situation, just as the Evangelist intended. When the second review with the commentary is done, perhaps in a small group over several meetings with discussion periods, it will tend to separate the Gospel material into smaller sections. However, seeing the material in a unified format as a starting point, rather than a series of short readings, is important to understanding the whole Gospel message. The Evangelist has written the more complete message for responding to the needs of a special community, and that should be remembered as the special context of the writing itself.

When the Gospels of Matthew and Luke are reviewed, the initial reading should be of the additions which these two Evangelists made to Mark's composition. There is no need to again read Mark's Gospel embedded in Matthew or Luke, since that belongs to a different context. The purpose of Matthew and Luke will be seen more clearly in their additions alone, rather than in combination with the text they gained from Mark. These additions for each Gospel are listed in Appendix A, and the commentary also will be limited to the additions.

John's Gospel should be addressed in the same way as Mark's Gospel with a full reading before starting on the commentary. This presents some special problems not found in Mark since, instead of separate pericopes, it includes long discourses which are difficult to read and understand without a commentary. This is especially true of the discourse following the Last Supper, which is presented as a long statement to the disciples at the Last Supper, but in reality addresses questions of the early Church near the end of the first century. The reader or the study group might consider that the initial review reading could be done separately for the Book of Signs (chapters 1 - 12) and the Book of Glory (chapters 13 - 21). This would shorten the initial reading and make the first part easier to read since it does not have the Last Supper discourse. Then, after going through the commentary for chapters 1 to 12, the initial reading of the Last Supper discourse will be more understandable since it builds on what has been revealed in the first section.

In following this pre-reading approach, the reader will more easily focus on the context of the Evangelist, rather than the individual pericopes which most readers are familiar with from Sunday readings and homilies. The special meaning of the Evangelist will come through in viewing the full composition in a way that can hardly be seen in a random review of pericopes even with a commentary. The Church canonized the individual Gospels rather than a list of pericopes. The pericopes clearly are declared inspired in the same action. Yet the meaning of the whole composition, or in the case of Matthew and Luke the complete additions by each Evangelist, also is the focus of the Church's declaration.

The intent of the Church in using Scripture, and especially the Gospels, is not just to look at historical writings but to apply the words of Christ to our lives. The use of the writings for Sunday readings and homilies accomplishes that for the situation of Jesus speaking in Palestine and that was the original intent of their use by the very early Church. However, the use of their writings to address later major questions also shows how the Church intended the information to be viewed. Yet, that view is more difficult to project in Sunday readings and homilies. The Church's encouragement of bible studies is an instruction to search for, understand, and be spiritually nourished by the whole writings and ultimately the whole Old and New Testaments. Bringing all four Gospels together in a common introduction and a presentation and commentary that follows the historical progression of development is intended to promote that same goal.

There are a small number of terms in the Gospels that have specialized meanings and are important to the overall understanding of the Gospels. These terms are translated quite directly into English but result in different meanings from what were intended in the original writings. A short explanation of the meanings that existed in the first century should be helpful before starting the commentary.

Messiah refers to one who is anointed into a special relationship with God. Priests would be anointed, as was Elisha the prophet (1 Kgs 19:16). Kings also were anointed and when a king was not in the hereditary line for the throne, the anointing showed the selection to be directly from God.

Son of God is a term that could be applied to angels in heaven (Ps 29:1-2) or any Jew who kept the Law (Dt 14:1-2). It was a title applied to King David most directly (Ps 2:7-8) and with the term messiah it probably always would mean a king. Since in the time of Jesus there was no hereditary line of kings, the two terms together meant a restoration of the kingship of David and with it the kingdom in Palestine. The term often is applied to Jesus by others in the Synoptic Gospels and in those applications the term would never carry the connotation of a divine being. Jesus does not apply the term to himself, but accepts it when asked by the high priest (Mk 14:62-63). Jesus' answer would, of course, include the meaning of Divinity even though the high priest would not have included that meaning in the questions. However, it is clear from the text of John's Gospel that the term means Divinity at the end of the Gospel (Jn 20:31). In between, from the time of Jesus' public life until the Gospel of John, the term will have a meaning which is not clearly defined.

The Resurrection changes the meaning of the term beyond any previous meaning because it moves the meaning beyond the Law. In addition, the Ascension, although it is introduced by Luke relating to a kingly messiah (Acts 1:6), would show that Jesus has a very different relationship with the Father than anyone else. So, when the term is used in the Synoptics by others, it may be seen as the definition given here but only during the time of Jesus' public life. However, the Synoptics are written to the Church at a later time and the meaning of the term at any time after the Ascension would go beyond that of the pre-Ascension meaning.

Son of Man is a non-messianic term which probably means no more than human representative. It is used most often in Ezekiel when God orders the prophet to do something or to carry a message to the Israelites. In Daniel 7:13, a human figure in heaven is described as "one like a Son of Man." Since that being is in heaven, it is uniquely different in that humans are creatures of earth, being born on earth, living on earth and going to an existence under the earth in Sheol after death. Therefore, the image in heaven is undefined as far as Daniel is concerned. However, angels are in heaven and they can bring messages to earth or even appear on earth in a human form. The term angel means messenger, so undefined doesn't mean not understandable.

Jesus applies the title Son of Man to himself in his public life and with a meaning of prophet might be how it was accepted. However, in the trial before the high priest, Jesus identified himself with the Son of Man from Daniel and was immediately convicted of blasphemy. The conviction was made because Jesus had placed himself near the throne of God, not that he had claimed divinity in the use of that term. Likewise, Stephen (Acts 7:55-56) described a vision with Jesus standing near the throne of God with the same result of being condemned and executed.

Kingdom or reign is designated more by the willingness of people to accept a ruler rather than from a geographical representation of power. In secular terms, a powerful ruler might be accepted as one who could provide protection to a greater extent than a weaker ruler. The kingdom would expand to the limits of that protection. It is this acceptance of the reign that describes kingdom. Such an understanding of the reign of God is important since it is that acceptance of the power of God which creates the kingdom. The power of a pagan kingdom is considered to be the power of the gods of that kingdom. The acceptance in Judaism that there was only One God for all of creation meant that the kingdom of God would spread to the whole world. The only need would be to make it understood that pagan gods did not exist. Then there would be no doubt about the Divine power protecting the kingdom of God; it had to be the totality of Divine power in the universe.

While kingdom is a very important concept in the Synoptics, it all but disappears in John's Gospel. Clearly the Synoptic Gospels build on Jewish thought about the expected kingdom as one ruled by a new King David with divine protection and open to Jews. That would be the misunderstanding of Jesus' teaching on the kingdom even immediately after the Resurrection (Acts 1:6). In John's Gospel, the revelation of Jesus' Divinity creates a different understanding of Divine protection and kingdom through a careful selection and arrangement of teachings from Jesus. The term kingdom can hardly be applied in the same way as before that exposition. But the transition to a fuller meaning of the term started before the writing of John (1 Thes 4:13-18).

Parable is not a term that requires explanation like the terms above. Rather, it is a means of explaining concepts that could not be done easily in the language used by Jesus. Aramaic was the language spoken by the Jewish people in Palestine. Hebrew, a language related to Aramaic, was overshadowed by Aramaic for everyday use in the last few centuries before Christ. However, Hebrew was still used for most of the last books of the Old Testament including Sirach and Maccabees in the second century BC. Aramaic was used in Tobit and most of Daniel in the second century BC while the texts relating to the Qumran community at about the same time were in either Hebrew or Aramaic. The conclusion could be drawn that Hebrew was still used for some writing, but it is almost conclusive that everyday speech was in Aramaic for Jewish people.

The use of Aramaic is quite adequate to describe what exists and is known in everyday life. However, to describe something unknown at a present time or something new or abstract would be difficult or impossible. Yet, the message of Jesus involved a revelation far different from anything found in the Old Testament or any place else during his public life. Almost to an extreme, it is both new and abstract. To make matters more difficult, the revelation relates to concepts that had been raised in the Old Testament. So the discussions Jesus has with Jewish people involve their religion and messianic expectations but entirely in a great change of meaning.

To cope with such a situation, Jesus often reveals his message using parables. These are stories that start from a situation known and understood by the people, but which come to conclusions those hearing the stories would not expect. If they followed the story carefully, the ending would be a surprise. Then they would have to rethink the story to determine how a new understanding could bring them to the conclusion selected by Jesus. The example of Jesus explaining the parable of the sower (Mk 4:13-20) illustrates how a parable works. Jesus puts a different meaning on all the points of the original story in order to make the parable clear. Without those changes, the conclusion could not be grasped.

The entire message of Jesus is somewhat of a parable. The disciples are shown in Acts as coming to new conclusions about the meaning of Jesus' message. When a major problem arose in the early Church, someone sees that it could be explained by examining the remembrances of Jesus for the means to explain the problem, and in the process a written Gospel is created. Therefore, the four Gospels themselves act like parables in addressing new situations as great parables or, more correctly perhaps, as seeing a new and deeper message in the actual words of Jesus.

Sin is another term which should not require any special definition, but its meaning in Scripture often is related to the Law. Judaism has a relationship with God in the Law which encourages certain actions and discourages others. When a Jew does the opposite of what the Law requires, the Law has been broken and the relationship would be broken as well. To reestablish the relationship, the person must again follow the Law. Even though the illegal action itself could be called a sin, the clearer meaning of sin in Scripture is the lost relationship with God. In most cases, it may be more meaningful to say "separation from God" when one sees the word "sin" in Scripture. The same substitution could be meaningful in the New Testament as well. That situation changed for Christians after the first century, and this suggestion is not meant to redefine sin. However, it is a meaningful approach to gaining a more complete understanding of the text of Scripture.

THE GOSPEL OF MARK

CONTEXT OF MARK

The context used in the introduction for Mark's Gospel can be summarized as follows:

- Written in Rome, perhaps in 68-70
- In response to Nero's persecution
- By Mark, a disciple of Peter

Subjects addressed are:

- Why did Christians have to suffer in the persecution?
- Why has no Second Coming occurred?
- Was salvation meant for the Romans, especially for Gentile Christians?

While these are not the questions or the context of Jesus' time, they are addressed in this Gospel writing by a careful selection and arrangement of stories and teachings of Jesus. This commentary will point out the relationship between these stories and how they fit that context.

In using the commentary, it is recommended that the Gospel of Mark be read through at a single sitting prior to looking at the commentary. Most readers will have to check back with the Gospel as they progress through this commentary. However, the initial reading will result in a familiarity with the Gospel that greatly assists in connecting the commentary remarks to the Gospel text.

The intent of going through both commentary and the Gospel text rather quickly is to develop a view of the entire Gospel rather than to focus on individual readings. The whole Gospel writing is Mark's response to the persecution and its questions, since the questions could not be answered in individual accounts about Jesus or even a small group of accounts. The reader should attempt to use the same view of the whole Gospel to understand Mark's purpose in writing.

OPENING OF THE GOSPEL

Chapter 1

The Gospel writing of Mark is developed around two basic questions. The first question is: Who is this Jesus? The answer given in the first half of the Gospel is that Jesus is the Messiah (8:27-30). A second question is then raised: What does this Messiahship mean? That question is addressed in the second half of the Gospel and answered by showing that Jesus must suffer and die and be raised from the dead. The suffering question of Mark's Roman readers arising from Nero's persecution is answered at the same time. Acceptance of Christianity is acceptance of the life of Christ. That life contains suffering and death which the Roman readers had experienced in the persecution.

The opening verse of the Gospel gives the answer to the initial question with Jesus being designated by the title Christ, the Greek form of the Hebrew word Messiah. The reader is told the answer to the first question even though the disciples with Jesus were not asked to answer until chapter eight. Yet, it was apparent to the first disciples with Jesus and was fully clear to the early Christians in Rome who knew the Gospel stories before they were collected into a Gospel account by Mark. Son of God, which is added to Jesus Christ as a title (1:1), had been given to King David in the Old Testament (2 Sam 7:14 and Ps 2:7). This represents a Jewish understanding of messiah rather than the Divine attribution of Christianity.

John the Baptist's announcement of the Messiah (1:2-11) carried an importance for Jewish verification of the Messiah more than for Christians of today. Jews would want to be sure that the messiah had been chosen by Yahweh since their concept of messiah would not include a divine messiah. For them, the messiah would be an instrument to obtain freedom and protection from foreign rule. If the messiah were from Yahweh, divine power would assure success. However, a messiah without divine backing might cause an uprising not supported by divine power which would not succeed and could result in the destruction of Judaism. The Roman Christians would realize that the special calling of such a witness as John the Baptist was a statement from God that the message revealed by Jesus Christ should be believed.

John the Baptist is introduced as a prophet (1:2-3) who was expected in the prophecy quoted from Isaiah (Is 40:3), which also includes words from Malachi (Mal 3:1). The description of John is taken from a description of Elijah in 2 Kings 1:8. John received no personal gain from being a prophet since he would be imprisoned prior to Jesus' public ministry and would be martyred before it ends. Finally, John proclaims the need for repentance, a turning back to Yahweh, which was the traditional message of Old Testament prophets. The description may mean that if a prophet was supposed to announce the Messiah and someone was present who looked like a prophet, acted like a prophet, and spoke like a prophet, surely all the conditions were fulfilled.

The baptism of Jesus (1:9-11) could be seen as an indication of his Divine nature, however, the voice from heaven gives almost an identical wording as the statement given in Psalm 2:7-8 about King David. The possibility of Jesus having a divine nature would never be indicated to the ones present at the event when the connection to King David was so obvious in what was said.

The temptation scene (1:12-13) has little of the drama given in the Gospels of Matthew and Luke. However, it carries the understanding that evil forces were opposed to the coming of the Messiah, as might be expected, and that Jesus successfully resisted such forces. The resistance is not just a trial of strength, but comes in the same context as the Exodus event. After passing through the water (as occurred in the Exodus), a symbolic 40-day period was spent in the wilderness in which the only protection during that period was from heaven (as also occurred in the 40-year period in the desert by the Israelites). The symbolism points beyond a continuation of the old revelation and points toward a new relationship with Yahweh as occurred with the Israelites. That would be important to the Roman Christians who did not understand that Jesus was not just the last step of the Old Testament revelation but a dramatic move beyond it. At Mark's point in time, when a union still existed between Judaism and Christianity, the difference between the two was not definite. However, the opening of Christianity to Gentiles was the seed of a very separate understanding which had been planted, and the destruction of the Temple in 70 would end the union.

JESUS' PUBLIC MINISTRY IN GALILEE

Jesus' public ministry began (1:14-15) after the Old Testament introduction by the prophet was completed and John was removed from the scene. There is not an overlapping period and early Christian teaching probably emphasized that there should not be an overlapping period in which Judaism exists without acceptance of the Messiah. However, that is the reality during the time between the Resurrection and the writing of Mark. The placement of this short summary statement about the kingdom seems to indicate almost no activity prior to choosing the first disciples. The other Gospel accounts will indicate that this initial ministry period may have been more extensive than described by Mark.

Mark's writing opens with a burst of activity that seems to reflect an early acceptance of Jesus, yet is devoid of a complete understanding of the mission of the Messiah. Therefore, he shortens the early descriptions to emphasize the quickness of the steps taken by the Messiah. The Romans would recognize their own experience from this in how they quickly accepted the Second Coming expectation which was the earliest understanding of how the kingdom would be formed.

Jesus called the first four disciples (1:16-20) very abruptly and the response of Simon, later renamed Peter, Andrew and the Zebedee brothers was without question or hesitation. It is very unlikely that anyone would choose to follow an itinerant preacher and leave an established livelihood without a question or clarifying statement of any kind. Yet, Mark's Roman readers, and later readers elsewhere, could relate to the incompleteness of the first disciple's understanding of Jesus and the extreme suddenness of their response. If the experience of the Romans was to accept an invitation to become disciples and immediately accept the kingdom before the Second Coming, the severity of Nero's persecution would remind them that more than a quick Second Coming was involved. They had not asked about the full importance of accepting Christianity in their lives. Only after the persecution would real questions be raised about the details and probable results of such a choice.

In the synagogue on that first recorded Sabbath (1:21-28), Jesus taught as one especially sent by Yahweh, as might be expected. However, Jesus went beyond teaching to cure a man by casting out an unclean spirit. The people were overwhelmed by the action and it seems likely that synagogue officials also must have been too astonished to question such actions on the Sabbath. The result was amazement and acceptance throughout the countryside.

A little reflection might have raised the question of how this Messiah could be so different from the earlier anointed one of Yahweh, King David. He was not known to cure by casting out evil spirits either in or out of a synagogue on the Sabbath or any other day. The very events which caused Jesus to be accepted as an anointed one should have raised questions about the nature of his Messiahship. If he was different from King David, this could mean that his mission was more than just producing a free homeland for Jews.

Peter's mother-in-law was cured at a touch (1:29-31). This occurred at home, rather than in the synagogue, yet it was still on the Sabbath, and without an evil spirit present. It had the appearance of an infringement of the Law concerning Sabbath activity, especially when it was followed by her waiting on them. It might be expected that Peter would begin to have some questions about the Messiah, but the account doesn't include any.

After sunset, when the Sabbath had officially ended (1:32-34), Jesus worked a number of cures. Many of those who were sick and possessed were cured and the whole town was present to accept Jesus. King David never was involved in such activities nor would that be expected of an earthly ruler. Jesus prevented any witnessing by evil spirits even though they recognized that this Messiah was not the one expected. The works of Jesus alone should have witnessed to the broader meaning of this Messiah, yet those affected by the works did not comprehend fully any new meaning of the Messiah from that witness. The Romans would remember they were impressed by stories of such events, yet they also did not question if it pointed toward a different expectation. Just considering a few events set together in a single day gives a different view from the separate individual pericopes. However, the Roman Christians would have only known the individual accounts until Mark arranged them together in this form.

Another side of Jesus was presented the following day (1:35-39). He got up before dawn and went to a private place to pray. While the Jews are a very prayerful people, this would not be a description of their normal method of prayer nor does it describe King David, their model of a messiah. Keeping the Law requires a doing of something, so prayer would be said aloud as a witness to people, while Jesus prays alone as if in meditation. This Messiah is not just sent by Yahweh or anointed by a divine representative, he projects a different relationship with Yahweh than the requirements of the Law. The disciples did not seem to notice the difference, but were more interested in finding Jesus to pursue a continuation of the activities of the previous day. Surely no one would have thought that a new anointed king would say that such actions were why he "had come." The original understanding of messiah must have been to establish an independent kingdom.

The initial introduction, which seems to be a 24-hour period, has the appearance of great success. Jesus gained instant disciples, he was a sensation in Capernaum, and afterwards was triumphant throughout Galilee. Everyone accepted him and, seemingly, no one questioned or tried to understand. In the minds of Mark's Roman readers, the first disciples were not seeing the differences between this Jesus and their historical model of a messiah.

Jesus' cure of a leper (1:40-45) introduces far more directly the question of the relationship between him and the Law of Moses. The religious authorities, who would have great concerns about a messiah who does not live within the Law, as defined by rules governing almost all activity, were the first to question the actions of Jesus. Leprosy was a disease controlled under the Law. A leper was to be separated from the community, to live apart, to dress and maintain an appearance that would tend to keep people away, and to call out "unclean" to warn anyone who approached (Lv 13:45-46). The Law gave no prescription on how the disease could be removed from a person.

Jesus' response was the opposite. First he touched the leper in opposition to what the Law stated and, in this action that went beyond the Law, cured him of the disease. He ordered compliance with the Law from the man in showing himself to the priests only so that the cured man would be accepted by the Jewish community. Jesus had not just gone beyond the King David ideal of messiah, he had gone beyond the Law itself. If the messiah was expected to proclaim the need to follow the Law rigidly, Jesus, in this act, had proclaimed something beyond that. Then he cautioned this cured man not to become a witness to his being the Messiah. His kingdom and relationship with God would be quite different. Mark included Jesus' statements, but not to promote Jesus' works as a great messianic secret. For Mark's readers, it was not so much a deliberate secret as something not understood immediately by the early disciples or themselves. Until it was searched for in the whole collection of Gospel stories, the real understanding of the kingdom would not be clear to those who expected so much less of a kingdom.

Chapter 2

Chapter two starts with a series of conflicts between Jesus and the religious authorities. The authorities preferred a very narrow interpretation of the meaning of the messiah and one fully consistent with their understanding of the Law. The people as a whole were amazed and accepting, but for those who were determined to remain within a narrow definition of the messiah, only questions were raised.

The issues raised by the paralytic being lowered through the roof (2:1-12) concerned how Jesus acted for Yahweh. Probably Jesus was preaching to a group of people who filled a courtyard and prevented the paralytic from being brought to him. Those carrying the paralytic went to the roof of the house, most likely pulled aside vines or thatching providing shade to the courtyard, and lowered the paralytic on his stretcher. Cutting through a roof constructed of clay dried around cross-hatched poles would have dropped large clumps of hard clay on those below. Before a hole could have been cut in the roof large enough for a stretcher to be lowered through, it might have caused the collapse of the entire roof.

Jesus introduced the cure of the paralytic by saying the man's sins were forgiven. The Jewish understanding of good and evil coming into one's life was that they were a result of virtue or sin in the person's life deserving of a reward or punishment. If the man were paralysed, the view would be that he must have been punished for great sins. If the sins were forgiven, the punishment would disappear; or to say it in the more obvious way, if the man were cured, it was a sign the sins were forgiven. To forgive sins or to be healed would be the accomplishment of the same thing in the Jewish understanding of that time. However, sins could only be forgiven by God. Therefore, what might be expected of the messiah is that he would announce the cure and the people would thank

Yahweh that the man's sins were forgiven rather than that he was cured by the announcement. Jesus turned this around by announcing the forgiveness of sins instead of the cure. That said something quite different to the religious authorities since, then, Jesus was doing what could only be done by Yahweh. Yet, if Jesus could actually act for Yahweh, how the changed condition was announced would not matter and Jesus said as much.

The result was that everyone was astounded at the cure. They had never seen anything like that, because Jesus seemed to act for Yahweh and did not just announce a change which had occurred. They should have recognized that this was a different Messiah from the one they had expected. The placement of the story after the cure of the leper provided the second emphasis. Jesus did not act under the limitations of the Law in the first cure. Here he did not act as the agent of Yahweh in the same way as would be expected by the messiah anticipated in Scripture.

Conflicts continued with religious officials in the call of Levi, a meal with his friends, and in questions about fasting (2:13-22). A tax collector was an agent of a foreign government in the eyes of Jews and, therefore, was in constant violation of the covenant which gave Palestine to the Jews. In a strict keeping of the Law, the religious officials would shun such people as the equivalent of Gentiles and sinners. It would be expected that the Messiah would cleanse the country of the tax collectors, as agents of a foreign government, along with all other Roman agents and Gentiles.

Jesus' choice of Levi as a disciple, a person important in the work of the Messiah and, therefore, an agent of Yahweh's choice, would be seen as a disregard for the Law. Such disregard would not be viewed as a change in understanding the Law so much as proof to the Pharisees that Jesus was not the Messiah they had expected. Only if someone recognized that the Messiah was different from what was expected would the message have a positive meaning that the kingdom was open to those outside the Law.

The initial establishment of the covenant was in Yahweh choosing the people of Israel who were outsiders living in Egypt. Jewish thought would tend to understand those Israelites as being outside the Law and similar to Gentiles. The Messiah's proposal of a covenant change, which opened the Law to outsiders, could have been viewed as a reason not to believe in him. After the exile, Judaism had accepted a very strict interpretation of the Law which in its daily rules governed essentially all actions of life. Separation from Gentiles was an important part of Jewish witness to being a people who lived the covenant. The conflict which Jesus' actions raised was not due to the original understanding of the covenant relationship at the time of the Exodus, but in the narrow framework of these rules that had developed in the later Jewish history.

Viewing the Messiah as a new King David could mean that the Law remained untouched and the Messiah's role was to free the land of Israel. However, Jesus avoided the King David concept and titles and, in so doing, opened the question of possible changes in understanding or applying the Law. When an outsider was chosen as a disciple, the covenant relationship was opened to those who needed salvation the most. That would be a very major change from the directions to be separate from such people. It was not the same as an adjustment where minor fasting rules were set aside. If sinners were those separated from the Law, then clearly many Roman readers who were Gentile Christians were outsiders as well.

Questions could be raised about how such a change could be accomplished within the old established framework of rules related to the Law. The answer by Jesus was that such a change could not fit the Law or its extension into rules because it was nearly the opposite. The old wineskin of rules, which contained Jewish understanding of the Law, could not contain a much broader understanding of the relationship with God. Such rigid rules could not be used for a new revelation anymore than the covenant understanding from

Abraham was adequate to live the new Law relationship given to Moses and the Israelites. The Apostles with Jesus should have realized that and the Roman readers should have been aware that Christianity had gone beyond the Second Coming meaning of Christianity they had accepted from the time of the Resurrection.

This process of opening the understanding of the Law continued in the account of picking grain (2:23-28) and the cure of a man with a withered hand (3:1-6). Picking grain as the disciples walked through a field on the Sabbath was not a violation of the Law if it were just picking up food and eating, but would be a violation if the picking was harvesting. The Pharisees raised an objection to this marginal issue even though Luke's version included the rubbing of chaff off the grain to emphasize harvesting. Jesus moved it to a very major point by suggesting that he could change the meaning of the Sabbath. This was no longer a minor rule, but a different understanding of one of the ten commandments. His quote of the Sabbath being made for humanity (2:27) would be accepted by Jewish scribes; however, the claim that the Messiah was master of the Sabbath was something very different since it modified a commandment.

Chapter 3

Curing the hand of a man on the Sabbath (3:1-6) in the synagogue is not just a related story. It is intended to prove the master of the Sabbath claim. That infirmity must have been of long standing and, therefore, in Jewish terms, represented a sinful condition in the man's life. There was little reason to cure a long-standing ailment on the Sabbath. The man certainly would not have objected to waiting until sundown for the cure after bearing the burden for years and probably accepting it as a permanent condition. The immediate cure tended to prove Jesus' claim as master of the Sabbath by changing the understanding of a commandment ordained by Yahweh and yet showing divine acceptance of the claim by using God's power in the healing.

The Pharisees became angry because they did not believe that someone who had broken the Law, especially concerning something on the Sabbath, could be from Yahweh. However, Jesus had proved to all those who witnessed the event that he could go beyond the Law. The Pharisees and Herodians started plotting against him because, unless Jesus could be killed, these witnesses might follow this Messiah into an uprising that would result in the destruction of Judaism. The religious authorities would not look beyond a King David-type messiah even though the signs pointed so strongly to that conclusion. However, for the Romans, only in tying the two Sabbath readings together did the claim of Jesus become so obvious.

The context of Jesus' public ministry is very much the difficulty he faced in attempting to change a covenant relationship. Yet, that was the very basis for gaining acceptance as one sent from God. A new relationship could not be exposed to those who equated authenticity with explicitly following the guidelines from the old relationship. Mark used the events of the public ministry to answer later questions about why so many Jews, and especially official Judaism, did not accept Jesus as Messiah. If signs which signaled a new relationship were ignored and only the narrow rules of the old relationship were used as the basis for deciding, the relationship with God could not be expanded even by Yahweh's agent.

Those who were less focused on the rules of the Law and, therefore, more open to the signs worked by Jesus, accepted Jesus very completely (3:7-12). This summary statement by Mark showed acceptance by people throughout Palestine and even in non-Jewish areas beyond Palestine. Jesus had not visited these areas yet in the way the Gospel unfolds, so the summary of success would not have occurred by this time in his public life or at any time in the Gospel accounts. Therefore, even the summary statement must have been a remembered and recorded story for the disciples in Rome. However, the comparison is clear and where people were open to what was being revealed in God's name, the truth was recognized. The evil spirits recognized the Messiah, even though they also used the Son of God title that Jesus avoided because of its King David connection.

Jesus appointed a new Twelve (3:13-21) to replace the twelve tribes that provided the foundation for the Israelite's covenant. The appointment was a sign that more was being changed than just a few rules attached to the Law. These twelve would be the basis for a very new covenant, and for those in Rome, it would be understood as a new Exodus journey as well. However, those who were closest to Jesus, who knew him best, and even those united with him as family (3:20-21), were not as accepting as the faraway Romans. Those who shared a blood relationship in addition to a religious background with him thought he might be insane.

Up until this point Mark had told his readers that people were astonished by the teachings of Jesus and now a section gives some of those teachings. The first teachings are a series of very simple parables (3:22-30). Those who opposed Jesus must explain away the signs before their opposition could gain credibility. If the power exercised by Jesus were not from God, it must be from evil spirits, since such signs could not have only a human origin. Yet, the actions of Jesus recorded so far were often in opposition to evil spirits, which suggested a kingdom or household divided. It is obvious that nothing could be accomplished by evil spirits if their actions were in opposition to themselves, and those who would make such a charge could be considered as representing evil.

Those who opposed the Holy Spirit, who brings salvation, would act in opposition to salvation for themselves. Yet the Holy Spirit called the Roman disciples to witness to the world, and if in the persecution they stopped witnessing, wouldn't that constitute a rejection of the Holy Spirit? Not doing what is required of a disciple is a rejection of discipleship and of the union that comes with discipleship. The presence of God must be accepted before the gift from God is accepted. Jesus' opponents would play a dangerous game if they opposed him without justification.

The relationship anyone has with Jesus is based on how they accept him. Therefore, those as close as family members (3:31-35) would gain nothing if they did not accept him as the Messiah who had come. Those who did accept him, even if they were as distant as the citizens of Rome, would be as close as his immediate family. Those Romans who wondered if the coming of the Messiah was for them as well as the Jews were given an answer in the words of Jesus. Those who accepted the will of God revealed by Jesus gained everything, while those remaining in relationships as close as the historical relationship of Judaism with Yahweh, or even as blood relatives, might gain very little.

Chapter 4

The series of parables given in chapter four were important in Jesus' public ministry, but Mark gathered them together for what they said to the situation of his readers. The parable of the sower (4:1-9) fits the agricultural practices of Palestine. Unlike American planting methods where the ground is prepared in the spring when moisture is present and then planted, Palestinian practice in the time of Jesus would be almost the opposite. Seed was scattered throughout a field in the fall, then lightly plowed to cover the seed, and left until the winter rains started the growing process. In scattering the seed on all the fertile soil, some seed would get on the path or too close to the briars to grow well. An area of shallow soil might be planted and produce during a wet winter but might die out if the rains were interrupted by dry periods occurring during the winter. Therefore, a farmer could not expect that every seed would produce a stalk of grain with, perhaps, thirty new seeds which could be harvested from it.

The conclusion of the sower parable is in the yield which could be expected. When Jesus mentioned a thirty-fold yield, he sounded like a city dweller to Palestinian ears since that yield would require almost complete germination and growth with no losses. When Jesus said sixty-fold or a hundred-fold, the hearers knew it was a parable that carried some other meaning than raising barley or wheat. The original setting could well have been a response to how Jesus as a King David-style messiah was going to free Palestine from Roman rule with such a small group of followers. The parable indicated that it would be done with Divine rather than only normal human power. Jewish expectations were that the messiah was a sign that God would provide a victory over foreign rulers, not that the messiah would provide it.

Mark's explanation that parables might not be easily understood (4:10-12) has the appearance of a deliberate attempt to hide the meaning from the people as a whole. The nature of a parable is that it points beyond the actual language and might not be understood easily or immediately. To accept what appears to be an obvious meaning is to miss the real message. What is being addressed is the "mystery of the kingdom of God"[21] which is not easy to grasp. The Roman Christians had not attempted to see the deeper meaning of the mystery of relationship with Christ in the time of the persecution. Now they must read these stories once more to "see and see again" in order to gain the meaning of salvation. Mark reminded his readers that these stories were known by them, but they had to turn them over in their minds again to find an application for their problems in Rome under Nero.

The explanation of the sower (4:13-20) is usually considered to be a later teaching by the Church rather than an explanation by Jesus. Almost certainly the disciples asked for explanations of the teachings of Jesus in the evening as they dined together or afterwards. These kinds of explanations would have been used to apply the teachings of Jesus to new or at least non-Palestinian problems as the Church spread.

What is given here may be explanatory material started by Jesus and modified over time to clarify the meaning. Mark may have added words or phrases such as "or some persecution on account of the word" (4:17) to apply it directly to the Roman readers. However, the meaning could be to remind Mark's readers that the parables have their importance only when disciples look beyond the initial words and make the application to themselves. The message had come to them but their own situation – on the edge of the field, on patches of rock, among the thorns – made it difficult to see the full meaning. Yet, they had been faithful in the time of trial and a great yield would come of it, in the form of salvation, even though questions remained.

What follows is a series of short parables (4:21-32) which, with the sower parable, would speak to Mark's readers. In the public life of Jesus, the parable of the lamp probably meant that hiding revelation, as the Jews did from the Gentiles, meant that they robbed even themselves of the full light. Light can never be saved by covering the source of the light with a basket. It must be allowed to shine to everyone in order for anyone to gain a benefit.

The measure of grain parable is a teaching that everyone is judged as they themselves judge. The same basket is used to measure what is sold and what is purchased back. To use a smaller basket to short the buyer would result in a loss to the seller when he refills his inventory.

The parable of the seed growing by itself points to the need for starting the process of growth by planting and, if done, the process will complete itself under God's plan. Certainly the mustard seed points out that small human input does not describe the full result of any action of a disciple.

For Jesus' listeners in Palestine, the parables point out that the kingdom is different from what was expected by the Jews and the result greater than the human effort expended. If Jesus had only a few followers, that small number said nothing about what God can accomplish.

Mark's situation is quite different as the Roman Christians think about the persecution they had just endured. They were persecuted because they were Christians; their own witness of Christ marked them as victims. Almost certainly, they must have quickly realized that witnessing in public, especially before Roman authorities, was best avoided. Witnessing before other Christians might be beneficial for maintaining morale, but what good could come of trying to change the mind of the persecutors who perhaps were already condemned because they would reject Christ. Such witness would only bring the death of the person witnessing. How little good could possibly result from the tiny efforts of members of the small Christian community against Roman power? Yet Jesus' revelation was for the whole world and neither the Jews nor the Romans had the right to restrict the witness from some people who were judged to be unacceptable by the disciples.

The parable of the sower would contradict the conclusions that some should not receive the witness by reminding the Roman readers that Jesus' command was for the entire field to be sown, even the unlikely places for growth (4:1-9). Wouldn't the Roman disciples recognize that when the message of salvation was only given within Judaism, many Romans of Gentile origin would have been the most unlikely places for the message to be proclaimed? It may not have been the clearest meaning thirty-five years earlier when Jesus spoke or in the original proclamation of the parable in Rome. However, in Nero's time, this is how it could be perceived and understood in its hearing.

Witnessing only within the Christian community was described as putting a basket over the lamp of faith in the same way Judaism hid revelation (4:21-23). If the meaning of salvation was in living a discipleship that brought the message to the whole world, anyone who restricted the message to some could hardly claim to be living discipleship. To judge that the persecutor could not be saved was to reject God's plan of offering salvation to everyone. Such a rejection of God's way could bring the same judgment on oneself as in the measure of grain (4:24-25). It is true that persecution brought death in some cases, but if the word of God was planted by the witness, the process of salvation was started (4:26-29). It was not just the smallness of human witness that describes the result but the greatness of God's plan that grows from it (4:30-32).

The Roman Christians must see through the first layer of meaning expounded on the Palestinian hillsides by Jesus and grasp the deeper layer as Jesus' words spoke to their own situation. The repetition about those having ears should listen (4:9, 23) may be Mark's addition to drive the point home to those with Roman ears. Yet, it sounds like words Jesus would use to Jewish listeners and fits the Isaiah quotation (4:10-12).

In closing this section, Mark included the miracle of the calming of the storm to drive his point home more directly. He made it less a miracle event and more of a teaching. As the storm raged, Jesus slept, just as there appeared to be no answer to Roman prayers during the persecution. With what appears to be almost a Roman voice, the disciples in the boat asked Jesus, "Do you not care that we are going down?" The meaning to the Romans was that they were going to die. Jesus finally arose and calmed the storm just as the persecution fury was calmed with the death of Nero, which was God's action in Roman eyes.

Jesus asked his disciples and the Roman ones, "Why were you so frightened? How is it you have no faith?" The Lord can control all storms and can surely remove a single ruler if that is necessary. The death of Nero in 68 cancelled the edict of persecution, and how difficult was that for God to arrange? Faith is required for difficult times. The disciples, filled with awe, say to one another, "Who can this be? Even the wind and sea obey him." They have begun to realize there is something different here and after looking at the meaning of the persecution, the Roman disciples should do the same. Just as the kingdom was different from what the first disciples understood, so was persecution different from what the Romans first understood in the time of Nero.

Chapter 5

Jesus' venture into Gerasene country (5:1-20) was a visit to Gentiles in a non-Jewish area or an unclean land. He had control in those areas, even in the place of the dead, a place unclean according to the Law. Finally, the man he was to cure was under the control of an unclean spirit. The use of the name "Legion" for evil spirits reminded the Romans of who was in charge of the persecution and suggests the term was added for Rome especially. Jesus could still control such evil even when it was great enough to take over the exceedingly large herd of swine.

In Jewish lands, Jesus ordered silence about his actions since the Jewish understanding of messiah was so tied to a new King David that the actions would be misunderstood if made public. However, among the Gentiles, such as at Rome, his directions were, "Go home to your people and tell them all the Lord has done for you." The newest disciple witnessed to others throughout the Decapolis and the Roman disciples should do the same in their land.

The stories of Jairus' daughter and the woman with a hemorrhage (5:21-43) seem folded together by Mark to give a meaning which is greater than in treating them as separate events. It is possible that the two events were intertwined from the start, but Mark has a technique of inserting one story into another, and so the meaning should be found in the relationship of the two rather than in ignoring the connection. The double miracle is a teaching about faith.

Jairus, as a synagogue official, would be expected to be skeptical of Jesus. If the Pharisees opposed Jesus, it would be politically wise for a synagogue official to do the same. However, his daughter was dying and he recognized it. Therefore, he must judge Jesus on the basis of the signs and, in doing so, recognized he was from God. Only God, the owner of life, could keep his daughter from death, and so Jairus made the faith decision that Jesus could act for God here on earth. He accepted the reality of Jesus and the signs of his public ministry, and his life changed because he accepted.

The woman with the hemorrhage treated Jesus more as someone who had magic power. Her faith did not require full acceptance of Jesus or a change in life. Her view only required that she make contact with a somewhat magical power and it might bring results for her ailment. In fact, any faith and contact with the Lord is rewarded and she gained the relief she desired. Jairus, on the other hand, with his more complete faith which caused him to change his life, received the gift of his daughter's life. All faith is rewarded, but complete faith brings life, the resurrection.

Chapter 6

In Nazareth (6:1-6), however, Jesus worked no miracles even though he cured a few people (similar, perhaps, to the woman with a hemorrhage) because he found so little faith. The plan of God is carried out by those who through faith accept Jesus as the Lord of their lives, rather than someone who can bring about preconceived ideas of kingdom. Least important of all would be only belonging to a people with a history of relationship with God. That relationship would count for little if salvation comes from accepting a new revelation.

If the Romans wondered about the result of Judaism not accepting the Messiah, they would have understood that salvation comes on the basis of who has faith, not who had a religious history with the Messiah. The great result did not come from knowing about Jesus in the collections of stories about him or in the faith that accompanied baptism before the persecution. When their faith reached the level where they changed their lives or even lost them, they would be blessed with the resurrection.

Sending out the Twelve to preach (6:7-13) and the death of John the Baptist (6:14-29) are also related, even though the connection occurs in verse 30 where the return of the Twelve is later recorded. The mission of the Twelve is similar to the ministry of John the Baptist in that they preached repentance throughout the land. The disciples went without preparation and accepted what came to them just as John seemed to have done. John the Baptist was imprisoned and finally beheaded because he had spoken his simple message of repentance to everyone, including important officials

whose lives were not turned toward God. He witnessed even
in a situation that was at least as dangerous as witnessing to a
centurion in Rome.

The inter-tie between the two readings suggests that the
Apostles would have recognized the similarity and could have
expected the same result for their work. It could be concluded that the persecution of Nero and the death of Peter and
Paul, especially Paul who like John the Baptist was beheaded,
should not have been a surprise to disciples and, to some
extent, should have been expected. The Romans should
have recognized that such a result, being close to the type of
witness suffered by Jesus, was a sign of the kingdom, not of its
failure.

Jesus' multiplication of loaves (6:31-44) is the great
Christian miracle of the early Church, the only miracle
account found in all four Gospels. Those who follow Jesus
looking for life will be fed this meal of bread and ichthus or
fish. However, the small dried fish that would likely be available was called opsarion. Ichthus is a word for a live fish and
has its strong Christian connection because its Greek letters
were used as the initials for "Jesus Christ, Son of God,
Savior." The line drawing of a fish became a widely recognized Christian symbol. As a meal then, of "bread" and
"Christ," the event is identified with the Eucharist in
Christian tradition. The language of the story supports this
Eucharistic description with Jesus' actions being a prayer,
blessing and breaking of the bread, and its distribution, the
same actions as that of the celebrant in a Eucharistic liturgy.

Commentaries on this passage often have a tendency to
explain away the miracle as a distribution of a small amount
of bread as at communion or the sharing with everyone of
bread that was present among the crowd, rather than admit
that a ton of bread was produced, as the story requires. The
use of this story by all four Evangelists argues strongly against
any attempts to explain away the miracle. Its universal
acceptance speaks for an early and widespread telling of the
story when it would have been impossible to either invent a

miracle of such a magnitude or change the details of an important event. The early availability of 5,000 witnesses for the story more than offsets the modern tendency to explain away miracles. This is the Jesus the Roman disciples knew from the Eucharist. This is the food they always have for the real life they were now living and it can never be brought by them in knapsacks.

Following the feeding of the multitudes is the walking on water event (6:45-52) which probably was especially important to Jewish disciples. Water is viewed in the Old Testament as something controllable only by God. The restless water had to be controlled for the land to appear in creation and again in the Exodus event for the rescue of the Israelites. The language of Jesus going to "pass them by" is similar to Yahweh's instructions on Mt. Sinai (Ex 33:22) where the splendor of God will "pass by" Moses. Jesus' response, "It is I," is literally "I Am" ("ego eimi" in Greek), the name of God revealed on Mt. Sinai (Ex 3:14). So there is a unity between the Old and New Testament images of covenant in the two stories which shows up when the Greek text is used for both Testaments. For Mark's readers, this would give an emphasis on the divine presence in the kingdom work of the disciples.

It is likely that these two stories already were attached before they were used by Mark. The feeding in a desert place through the multiplication of loaves also has a tie to the manna supplied in the desert after the Exodus event, which complements the control over the water theme. In John's Gospel, which comes from an independent source, the two miracles are combined which was not necessary for John's purpose. Even though there is a divinity connection in the use of "I Am" by Jesus, the conclusion at the time, and for the Romans, is that the disciples were "utterly and completely dumbfounded." A summary statement (6:53-56) has been used by Mark to close off this section just as he did earlier (3:7-12).

Chapter 7

A meal with Pharisees contrasts the reaction of those open to signs with the response of the religious authorities. What follows is not just a discussion about rules established by the Pharisees. Instead it is a question to the Romans asking if they too had been caught up in minor issues rather than seeing the more important meaning of Jesus' message (7:1-23). No matter how great and widely recognized the signs were that Jesus worked, the religious authorities worried about the detail of rules associated with the Law. Jesus' response to scruples concerning the details of washing fruit and one's hands was to compare such minor practices with the major failure of the authorities in keeping the basic commandments of the Law.

The corban issue (7:11) allowed the use of a gross distortion of a commandment which called on everyone to be responsible to one's parents. The ruse of dedicating one's wealth to religious use in the temple but retaining the right to use it personally was simply a means of gaining a short-term personal advantage. The one who dedicated the wealth could use it during life, but the residual would remain in the temple treasury when the dedicator died. To allow other than personal use of wealth would be seen as removing something from the temple because it reduced the final residual. Clearly the intent is to have a means of denying aid to one's parents.

The following discussion on food laws was taken to be an official setting aside of the theory of unclean foods (7:14-23). That may have been a conclusion added by Mark or an early explanation that worked its way into the basic story but it clearly is not from Jesus. As Jesus originally spoke, this story was probably an explanation of how one must go beyond simple regulations to fulfill the Law completely. Bringing the divine relationship into life involves more than simple restrictions on what humans might determine is incompatible with the very covenant which produced the relationship. The kingdom brings a different understanding of life and religion. During the persecution Mark's readers had seen a difference so great they had difficulty accepting it, yet the message had been given earlier to people who could not make the change necessary to accept it.

With the account of the healing of the Syrophoenician woman's daughter (7:24-30), Jesus moved out of Palestine to a more Gentile area which we call southern Lebanon today. The Syrophoenician designation would be necessary for Roman readers since the Phoenicians also inhabited Carthage and the coast of Tunisia. Those would be the Phoenicians known to Rome without the added distinction. Mark may have included these accounts to address questions about the possible need for Gentiles to become Jews when accepting the Messiah or the possibility that a Christian opening to Gentiles occurred only after the failure to fully convert Judaism. The stories tend to show that even in the public life of Jesus, the Christian message was directed partly toward Gentiles.

A problem with the account of the Syrophoenician woman whose daughter had an ailment is the use of the term "dogs" to designate Gentiles. Often the term is softened to "house dogs" or even "puppies." However, the harshness of the term "dogs" should be retained. In Palestine, as in Arab areas of the Middle East today, dogs are often wild scavengers rather than pets. Feeding in garbage dumps, they are often diseased, and would be an example of being unclean and causing the land to be unclean, just as the Jews thought of Gentiles.

The woman asked for the Messiah to help her, but Jesus responded by reminding her of the Jewish understanding. Her response has the tone of "I did not ask because I am so great, but because you are great." She had judged on the basis of the signs rather than Jewish tradition and, in doing so, saw more than anyone else. She claimed no position with regard to the Messiah, but responded from a position of faith and gained healing for her daughter. The cure was done at a distance rather than by the Lord actually coming to the daughter. The people of Rome who also were distant in both space and time from the public life of Jesus would recognize that Jesus would reach out to them when they were beset by evil forces.

The healing of the deaf man (7:31-37) occurred after a return to the Decapolis region, a Gentile area southeast of the Sea of Galilee. It should be paired with the cure of the blind man at Bethsaida (8:22-26). The coming of the Messiah was foretold by Isaiah (35:5-6) as a time when the deaf hear, the dumb speak and the blind see. This prophecy was fulfilled in this pair of events done among both Jews and Gentiles. If the prophecy to Israel also related to Gentiles, then surely the plan of God from the start must be for the Messiah to bring a new relationship with God to all people, including Roman Gentiles.

Chapter 8

A second multiplication of loaves is recorded among Gentiles as well (8:1-10). It is difficult to determine if this is a repetition of the original or if it is simply a different tradition relating to a single event. The second multiplication is not recorded in the Gospels of Luke or John, and the Matthew version is taken from Mark rather than supporting a second event. However, Matthew had no reason to include the second account if his own sources did not include it. The clear intent of Mark is to show that the cornerstone of unity between Gentile disciples and Christ in the Eucharist has its roots in Jesus' public life rather than something added later to the Christian understanding.

The multitude was made up of people who had been with Jesus three days (the period in the tomb and, therefore, after the Resurrection), had come from a great distance (incorporating the faraway Romans), and had seven loaves to start and seven baskets of fragments afterward. The seven tends to relate to the special disciples chosen in the early Church to minister to the Greek-speaking Church (Acts 6). There are fewer people in this feeding (4,000) than in the first (5,000). Yet, that is a significant number and may be an indication of the relative numbers of Gentile and Jewish Christians in Mark's Church or in Christianity as a whole when Mark is writing. However, there is little about the account relating to Gentile Christians except that it is placed in a section of the Gospel relating to Gentiles.

Pharisees representing Jewish religious authorities (8:11-21) witnessed nothing but great signs from Jesus and, yet, they requested a sign before accepting Jesus as the Messiah. The question of the Roman Christians about how the message came to them while not being accepted by Judaism was answered in their exchange. Those open to the message of the Messiah accepted it from the first, but some who would not accept the signs also were present. For Rome at the time of Mark, Jesus seemed to be saying, do not ask for more signs as if that were a substitute for faith. Understand the signs already given, make a faith decision from that, and live that faith even if difficulties come. The signs may be very valuable in order to start the faith decision, but the true response results from a life in Christ rather than a full understanding of everything which occurs in life.

The cure of the blind man (8:22-26) provided a different view since being illuminated is a characterization of baptism. Even those who have had their eyes opened may not see everything clearly at once. The questions raised by the Roman Christians were indicative of the process of growing in faith rather than a failure. Then, to underscore such a conclusion, Mark returned to the original disciples who had lived with the Lord, witnessed the signs, and had been the recipients of special explanations. How well did they understand the full meaning of the Messiah when they were with him in his public life?

The questioning of the Apostles and Peter's confession of faith (8:27-30) answers the initial question of the Gospel of who is this Jesus. Peter proclaimed, as spokesman for them all, "You are the Messiah." He was told by Jesus not to tell anyone since, even though he knew the correct answer, he did not understand what the term Messiah meant for Jesus.

The second question, which opens the second half of the writing, is precisely that: What does this Messiahship mean?

An answer to the question is given immediately (8:31-33). It means that Jesus will be rejected by the religious authorities, suffer and die, and then rise again. Peter displayed his misunderstanding by seemingly trying to correct Jesus' conclusion. It could be assumed that Peter attempted to reassure Jesus that, far from being rejected, he would be welcomed in Jerusalem. There he would be crowned as a new King David, as the type of messiah expected by Jews. With divine assistance, the expected clearing of the land of foreign rule would be successful. Peter had accepted the Jewish concept of messiah completely and had interpreted the signs as a confirmation of that view.

Jesus rebuked Peter severely in front of the other disciples and, through Mark, in front of the Roman Christians who had accepted Peter as their leader and had witnessed his martyrdom for being a loyal disciple of Jesus. Surely, Peter knowing the answer to Jesus' question but not knowing the real meaning of the answer, or even accepting Jesus' response at that time, tells the Roman readers to look more deeply for their own answers.

Five great sayings of the Church are then included (8:34-9:1). Everyone reading this Gospel would know and accept these sayings and, yet, Mark may be showing that even the most straight-forward of the sayings would not have been understandable at the time of Jesus. A follower taking up his cross (8:34) was the opposite of Peter's understanding. Crucifixion was the Roman punishment for sedition, and to be on the cross could only mean that an uprising had failed. It could be interpreted as meaning that God had not supported the Messiah. Losing one's life for the Gospel (8:35) would also be without meaning before the Resurrection. There was no Gospel before then except in the life of Jesus and that Good News would be associated with success, not losing one's life. Gaining the whole world (8:36-37) was hardly a consideration since the expectation of a King David-style messiah

was to free Palestine. The goal was to make it a Jewish homeland and separate it from the world rather than make the
world a goal for the kingdom. Instead of a generation
ashamed of Jesus (8:38), Peter was saying the opposite. This
generation wanted a Messiah, and they were proud he came
in their time. Yet, the meaning of the one who came was not
the meaning of the one expected.

Chapter 9
Finally, those who would not see death until the coming
of the kingdom (9:1) was the basis for a Second Coming
expectation to occur while the disciples lived. Peter had just
been martyred along with Paul in Nero's persecution and,
perhaps, nearly all of the original disciples were dead. For
Roman Christians, this seemed to mean that the kingdom
had failed because the Second Coming had not occurred.
Mark told them that the kingdom had not been understandable for the first disciples either, and the Roman Christians
should reexamine what was really meant by the kingdom and
not use the old understanding.
One could argue that the last saying is incorrect or that
Jesus was wrong in this saying. However, the clear alternative
is that the time of waiting was over because the start of the
kingdom had already occurred and had not been recognized.
Mark's conclusion, later reinforced in Luke's Gospel, was that
the kingdom had already been established and the Second
Coming would be a judgment at the end of the world (Mk
13:24-32). The Roman Christians should not have been
waiting for nearly forty years for a Second Coming, but
should have been expanding the kingdom already formed.

JOURNEY TO JERUSALEM

The journey to Jerusalem is known as "the Way" or the
journey with the Lord. It is presented by Mark as the time of
Jesus teaching disciples and, therefore, directed at Roman

disciples in the Gospel. Since the destination is Jerusalem and the cross, it gives emphasis to persecution as being something disciples should expect. There are a few notations by Mark that indicate a journey that ends in Jericho and Jerusalem. Otherwise, the journey is about discipleship with no other indications of an actual itinerary.

The Transfiguration event must have been seen as an opportunity to give a clear understanding of the Messiah (9:2-13). Jesus is shown with the prophets of the Old Testament who brought a dramatic change in relationship with Yahweh. Yet Peter did not know what to do or say about it and coming down the mountain all the participants were quite ready to keep quiet about the event. It may seem to be a means of producing a clearer understanding in the early Church, but its place in Mark's Gospel would indicate it too was subject to misunderstanding. This event also might point toward a Divine Jesus. However, Jesus also seems to have an equality with Moses and Elijah who were chosen by God but were only human. The disciples coming down the mountain were puzzled about the "rising from the dead" and they were not sure about the signs that would proceed the coming of the Messiah. The question asked is: Should the Roman Christians worry about their own questions when the original disciples who were closest to the revelation of the Messiah also were bothered by misunderstanding?

At the foot of the mountain, the remaining disciples fared no better. A father's plea for a cure of his epileptic son (9:14-26) could not be granted by the disciples through their own or the father's faith. Jesus would expel the evil spirit only after making it clear that it is through the faith of the boy's father that help would be given.

Gifts cannot come from God without human acceptance, yet the ability of the disciples to cast out evil depended on prayer. The power of prayer is the power of a connection to God. Divine power is not put under the absolute control of the disciples to use as they please. Rather, it comes through disciples who act as a pipeline for transmission of

God's power rather than as independent operators. A life of prayer is the necessary means of retaining the connection. It is essential to living that connection. There could be no better starting point for disciples than prayer.

As Jesus started for Jerusalem (9:30-32), the journey included teachings on how Jesus reacted to situations that arose, and disciples should imitate his responses in their own situations. Jesus gave a second prophecy concerning Jerusalem but the disciples missed the warning completely and were afraid to even question what Jesus meant by the prophecy. Probably they were not interested in being corrected as Peter had been earlier.

The fact of a foretelling of Jesus' suffering and death must have been known by the Roman Christians, and they knew that their relationship to Jesus was as the Body of Christ. Yet they never asked if that meant they would experience the same. They were surprised by Nero as the first disciples were surprised by the passion and death. Each could have averted such surprises by examining Jesus' view of the Messiah. The Roman Christians had stayed with a Second Coming-type of kingly messiah just as the Apostles with Jesus had retained the King David-style messiah. The teachings of Jesus pointed in a different way for both groups.

The disciple's discussion of who was the greatest (9:33-37) comes from their concept of messiah and kingdom. If they thought of a royal kingdom, they may have wondered how the positions of importance would be divided among them. Based on their own abilities and skills, they could have made arguments about why each deserved a particular position. Jesus' argument about one-like-a-child being the greatest is not an argument against the line of reasoning of the disciples, but an attempt to explain the different concept of kingdom. Being a servant in a kingdom was not what the disciples desired or expected as early followers of the Messiah.

Relating to others who accepted the Messiah in their own way (9:38-41) produced difficulties for the disciples.

Others who changed their lives in response to Jesus would be welcomed in the early Church. However, at this point, such followers may have looked like competition for the best positions. Anyone who turned toward the Lord should be seen as a supporter of the kingdom even though suspicions toward less orthodox responses would be a historical problem for Christians. However, anyone who tries to put on the life of Christ in even the simplest way would "not lose his reward" (9:41).

Obstacles to spiritual growth (9:42-50) were to be dealt with in a way that might not have been as dramatic as giving up life, limbs or eyes. Perhaps the Aramaic language of the original carried the concept of overreaction due to its own limitations in addressing such problems. However, Mark's Roman readers had accepted Jesus as the Messiah, and the ones reading this Gospel writing had persisted in their beliefs during a persecution when such persistence carried the risk of great suffering and death. So this reminder that said if one came down to the choice between eternal reward with the loss of a limb or an eye or the keeping of limbs and eyes but no eternal reward, surely the choice would be the eternal reward. Those who had not survived the persecution had carried the choice further to include life itself. So, as difficult as the choice may seem in the crude language of this pericope, the Christian does make the choice of the living relationship with Christ as most important of all alternatives. The early understanding of baptism was the act of going down into the tomb with Christ and giving up this life and rising up to put on the life of Christ (Rom 6:3-4). The disciple should see that if such an understanding is lived out, a disciple has already made the choice of giving up this life. Persecution was difficult to accept, until the option of no reward is faced, and then the Romans would see suffering in a different light.

Chapter 10

A divorce question (10:1-12) seems to interrupt Mark's discussion of discipleship. It is almost as if he decided something should be said about marriage to the Romans and this was as good a place as any to do just that. The real meaning was probably a way of putting the chosen life with God into a familiar context rather than to say anything specific about marriage. The marriage vow does not just tie two people together, but it makes their lives one. The annihilation of that united life by divorce brings death if divorce means adultery since that is expressly condemned in the Decalogue. The life of baptism is the same; it is a life we have chosen, because it is eternal. To later reject the life is quite possible, but then the person retains only a very temporary life on earth. A separation from eternal life is the complete death.

The statement about children (10:13-16) continued this theme from a different viewpoint. A child can never earn anything, but is willing to simply accept what is given. The life of baptism must be accepted in the same way as a gift from God that is clearly given, but cannot be earned. Mark's community may have questioned a gift they did not understand, but in accepting the gift, the plan of God was fulfilled.

Sometimes this section is seen as a defense of the practice of baptizing children. Jesus did not baptize others so there would be no direct basis in his public life for that practice. The baptism language here of not hindering, putting arms around them, laying on hands, and blessing them could be interpreted as baptism and used for justifying such a practice. Such an interpretation may have been related to the account, but in Mark's Gospel it would seem that it relates to accepting and living the free gift of eternal life.

The rich young man (10:17-22) did not raise a Jewish question about inheriting eternal life, since he would know the answer would be to keep the Law. Wealth was considered a sign of being rewarded for living a good life. A rich person would seem to be the sign of salvation already given since he was rewarded so well. Jesus gave the Jewish answer in mentioning the commandments because that answer is to keep the Law which defined the relationship with God. However, the man had kept them and also had wealth, so he seemed to want to go beyond the Law in approaching God. Jesus' answer, which was to give up the very signs of divine reward, was shocking to those who heard Jesus advise the giving up of gifts from God rather than using them to witness. The choice would be difficult, also, for anyone who wanted ties to the world and had accepted discipleship with the Lord.

This section brings up a situation of calling Jesus "good" while Jesus' response is that only God is good. Here is a case where the divinity question is raised and Jesus responds in a way that gives a negative reply. It would not seem that Jesus' Divinity was understood by Mark, or at least by the original recorder of the account.

The disciples were astounded by Jesus' teaching on wealth (10:23-31). Their desire for a high position in an earthly kingdom may have been shown in their lack of acceptance. If the rich young man was asked to give up everything to follow the Messiah, what could it mean to those who already followed him? The separation between heaven and wealth probably does not condemn the affluent of this world so much as it condemns the concept that earthly reward reflects spiritual accomplishment. Yet, the subject returns to the nature of the spiritual life. The disciple must actually choose a life with Christ, but to retain that spiritual life, that life must be lived.

Those who choose wealth in this life, especially the ones who dedicate their lives to earning wealth, have chosen something different from the life of Christ. On the other hand, disciples who have given up the rewards of this life or are willing to do so in choosing the Lord, gain a reward of eternal life in heaven. God seems to grant whatever life is chosen. Perhaps Mark added a reminder about persecution (10:30), since Jesus' life included persecutions and they may be part of the life chosen by the true disciples.

Just how the disciples related these teachings to the journey at hand and a third prophecy of the passion and death in Jerusalem (10:32-34) are the subjects of the next section. The disciples were again considering who would gain the most important positions in a royal kingdom (10:35-40). James and John seemed willing to accept any sacrifices, which they imagined likely with the Messiah, to gain the seats of greatest power among his followers.

The Roman readers recognized the humor in Mark's placement of this story. They too had said "Yes, Lord" when discipleship seemed to mean little chance of loss and a great opportunity to be on the bandwagon before a Second Coming that was expected early. Now the Roman readers knew what was in the "Lord's cup" and were fighting a confusion of their own. Yet, the Roman disciples were making the choice anew and were repeating the "Yes, Lord" with conviction. The seating arrangements in the eternal kingdom seemed different from what the early disciples expected.

Those who complained that James and John had attempted to upstage them (10:41-45) received a lesson just as confusing. In their minds, people attempted to gain the important seats in order to be served. It is from those seats that the occupants had the power to "lord it over" the others in the kingdom. Jesus seems to use language that misunderstands the situation. The disciples echoed the protest among the Romans: Why should anyone witness in public to show the kingdom to the Roman officials who persecuted anyone identified as a Christian? The first disciples did not understand the meaning of these teachings before the Resurrection nor did the Roman disciples before the persecution.

At Jericho a blind beggar, so poor he didn't even have a name of his own, called out for a Jewish messiah (10:46-52), "Son of David," who as a royal messiah would be what the disciples of Jesus expected. When he was brought before Jesus, he asked for sight, the sign of baptism, indicating he recognized that Jesus brought more than what would come from a royal messiah. When he received his sight, he became a disciple, a follower of Jesus. The son of Timaeus had chosen correctly because he was blind to everything else. This is the end of the discipleship instruction which shows how a disciple should see the world and respond to the Lord.

THE JERUSALEM MINISTRY

Chapter 11

This section which maintains a connection to Jerusalem is more of a conclusion than a chronological continuation of the first ten chapters, with chapter thirteen being a special summary statement. Mark's composition ends as his collection of stories and teachings connect to the preexisting passion and death narrative. Jerusalem is the place of the Temple, the spot where Yahweh dwells on earth. In Jewish understanding it is the center of the universe. Yahweh visits the chosen people especially in Jerusalem. Therefore, for Jesus to address the Jewish people about a relationship with Yahweh means it must occur at a meeting in Jerusalem. Any place else could be seen as a relationship in opposition to Yahweh.

Jesus' entry into Jerusalem (11:1-11) was by riding on a donkey, rather than as a pilgrim on foot. For so long Jesus had separated himself from any messianic identification, but in Jerusalem he proclaimed his difference. For this meeting he came as Messiah; what had been hidden would now be made clear to the disciples and everyone. However, the welcome was in the form of the title "one who comes in the name of the Lord," which expressed the understanding that the people expected a King David-style messiah.

Jesus' return to the Temple the following day was told in one of Mark's insertion stories where the cleansing of the Temple is contained within two parts of a barren fig tree parable (11:13-25). The fig tree with no fruit out of season was condemned by Jesus without explanation. The expulsion of those who provided birds, animals and proper coins for sacrifices and gifts is often seen as an equating of such business with a "robber's den." The real meaning is quite different since a robber's den is not a place of robbery, but a place of refuge where robbers go after committing a crime, where they are safe from legal justice.

In the book of Jeremiah (7:1-11) the religious authorities of Jerusalem were condemned for not following the Law.

They believed that Yahweh's promise to David that his sovereignty would always be secure (2 Sam 7:16) meant that Jerusalem would never be conquered. Jeremiah accused them of acting with impunity against the Law because they feared no punishment so long as they were in the Temple, which they called the Sanctuary of Yahweh. That was misleading to the people of Jerusalem at the time. The temple leaders should have been calling for a return to living the covenant relationship but failed to do so. They used the Temple as a false haven from punishment for their failure or, in the words spoken by Jeremiah, "a robber's den." The meaning of Jesus' condemnation in Jerusalem in Mark's Gospel was not focused on the sellers of animals for sacrifice or those exchanging one currency for another. It was on the Jewish leaders who promoted the practices that required the sellers instead of looking for the true relationship.

The withered fig tree that did not produce became a symbol for the temple leaders. They had the duty to recognize the Messiah and to interpret the early prophecies about the Messiah to the people at the time of the coming. Their season to produce fruit was not determined by the time of the year but the time of the coming of the Messiah. They were more concerned with the protection of a temple building than in the message from Yahweh and, in being that way, emulated the priests of Jeremiah's time. The Roman readers may have recognized that their own interpretation of the mission of the Messiah was concerned only with waiting for a Second Coming and not the real message of spreading the kingdom. Therefore, the story is not simply included by Mark to condemn Jewish leaders, but to correct similar faults among Christians. Christians live in the season of the Lord; they are called to always bear fruit.

The remainder of the Jerusalem ministry continues this theme. Jesus confronted each group of religious leaders individually and found them wanting. They had not recognized the Messiah because they had not understood the Scriptures. Judaism's failure to fully accept Jesus as the Messiah relates to the failure of the Jewish authorities to accept a revelation which would move their relationship with Yahweh beyond the Law.

A conflict with the chief priests, scribes and elders (11:27-12:12) started the parade of confrontations. The leaders wanted to know the authority for the teaching of Jesus. A prophet would be the most direct authority for any new teaching from God to Judaism with the signs of Jesus being confirmation of the divine message. The leaders refused to accept John the Baptist as a prophet since it would have required them to change their position as ultimate religious authorities of the nation, the Scriptures, and the synagogues. Yet, if they did not accept the witness of a special prophet or the signs, there would be no answer for their questions.

Chapter 12

The parable of the wicked tenants of the vineyard illustrated the position of the leaders (12:1-12). Anyone who completely and deliberately failed to produce when given a responsibility would lose their position. The parable said that if the leader's actions were opposite of their responsibilities, they would have lost their opportunity to carry out the responsibilities in the kingdom at a later date. They would be swept aside in the same way as those who misused their positions in the vineyard.

A second group being addressed consists of Pharisees and Herodians (12:13-17). Since Herodians would have authority only in Galilee and on the other side of the Jordan River in Perea, this episode would more likely have occurred outside of Jerusalem. It tends to show Mark's use of accounts concerning all groups of authorities who rejected Jesus as the Messiah in composing the Jerusalem ministry, rather than presenting an actual description of Jesus' time in Jerusalem.

Since the Pharisees represent strict religious interpreters and Herodians represent civil power, the conflict over paying Roman taxes presented a lose-lose situation for Jesus. If he advised the payment of taxes, the Pharisees would say Jesus supported foreign occupation of the land given by Yahweh to the Jews and, therefore, was a traitor rather than the Messiah. If Jesus said not to pay, the Herodians might arrest him for opposing civil rule. Jesus responded by obtaining a coin of tribute from his opponents. The interpretation of his request was that the one whose image was on the coin was considered to be the owner of the coin, and whoever used the coin would accept the sovereignty of the owner. In providing the coin, the Pharisees and Herodians had acknowledged Caesar as ruler of Jewish lands and insulted themselves before the crowd. The account showed Mark's readers that the opponents of Jesus were not acting as Jewish leaders in their means of opposing him.

A meeting with the Sadducees (12:18-27), the only meeting of Jesus with them recorded in the Gospels, must have taken place in Jerusalem. They were temple-oriented and would not have been gathered officially elsewhere. Since the Sadducees tended to accept as authoritative only the Torah, or first five books of the Old Testament, their question and a response by Jesus must be framed in that context.

The question involves a silly extension of the Levirate marriage regulation of a childless widow marrying brothers of her husband to gain a child in his name and its effect on a life-after-death relationship (Dt 25:5-10). A less extended situation was possible and perhaps known at the time of the question. Yet the Law of Moses was intended to cover every situation of human life. Not finding anything about an after-life resolution in the Law to the question at hand would imply no afterlife or resurrection, which was the position of the Sadducees. Jesus' response of an Old Testament quote (Ex 3:6), which had its real meaning in a different context, was an acceptable way to use Scripture and the Sadducees were defeated.

In the period immediately after the Resurrection, Jesus is shown as being beyond the Law and, therefore, beyond Moses. Because he was raised to life by God while under the Law, he could not be seen as cursed by being crucified (Dt 21:22-23). This story would illustrate Jesus' teaching of being beyond the Law at an early date. In Mark's time, the teaching would be used to show that different meanings could come even from Scripture. Therefore, taking a single teaching of the early Church, such as the Second Coming, could easily produce a limited understanding.

Lastly, Jesus confronted the scribes (12:28-44) who should have been the most knowledgeable about the Old Testament writings, yet are shown to misunderstand their own specialty. The question about the greatest command-ment is answered from the opening verse of the Shema (Dt 6:4-5), a prayer which every Jew recited daily. The experts seemed to have missed the most obvious answer which was known to everyone. On the other hand, Jesus quoted from David (Ps 110:1) saying (in the Old Testament text), "Yahweh says to my Lord" indicating that the Messiah is above David in importance to the point that David would accept control of his own life from the Messiah by calling him Lord. Such an interpretation opens up a very different idea of Messiah from just a new King David, yet these scribes as experts had not grasped this meaning.

The scribes were then taken to task for not living out the second commandment of loving one's neighbor (Lv 19:19) used in their initial confrontation. Everyone was called upon to love their neighbor as self, and the scribes, who according to their position would know the meaning most clearly, should have been models in living out the com-mandment. However, their lifestyle was to live in a manner clearly above their neighbors and to treat the weakest mem-bers harshly, even extracting from the poor their last coins for the support of the temple organization. Yet the quote from the Law was the plainest evidence that the meaning of the covenant relationship went beyond even the temple func-tions and sacrifices (12:33). The Jewish acceptance of Jesus as the Messiah was stopped when his teachings seemed to infringe on the Law.

The conclusion for the Romans would have to be that the Jewish religious authorities failed in their greatest task of recognizing the Messiah, just as they did in the simplest and most easily understood directions spelled out in the Law. That the Jewish religious authorities are seen as rejecting Jesus as the Messiah was no basis for the Romans to doubt that Jesus was the Messiah or believe that his coming was intended only for the Jewish people. The meaning of the Messiah is lost to anyone who is not open to a very different relationship with God. It is shown in the stories as a failure within Judaism. However, those stories were included in the Gospel to show the Roman readers that their lack of understanding in the persecution of Nero was a result of not wanting to go beyond the Second Coming interpretation of Christianity.

Chapter 13

Chapter thirteen is the final section assembled by Mark to introduce the passion and death narrative. Like the Jerusalem ministry, it tends to be somewhat of a summary statement. However, its primary purpose was to clarify the Second Coming question. Was the kingdom supposed to start with a Second Coming of Jesus in person? Certainly that must have been a teaching of the post-Resurrection Church and those teachings seemed to emphasize that the Second Coming would be introduced and incorporated with some great signs and difficult times.

The difficulties of Nero's persecution triggered an expectation of the Second Coming and when the persecution passed without the occurrence of a coming, considerable doubts must have been raised among the Romans. Mark revisited some of the early Church statements of Jesus concerning the end times to show that in a more complete context a different picture would emerge.

Starting with the prophecy that the Temple would be destroyed (13:1-4), the four initial Apostles raised the question of the timing of the destruction and signs that would proceed it. Jesus' discourse on the end started by describing events that would occur before the end days. The description contained a list of events (13:5-10) which may have happened between the Resurrection and Mark's writing or could have occurred in any like period of time. It may have been even more than the readers had witnessed. The language probably would cover Nero's persecution and show that the end time, at least as it may have been associated with a Second Coming, had not occurred. The end would not occur until all the nations were evangelized (13:10).

Introducing a reference to a "disastrous abomination" as part of a particularly difficult time (13:14-23), Mark uses the image of profaning the Temple during the time of the Maccabees in 167 BC when the Syrians installed an idol of Zeus in the Temple. While the attempt of Emperor Caligula in 40 to install a statue of himself in the Temple also may be recalled, the overall language is from the book of Daniel, written in the 167-164 BC period.

The Daniel writing used language that could reflect the Babylonian destruction in 586 BC and would have been the natural source for Jesus to use if warning about a destruction. Nothing in the description would indicate that Mark was referring to the destruction of the Temple in 70 and, for Christianity, the description had no connection to putting down the Jewish revolt in 70. These texts could be seen as a warning by Jesus that such things were bound to happen, and they said nothing about the kingdom rather than being a prophecy of the Second Coming.

Finally, Jesus is quoted (13:24-27) concerning his coming as the Son of Man in the clouds of heaven which will come at some later date after the time of distress. The darkening of the sun and moon and falling of the stars is the time of the end of the world and final judgment rather than a Second Coming of Jesus to establish the kingdom. The conclusion to be drawn by the Roman readers is that what had occurred should not have suggested a Second Coming associated with the start up of the kingdom even though difficulties were witnessed in Nero's persecution. The failure of early Church expectations associated with Nero's persecution, or from any earlier problems, says nothing about a failure of Christianity.

The closing of the discourse (13:28-37) advises a reexamination of what had occurred and to reread the signs differently from the original Second Coming expectations. If Christians can figure out when summer is coming, they should figure out when the kingdom is to start. It would be before the generation with Jesus had passed away or, as a repeat of chapter 9:1, it had already started. Since the sun, moon and stars would still be present, there should be no waiting for Jesus' return to start the kingdom. Jesus' words are not going to change or be proven wrong. He never gave a time for the Second Coming because that time is known to "no one but the Father," not even to Jesus.

The instructions to disciples were to be alert and live each day as the last, rather than waiting for some last day to arrive. Salvation is to be found in a continuing union with Christ lived out in the world, rather than somehow getting in before the door to salvation is closed by a Second Coming.

PASSION AND RESURRECTION

Chapter 14

The Passion narrative starting in chapter fourteen is based on a tradition fixed before Mark composed the Gospel. Therefore, it has the appearance of a single, rather smooth narrative, especially starting with the Gethsemani account, rather than being stitched together out of a collection of individual pericopes. Mark was more restricted in adding material to this section of the Gospel, as were the other Evangelists. The Passion narrative reflects a Jewish-Christian view in Palestine rather than the broader Church of Mark's time or the Roman concerns. However, since the primary Roman concern was the meaning of suffering, there is a connection between the meaning of being a disciple and the passion of Jesus.

If accepting the Messiah is following Jesus, and the meaning of Jesus as Messiah is given in the Jerusalem experience, discipleship and Jesus' suffering combine to answer the Roman questions about their own suffering. This might be particularly clear after the Roman disciples had seen their own experience, in accepting baptism quickly and without questioning, mirrored in the acceptance and early misunderstanding by the original disciples.

The starting point of the Passion narrative is the introduction of the plot of Jewish religious authorities to arrest Jesus by trickery (14:1-2). There was no official Jewish action to kill Jesus. The conspiracy had been developed throughout the Gospel as Jesus moved beyond a rigid keeping of the Law as taught by the religious leaders. In their minds, Jesus may or may not be a messiah selected by God. As non-Jewish readers of the Gospel account, later Christians, up to the present, tend to be overwhelmed by the signs recorded in the Gospel accounts.

In Galilee where the signs were worked, a general acceptance of Jesus as Messiah tended to exist. Scrupulous Jewish leaders, who recognized that Jesus strayed from the rules associated with the Law, would have questioned his role as Messiah on that account. Reports that reached Jewish leaders in Jerusalem would have come from those who recognized the discrepancies, even though popular support and the astonishment of Jews would have received popular reporting. Even in John's Gospel where Jesus is presented as being in Jerusalem on other occasions and working signs there, a lack of real contact with temple authorities is shown. It does not take much imagination to recognize that religious bureaucrats would take more notice of clerical questioning of Jesus' actions than a popular appreciation of them by the people as a whole. Bureaucrats might well see their role more in protecting the nation from a false messiah than in supporting popular interest.

The plot was based on the following assumptions and courses of action. If Jesus were from God, he would succeed as Messiah under any circumstances. If he were false, any uprising that would occur against Roman rule without divine support would fail and destruction of the nation and Temple might result. Jewish revolts in 66-70 and 132-135 proved this hypothesis to be correct. It might well be that the religious leaders did not believe that Jesus was the Messiah and they would never have supported him. Regardless of such suppositions, they had to be convinced he was true and, lacking such conviction, their desire was to get rid of him and at the same time not be condemned for their action.

The plan that was developed, as shown in the Gospel accounts and Acts, was to accuse Jesus of sedition before the Roman authorities. That crime would be punished by crucifixion. Under the Law (Dt 21:22-23) a criminal who dies by being hung on a tree, or was crucified under Roman practice, would be cursed by God. People would recognize in his death that as one cursed by God, Jesus could not have been the Messiah, the one anointed by God.

The leaders must somehow arrest Jesus in secret, so as not to cause a public outcry and possibly cause the very disturbance at Passover time that would bring a Roman reaction. They must gain some kind of unified decision from a broad group of leaders to support his being turned over to Roman authorities and have him sentenced by the Romans for inciting a revolt against Rome. Without a strong show of support by Jewish leaders for such an action, it was unlikely that Pilate would have actually proceeded with the sentence of execution.

If the leaders succeeded in secretly condemning Jesus before Pilate and having him on the cross before the people gathered, the people would not intervene because Jesus would appear not to be the Messiah in his dying on a tree. The Jewish religious authorities then would be praised for unmasking a false messiah. If Jesus were, in fact, the Messiah from God, the crucifixion would be prevented by Divine power, and through the King David-type of messiah, the leaders expected that Palestine would be freed. Such a desirable conclusion would probably result in public forgiveness of the leaders for their action. The win-win situation allowed the Jewish leaders to make certain of Divine sponsorship of Jesus as Messiah before supporting him.

When Jesus was anointed at Bethany by a woman while dining at the house of Simon the leper (14:3-9), the event was presented as an anointing before burial. Jesus understood the plot and accepted the suffering and death he foretold earlier. He was not surprised at the outcome, just as the Roman Christians should not have been surprised with the persecution there. Judas joined the plan of the religious authorities (14:10-11) in providing the means of locating Jesus for arrest without public knowledge.

The Last Supper seems to be clearly identified as a Passover meal (14:12-16) which two disciples prepare in terms of having a lamb sacrificed. The identification of a man who would provide a room for celebrating the feast is given in the form of a sign since a man carrying a water jar would be a rarity. Such a sign may have had greater importance and meaning in opening the Passion narrative before being preceded by Mark's thirteen chapters of signs as an introduction.

Jesus arrived at the Passover meal with the Twelve (14:17-21) which does not identify the first two disciples who prepared the meal. We can guess that there were more than thirteen participants at the meal, yet the purpose of the narrative was to show that all twelve Apostles were present rather than give the actual guest list.

Details of the meal are essentially non-existent (14:22-25), so the identification of the meal as an actual Passover is open to question. In John's Gospel it is clearly designated as not a Passover meal. The Passover feast is more than a simple remembrance by Jews of the leaving of Egypt at the time of the Exodus. It is a memorial where a review of all the readings concerning the faith decision of the Israelites

tends to make the Exodus decision present for the participants of the meal.

The Exodus decision was not a simple escape, but it was
a defiant leaving of slavery in the face of overwhelming military strength that would be used to prevent the departure. It
was the leaving of a rich agricultural land to walk out into a
desert in which, under normal circumstances, they could
expect to perish. It was a decision to trust the promises of a
God, whose name they never heard before, that they would
be protected from the greatest military strength in the world
at that time. They also would be protected against the natural hazards of a desert, which they saw as a place of death, and
go to a country about which they had only vague traditions
handed down from centuries earlier.

In the Passover memorial, each Jew makes present that
situation and personally makes that same decision of faith in
Yahweh's promises as the Israelites. The Church at the Last
Supper, in the form of the Twelve, made that same decision of
following a new Messiah with a promise which they hardly
understood. So the meal included a Passover decision for the
disciples even if it did not occur on the same night as
Passover was celebrated that year. Since the Eucharist was
always celebrated weekly instead of annually, the description
as Passover seems to refer to its meaning rather than the date
on which it occurred.

Peter expressed the new Passover decision clearly
(14:26-31) when the possible failure to maintain faith in
Jesus was mentioned. He was determined to follow Jesus
under any circumstance even if everyone else lost faith. He
would accept death rather than disown Jesus. Every disciple
in the room must have echoed those sentiments. They had
been presented with the covenant words in a meal of decision
and made their commitment even when Jesus prophesied that
it would turn out differently from the crowning of a new king
as they expected.

At Gethsemani (14:32-42), Jesus was fearful but with
faith, while the disciples treated the situation as a normal

Passover. They had never understood or literally accepted the warnings of Jesus on the way to Jerusalem. Their "Yes, Lord" decision, like the Roman Christians, was to show they were ready to support their own version of the messiah, not the one proclaimed by Jesus. Israel was not prepared for the events of the day following the original Passover nor were these Jewish disciples ready for the test of a new one. However, the Roman disciples during the persecution would repeat Jesus' words at Gethsemani and then they lived out that position by remaining Christians when facing death. Their response was the true Passover acceptance of God's will, so they responded like Jesus at Gethsemani.

The arrest of Jesus (14:43-52) could hardly have been viewed as a prelude to a crucifixion. Mark does not indicate any real resistance except the loss of a servant's ear. Moreover, Peter, in following the group to the house of the high priest, hardly shows a great fear of death. An arrest would cause some difficulties and should be avoided since some punishment would be given regardless of the outcome of a hearing. Peter's caution is consistent with avoiding punishment rather than facing execution.

What is often called a trial (14:53-65) has no official status as such. A death sentence could only come from the Sanhedrin after two trials were conducted on different days and under Roman rule could not be carried out by religious officials. Such trials would have been carried out by the full Sanhedrin meeting at the Temple rather than in the high priest's home. This was not a trial, but a gathering of evidence to gain support from a large group of Jewish leaders in condemning Jesus to the Roman authorities.

However, to convince Pilate would not be an easy task since he would be aware of Jesus' popular following and may not have fully trusted even his own appointed high priest. An example of how a Roman proconsul acted in response to a condemnation of Paul by Jewish leaders in Corinth is described in Acts (18:12-15). Where the condemning of someone might be due to a dispute over Jewish religious Law, a Roman official would have no reason to execute someone. Where an uprising might result and cause the very problems that Pilate was present in Jerusalem at Passover to prevent, he would have reacted in the same way as Gallio. Having a great showing of support for the condemnation by the entire Sanhedrin was essential to the success of the plot.

The hearing produced nothing that would gain support for a condemnation by members of the Sanhedrin. Finally, the high priest asked Jesus directly if he was the Messiah, adding the title "Son of the Blessed One" that would have been applied to King David. Jesus answered in the affirmative and it seemed likely that a simple agreement would have caused no change in the situation. However, Jesus then added a quote from the book of Daniel (Dan 7:13) in which the figure of someone who shares a position at the throne of God was applied to himself.

The term "Son of Man" would not be considered messianic by Judaism and is a frequent title in the Old Testament, especially in the book of Ezekiel, as "ben adam" in Hebrew. Jesus' use of the term for himself during his public life would be in Aramaic as "bar enas" and would not draw special attention. However, the quote from Daniel (7:13) in response to the high priest's question (14:62) includes Son of Man as "bar enas" and tells the high priest what Jesus had meant in using the term during his public life. The book of Daniel in chapters two through seven was written in Aramaic and later translated to Hebrew for acceptance as Scripture by Judaism. However, that single "bar enas" was left in Aramaic. The response of the high priest shows he had understood Jesus' claim to be at the right hand of God. This closeness of himself to Divine power, rather than only as one on earth who is anointed by God, brought the charge of blasphemy. Suddenly everyone agreed that Jesus should be done away with by being denounced to the Roman authorities. The plot succeeded because Jesus agreed to it.

Peter, who had followed Jesus with some loyalty (14:66-72), found himself being questioned too closely in the courtyard and began to retract the passion pledge. First he claimed not to have knowledge, then denied that he was part of anything, and finally denied even knowing the Messiah. The ritual of pledging to accept a covenant relationship had been undone, even without the threat of death being known. The impression is given in Peter's denials that he was not consciously denying Jesus but merely trying to extricate himself from questioning. Peter was surprised at the cock crowing and the fulfillment of Jesus' words, yet there appears to be little intent by Peter to deny Jesus, and that will become even more clear in later Gospels. Roman Christians would have been tempted to do the same to get out of a bad situation during the persecution.

Chapter 15

The denunciation of Jesus before Pilate (15:1-15) often is portrayed as a Jewish rejection of the Messiah. A crowded plaza was presented in film versions of the life of Christ as if all of Jerusalem was calling for the crucifixion. Mark's account, echoed in the other Gospels, is much more private and quiet.

A group of Jewish leaders and some guards arrived with Jesus at about daybreak and apparently reported that Jesus claimed to be a Jewish king. No one else would be out in the streets so early, so only this official group constitutes what is called a "crowd." The leaders had probably warned Pilate that unless something was done, Jesus could cause a popular uprising just as Jerusalem was filled to overflowing with pilgrims for Passover. Pilate immediately asked Jesus about the charges (15:2) which provides the clue to their source and nature. Jesus hardly answered and did not bother to dispute the charges in any way.

There is little Jesus could say in reply since he would never agree he was king in a way Pilate would understand. However, if he said he was sent by God to reveal God's gift that was a sharing of divine life, Pilate might believe he was insane and wouldn't crucify him as was necessary in the plot to prove Jesus was above the Law. Jesus had an interest in the plot for his purpose just as the Jewish authorities had for their purpose.

Even though the high priest was appointed by Pilate and, therefore, acted somewhat as Pilate's agent, Pilate had suspicions about the truth of the charges. His suggestion to release Jesus as a courtesy at a major feast was put forward as a way of accepting the charges yet not having to act on them. This was his way to prevent real trouble if Jesus did have a following among the people.

The chief priests had made sure that everyone present, the so-called crowd, would not accept anything but crucifixion for Jesus. For the plot to work, Jesus must be put up on a tree to die. Any other result would allow the people present in Jerusalem for the feast to claim that the chief priests had been an instrument in rejecting God's anointed one. Pilate could make no headway with such a group of determined plotters and ultimately he agreed with what was proposed.

Mark may have added the names of the two sons of Simon of Cyrene (15:21) because of a connection with the two sons of Simon who were known in Rome (Rom 16:13). He gave the crucifixion time as 9:00 a.m. for a six-hour time on the cross (15:25), rather than the traditional three hours. Clearly the initiation of the plot was a very early visit to Pilate before Jerusalem was awake. That passers-by jeered Jesus (15:29-32) showed the effectiveness of the plot rather than any popular turning against Jesus prior to being put on the cross. Those jeering claimed that they might believe in him again, but only if he could get off the cross. So long as Jesus appeared to be cursed by God under the Law, there would be no support for him.

Jesus' only statement from the cross (15:34) was the first line of Psalm 22. Since Jewish practice was to use the opening words or verse as the title of Old Testament writings, the words can be seen as calling forth the entire Psalm. This Psalm is a Jewish song of faith in times of great trials. Jews sang this Psalm as they were marched to their death in Nazi concentration camps during World War II. The opening verses of Psalm 22 describe the most desperate circumstances. Yet the last half of the Psalm starting with verse nineteen is an overwhelming statement of faith and hope in Yahweh. To consider the quotation of the opening verse as a sign of despair by Jesus is to greatly misread its meaning and Mark's intent.

The meaning of the crucifixion coming from those words of Jesus would be in the conclusion of the Psalm (22:27) that the whole world would "come back" to Yahweh. The Roman persecutions had that effect on the Roman empire. Far from being a description of despair, the words restate the hope of early Jewish Christians who remembered this statement in relation to the crucifixion over all other traditions.

At death the veil of the Temple was parted (15:38). The veil separated the place of God, the holy of holies, from the part of the Temple used for sacrifice. With Jesus' death, that separation no longer was meaningful. The meaning of the veil ceased to exist since every disciple has access to the new "place of God" in the life shared with Jesus.

A centurion in charge of the crucifixion recognized Jesus as the Messiah, a Son of God, in seeing how Jesus died. For Mark's Church, the centurion was a Roman witness to the crucifixion. It is in Jesus' death that the Messiah was recognized, and for the Roman Christians who have witnessed Christian death in the persecution, the message should be clear. Suffering and death does not represent a sign of failure of Christianity, but a witness to its real meaning. Death has no meaning when Christians have accepted natural death in baptism and have put on and lived an eternal life. The centurion, to whom the Romans would not witness, was a witness who would convince them.

The burial (15:40-47) brought forth even members of the Sanhedrin who hoped to see the kingdom established (15:43). Women disciples who had followed Jesus to Jerusalem and remained with him at the crucifixion took note of the location of the tomb. This is not just a note of inter-esting detail but a statement that on Easter Sunday they made no mistake about whose tomb was found to be empty.

Chapter 16

The original ending of Mark's Gospel account is with the women going to the tomb to anoint the body of Jesus (16:1-8), which was buried with such haste on Good Friday. They found the tomb empty and were told by an angel the fact of the Resurrection. They were sent as witnesses to oth-ers of what had occurred. However, the text ends with the women, frightened out of their wits, running away and telling no one because "they were afraid." The ending is so abrupt, it is often presumed that somehow the final portion of the Gospel was lost. However, the ending expresses what the Roman Christians must have done at the time of the persecu-tion. Disciples are supposed to witness to the Lord but when identification as a Christian meant death, the Romans most likely stopped witnessing because "they were afraid." This abrupt ending is most likely the original ending which drove home the point to the Romans that without the witness of Christian disciples, there would be no continuation of Christianity. An addition of traditions from the other Gospels (16:9-20) may have been made to provide a more suitable ending, but a less authentic one for the Church at Rome.

For Jews, the Resurrection meant that the Law did not apply to Jesus. He was above the Law as he taught in these remembered sayings which had been collected by Jewish Christians. For Christians at Rome, their fears, confusion and temporary questions of faith had been shared by those near to Jesus. The original disciples had come to understand that suffering would occur and they never walked away from the Lord again, even when facing death in a persecution in Rome.

The Roman Christians would make the same commit-ment after seeing the teachings, which they all knew by heart, arranged by Mark as an account that responded to their overwhelming questions. They would never walk away again even though persecutions would be present for them and those who followed after them. In two centuries the Roman Empire would be converted. That conclusion could be taken directly from Mark's Gospel account. He could never have known as he constructed this account how true his inspired message would be to the early Church. Yet, he had the faith to believe it to be.

THE GOSPEL OF MATTHEW

CONTEXT OF MATTHEW

The context proposed in the introduction for Matthew's Gospel can be summarized as follows:
- Written in Antioch, Syria, in 75-85
- Concerning the impending separation of Christianity from Judaism
- By an unknown Evangelist designated as Matthew

Subjects addressed are:
- Christianity as the fulfillment of Judaism
- A focus on new teachings versus living the relationship
- Warnings that witnessing is essential for a disciple
- The disciple must produce fruit

The additions that Matthew makes to Mark's Gospel strongly urge Christians to remain Christian in this separation from Judaism rather than returning to Judaism. Of the four groups described in The Context of the Gospels (page 34), the fourth group would have made the additions to influence the other three groups to remain loyal to Jesus. Since Matthew's message is contained in the additions, the commentary will address only the additions. The sections of the Gospel that are additions are shown in Appendix A.

THE BIRTH NARRATIVE

Chapter 1

The additions of Matthew to the Gospel structure of Mark open with a birth narrative. It is not just a new way of beginning the story, but a basic introduction in Jewish terms of Jesus as the Messiah, the anointed one of God, sent to open Judaism and the world to a new relationship with God. Part of the introduction is in terms of a new Moses to express a radical change rather than merely a prophetic addition to the message.[22]

Moses was introduced in the Book of Exodus as a child out of a heritage starting with Abraham and so was Jesus in this Gospel. Moses was threatened by a royal decree; Jesus was similarly affected. Moses was taken in by non-Jewish royalty, and the acceptance of Jesus was by non-Jewish Magi. Both had an Egyptian connection that provided shelter against difficult circumstances.

So long as such similarities are not stretched too far, there is a valid, parallel series of events that would at least come to mind for Jewish readers of Matthew's writing. The conclusion would be that Moses was an instrument of God in bringing the new relationship in the Law, and Jesus should be seen as introducing a new relationship that went beyond the Law.

An opening genealogy (1:1-17) may be a least-read part of the New Testament, at least by modern readers. It starts with Abraham through whom all of the nations on earth are to be blessed (Genesis 12:23). The tie was essential to Judaism since it shows the Messiah to be part of God's plan, even as the relationship with Yahweh was being opened to Gentiles before the time of the Law. The tie to David in the list of ancestors probably carried more importance to Jewish Christian readers than the virgin birth, since some key promises of a Messiah in the Old Testament were related to him.

Four women are included in the list, even though women would not play a role in a legal document defining lineage. The four women are all Gentiles who were involved in irregularities in their relationships to members of the list. Tamar (1:3) was a Canaanite woman who seduced her father-in-law, Judah, to continue the line of the tribe of Judah, after the first two sons of Judah had died. This was the primary tribe existing in the time of Jesus and his own tribal connection. We might conclude that without Tamar's action there would be no Judaism by the time of the Messiah.

Rahab (1:5), also a Canaanite woman from after the time of giving the Law to Moses, is considered to be the prostitute who assisted the spies sent by Joshua to Jericho before it was destroyed. Jericho was a key victory in entering the promised land and resulted in the Israelites overcoming their fear of the walled cities of Canaan. Ruth (1:5) was a Moabite woman who married one of Naomi's sons and returned with her mother-in-law to the land of Judah after the son died. She later married Boaz, a relative of Naomi, and was David's great grandmother. Lastly, Uriah's wife, Bathsheba (1:6), was involved in an adulterous affair with David, which resulted in her husband, Uriah, being put in a dangerous place in battle by David which caused his death. Since Uriah was a Hittite, it would be assumed she was not Jewish. After marrying David, she became the mother of Solomon, who continued the royal line of David.

The addition of the women could be used to address questions about any irregularities in the birth of Jesus. It is more likely, however, that they are intended to show that the very important royal line of Jewish history was dependent on Gentiles and situations outside of the Law. The conclusion could be drawn that the greater meaning of the Messiah is beyond Judaism.

Matthew's version of the Annunciation (1:18-25) is given entirely through communication with Joseph, rather than with a record of any statement from Mary. Joseph knew of the virgin birth and officially adopted Jesus as his son (accepts him as his own) by naming him. There is nothing misunderstood or hidden in how Jesus gained a connection to the line of David. In the Jewish understanding, the Messiah would be the natural heir of David and be adopted by God in the anointing, in becoming the Messiah. The Christian understanding is that Jesus is a natural heir of God and was adopted as an heir of David in the naming by Joseph.

Chapter 2

The visit of the Magi with their gifts (2:1-13) presents a different scene from the one found in popular Christian tradition. There were not necessarily three wise men, rather there were three gifts. There was no stable, no census, no shepherds and no journey by Mary and Joseph. It would seem that Mary and Joseph lived in Bethlehem in a house. The Magi saw a star at some earlier time which probably was framed by a constellation. It was interpreted that the star was a special sign of a new king coming to the kingdom associated with that constellation. The constellation Leo would be a good candidate since the lion was a symbol of Judah and the constellation becomes visible in July a short time after a traditional spring conception. However, the spring date for conception is derived from the December 25 birth date which was set at the time of a winter festival. Therefore, the choice of that constellation is unsupported by factual evidence.

The Magi were Gentiles who recognized the sign and responded to the sign. However, they came to the Messiah only through Judaism, through Jerusalem. Their response was with homage and gifts and then they returned to Gentile lands. It was not necessary for them to remain in Judaism for salvation to come. This is a means to suggest that the Christians of Matthew's time need not consider that remaining in Judaism is essential either.

Historically, much speculation has been attached to this account and its relationship to Luke's quite different account. However, Matthew's meaning could start and end with these few points, and he may not have known about a different tradition. Certainly there is an emphasis that it is not Palestine or Jerusalem or Judaism that is important but the meaning of who had come into the world.

Herod, as the Jewish king, even though Idumaean rather than Jewish, responded very differently from the Magi (2:13-18). Being jealous of power would be typical for him since he murdered three of his sons on suspicion of treason in the last few years before his death. A grander interpretation is that the official response from Palestine was to not accept the Messiah. Herod was a false Jewish leader who did not want to lose his exclusive position. He was more than willing to kill the one sent from God than to risk a change, regardless of the signs.

For Matthew's community, Judaism did not want to accept a Messiah who changed the historical relationship the Jewish people had with Yahweh. Later in the Gospel, Matthew retained Mark's parable of the wicked husbandmen (21:33-46) which makes about the same charge against the Jewish leaders. This early emphasis on the non-acceptance of a Messiah, who would change the existing power structure in Palestine, was setting the stage for such an interpretation.

The escape to Egypt (2:19-23) tends to confirm that the plan of God includes a new covenant relationship, rather than simply a fulfillment of a promise of a new Palestine as would be expected from a King David-style messiah. The fulfillment text (2:15) from Hosea is used to focus the reader's attention on the Moses connection. Those in Matthew's community who would be content to remain in Judaism were not just being silent about the Messiah, but were rejecting the new covenant conditions as surely as if the Israelites following Moses would have decided to return to Egypt after the Exodus event. Matthew closed off the introduction by proposing a reason for the Holy Family to move to Nazareth rather than back to Bethlehem which, in this account, seemed to be their actual home before the birth.

JESUS' PUBLIC MINISTRY IN GALILEE

Chapter 3

John's baptism of Jesus starts the public ministry (3:1-17), as in Mark's account. Matthew used only Mark's quote from Isaiah (3:3), and included the words from Malachi later in the Gospel (11:10). Matthew lengthened the statement of John the Baptist (3:8-12) by including some harsh criticism of Jewish religious authorities.

The criticism that group four of Matthew's community may have had for an official Judaism that was rejecting them is not presented as a later criticism developed in Matthew's time as the relationship soured. Here it is part of the statement of the original prophet announcing the Messiah. The opposition of Judaism was not just from a Christian part of the Jewish community, but was recognized in the plan of God from the start.

Chapter 4

In the temptation scene (4:1-11) Jesus responded to the evil power, which attempts to change the course of the revelation, with quotations from the Old Testament rather than with his own words. If the Old Testament record of Judaism were read correctly, it would support the message that came from the Messiah. The record would associate with evil the actions of the Messiah's opponents. If the plan of God brings hunger or suffering for the Messiah, Jesus would not use his power to create bread to alleviate such hunger. If the plan means danger for the Messiah, Jesus would not use the relationship with God to avoid it or to force God through a test to make a change. Finally, the meaning of Messiah is not in one who conquers the world through an alliance with evil, but in one who brings people into the true relationship God has opened to them. These Old Testament quotations in the response are used in about the same way as fulfillment texts and could have been used by Jesus or come from a collection developed by the Church.

This section closes with a strange quote from Isaiah (4:12-17). The way of the sea is a road located between the Sea of Galilee and the Mediterranean and becomes a coastal road in southern Palestine. Therefore, the prophet would be standing outside of Palestine in Jordan proclaiming that people living in Galilee, the Gentile area of Palestine, would be the ones who see the light. Those Gentiles who are assumed to live in darkness, rather than those in Jerusalem who suppose they have the position of light, would be the ones opened to salvation. This prophecy seems fulfilled by the message being opened by group four rather than those remaining in an isolated Judaism not open to Gentiles.

The remainder of chapter four comes from Mark's Gospel even though the summary statement (4:23-25) has been modified to be more inclusive. Including Syria in the areas hearing the message (4:24) would tend to support Antioch as the place of Matthew's composition.

Chapter 5

The Sermon on the Mount in chapters five, six and seven is a major teaching section in which Matthew described Jesus as a Messiah who goes far beyond the Law. Matthew's view of Judaism is of a people who kept the teachings of the Law and saw Jesus as a messiah who brings additional teachings. For Judaism the correct course was to keep all of the teachings, both in the Law and those from Jesus. Matthew emphasized in this Gospel that the Christian message is not only some new teachings introduced into Judaism, but a radically different way of relating to God. Christianity is a relationship with God that goes beyond the Law. So, just as Jesus is beyond the Law in the Resurrection, after dying in a way that indicated he would be cursed, the message of Jesus is beyond the Law rather than only the addition of new teachings.

The Beatitudes (5:1-12) present a different view of how one becomes blessed or near to God. The Jewish people believed that good fortune in life was a reward for a good life and, therefore, a sign of being blessed. Misfortune in life would be seen as a result of a sinful situation. Jesus indicates that the opposite may be true especially if misfortune is accepted to make possible the kingdom.

Jewish thought would tend to stress a doing of actions related to keeping the Law as a means to move toward God and, therefore, be blessed. The eight beatitudes tend to reflect interior disposition more than outward acts. Moving away from desiring what might seem enjoyable in this world is the indication that disciples are putting all their desires in the kingdom to come. Complete fulfillment of the Law is going beyond rules and beyond everyday pleasures.

Judaism had fought for the land they saw as a promised homeland for themselves and that desire remains with Palestinian Jews today. The promise of God of a kingdom is as much beyond an independent land as it is beyond the small nation that received the original revelation. When people look beyond a simple homeland, they can recognize the real kingdom open to all people. Unless the focus of desire can be moved beyond the everyday meaning, the real promise of God cannot be seen.

For the groups in the Antioch Church to which Matthew was writing, the choice actually faced was one of giving up much of their Jewish traditions, history and culture to become Christians only. No one should underestimate how difficult that choice must have been for those groups that accepted Christianity while living within a Jewish frame-work and, at the time Matthew writes, were being called to move out of Judaism. Surely they would seem poor, meek, mourning and hungry for what they had to leave behind. Yet, that was the way the journey with the Lord was taking them.

The disciples who chose to remain Christian would have to put on the life of Christ with its attributes of being merciful, pure of heart, and peacemakers, but also accepting of persecutions from former associates. It was how "they" per-secuted the prophets who came to change the course of Judaism at some earlier times. This teaching was from Christians and to Christians. Those who did not accept the Messiah were the outsiders to this discussion with the desig-nation of "they."

Judaism had been the salt in the lives of those who were Jewish Christians and it gave their existence flavor. It had been the light in their lives (5:13-16) assuring them that they fulfilled the plan of God. Now a revelation had come which exceeded Judaism. The question of Matthew asks if the groups reading this Gospel believe they can return to only what they had in life before the coming of the Messiah. Jesus says that Judaism would now be a flat flavor and a hidden light, and that should not be the goal of disciples. With the revelation of the Messiah, true disciples must go beyond Judaism as salt and light and extend the full message to the whole world.

Then a line is drawn separating the action that seemed to be required of Jewish Christians and what Jesus really proclaimed as Messiah (5:17-19). It was not a matter of giving up the Law as if somehow the original revelations would be discarded, anymore than the Law given to Moses resulted in discarding the promises made to Abraham about blessing all nations. Rather, the new covenant relationship goes far beyond the rules that define the Law of Moses on an everyday basis. The relationship with God presented in the Law must be fully lived rather than only obeyed in rules. It is in living the relationship that a complete response is attained rather than the partial response of rule-keeping.

To describe the change, Jesus explained the differences between the Jewish expectation in keeping the Law and the new living of the Law revealed by Jesus. In six antitheses (5:20-48), the disciples are asked to compare this living relationship with traditional teachings regarding actions ranging from very evil to praiseworthy. The result is a new and complete teaching on fundamental Jewish commandments and actions.

The original disciples heard these teachings and initially remembered them as examples of going beyond the common practices concerning the Law. Matthew presented them here as the fulfillment of the Law, keeping the Law completely. Jews would have asked about the relationship of Jesus to their religion which is the Law. Matthew's question is about the relationship of the Law to his community's religion, which is the Lord Jesus Christ. The answer is that the relationship in Jesus Christ calls one to go beyond Judaism, rather than to oppose Judaism.

The first antithesis concerns the commandment against murder (5:21-26). Nearly all people would assume they could pay little attention to such a commandment because they would never be involved in killing anyone. That viewpoint would relate to those who only see sin as overt evil actions against the very words of the commandment. Jesus then contrasted that viewpoint with the position of someone actually living such a section of the Law and never even turning in the direction of such evil.

The starting point for breaking such a commandment is anger, which is the initial movement away from God who is love. Directing one's life toward God means never even allowing anger to be present in one's life. Living a relationship of loving God and neighbor leaves no room for anger and no consideration of coming to such hatred so as to murder. What appears to be a commandment which is of no concern to most people is, in a living relationship, the nearly daily concern of all.

Adultery (5:27-30) also is a relatively rare act for most people who attempt to live a religious life. In the lived Law its starting point is lust which is far more obvious as a temptation. Divorce (5:31-32) is similar except that there are conditions under the Law in which divorce was allowed. Living the relationship with God is not in using or being open to such loopholes. Faithfulness in the relationship with God requires the faithfulness to be lived and, therefore, it must be present in all dedicated relationships.

Oaths (5:33-37) are something not seen as evil and may have been very common among the Jewish people in the invoking of God's presence as a witness to their deeds. Living a relationship with God is in itself making the divine witness present in every part of a person's life and, therefore, makes oaths redundant and unnecessary. When others see God's love in the way we live, they can trust us without our calling on the Lord as a witness.

Returning similar actions to others (5:38-42) can be seen as having an element of justice. Yet, Jesus' response goes far beyond the often-quoted offering of the other cheek. The tunic or shirt is the long, white gown worn in the Middle East even today. To give it up would be uncomfortable since the rough outer cloak then would be worn next to the skin. However, to give up the heavy outer wool cloak could mean death due to exposure. So the lived situation is to put one's life on the line for anyone, even an opponent.

Loving one's enemy (5:43-47) is the final step, especially for Judaism. In their history they had come to believe that loving those outside of Judaism would be a failure to be loyal to the covenant. They allowed that view to rule their lives because loving anyone else could be considered as a rejection of Yahweh. Now Jesus had opened a question Judaism had answered, since the time of the exile a half-millennium earlier, by maintaining their distinct separateness from Gentiles. In effect, Jesus said love the whole world and in doing so one would witness to God's love for the whole world. Living the relationship which Yahweh brings to creation is very clearly taught as these antithesis are thought through. The conclusion of taking on perfection (5:48) is living a true reflection of how God should be seen by everyone.

Chapter 6

Sections on almsgiving, prayer and fasting (6:1-18) appear to open a new topic, yet they follow the same line of reasoning even though the format is different. Matthew brought the teachings of Jesus to bear on his Gospel answer in the format in which the early community remembered the teachings rather than in a format of Matthew's own composition. Here, even the practices associated with holiness are reviewed in concept.

Almsgiving (6:1-4) is not just an action performed with some fixed percentage of wealth to determine an obligation. Living a relationship means a living of charity. The most obvious fact of creation is that it is entirely a gift. The world is seen as having been given before human life, and even science agrees with that procedure, if not the reasoning behind it. Judaism would witness by giving, yet Jesus' witness of the relationship with God is an openness to giving everything.

Prayer (6:5-15) in a close living with God is speaking within a shared life. It is not something done because of a rule regarding time, content, place or position. It is not the speaking to someone so far away as to require shouting from a street corner or even speaking out loud in a synagogue. People reflect on their own feelings in their innermost thoughts rather than publicly. If there is a unity of life with God, prayer should have the same internal intimacy. The witness of a relationship with God is not in what is broadcast or stated to a distant person, but in the witness of a life built on internal communication with God.

The Our Father inserted here was not intended by Jesus to become a rote prayer, but to show in Jewish terms that the relationship to God should be as close as a family relationship. Prayer would be speaking to God in the same way we share intimate needs and desires in the privacy of a home where no ill feelings or conflicts can be perpetuated and all life is shared and celebrated. In Matthew's time, this prayer must have already developed some liturgical usage in community celebrations. Matthew asks his readers if they will walk away from this intimacy and stop using a community prayer which could not be repeated in the synagogues. To choose the synagogue would be to accept a prayer asking God to curse the deviators, which means the Christians who by then had been shut out of the synagogues.

A teaching on fasting (6:16-18) ends the sequence of changed conditions proposed by Jesus. Fasting is used as a tool to change one's behavior, to correct one's desires to some extent. To dress or present oneself publicly in a distinctive way while fasting would be to advertise the tool being used. Spiritual development is part of the process of trying to live closer to a desired relationship with God. What the world should see is the results of such development rather than the tool or process. Only God should know of the steps we take; the world should witness a life that is changed.

The meaning of fulfillment, or of living the Law, was important within Judaism, but it tended to be seen as a literal following of the words of Scripture. Yet, those writings were always recorded in human words and culture. They carried the human limitations of people trying to understand revelation. Jesus, as the one who fully lives the Divine life, reveals that God intends for us to become a reflection of Christ. Rather than rules to follow, Christians have to put on and live the life of Christ and witness his invitation to all of humanity. As Matthew shows the contrast between the Jewish understanding and Jesus' teaching, a very different view of fulfillment is made clear. Only in understanding the greatness of the gift offered through Christ could one make the decision to live what appears to be a difficult life or, for those choosing perfection, a seemingly impossible one.

The living of a relationship with God must be centered on a total trust in God even in the difficult situations members of Matthew's community would face as they become separated from their Jewish heritage. Treasures that come from life on earth have limited value (6:19-21) because sooner or later they are clearly lost. Being able to see the light of complete revelation from God (6:22-23) is the only means of receiving complete life. Attempting to serve two masters (6:24), like trying to live two different lives, is clearly impossible.

That is especially so in the impossible situation of remaining within a Judaism that had rejected its Messiah, and being forced to live a quiet and unwitnessed Christianity, when the life of Christ was meant as a witness to everyone. Jesus' original words may have arisen from a somewhat different situation, relating to a choice between the life with God or only following the world. However, the words could not be more clearly applied than to a choice between two different approaches to a God who is love.

Creation itself is rich with the examples of God's love and care for humanity. So who could stand in the work of creation surrounded by the examples (6:25-34) and worry

about possessions? Matthew called his split community to
stay with the great revelation in their own time. Did any of
them need to worry about the loss of the revelation that came
out of their history if they accepted a life presented in a revelation of their own time? Does God ever take away from creation or only add to it? They could look around at what had
been given even before the first revelation to their ancestors;
had anything ever been diminished? Trust in God does not
mean being worried about possessions or heritage. The kingdom and holiness should be their first concern (6:33-34) and
everything for both tomorrow and the future will take care of
itself. A people whose only recorded history is a growing revelation of closeness to Yahweh should not suddenly stop and
fail to take the concluding step.

Chapter 7

How disciples should act was addressed in five short sections. Jesus said do not judge (7:1-5), while Jewish teaching
would be to judge leniently and never hold anyone to the
maximum accounting. Jesus taught that the only person anyone could change was oneself, so one need not judge anyone
else. The parading of beliefs or practices before those who do
not understand (7:6), rather than producing a benefit, may
mislead others to opposition, which would be to everyone's
detriment. Disciples should be persistent and trustful in prayer
(7:7-11), but not look for a response only in one's own words.
Prayer is always for a good to come and God is the source of
all good. If everyone trusts others every day, why should anyone attempt to hold God to only responding in the exact
words used in the request? Judaism would have cautioned to
avoid what one finds hateful; the golden rule (7:12) is stated
in the positive way because only God's acts are good and that
is the direction a Christian takes in living the relationship.

Finally, the call to remain Christian is a narrow and difficult way (7:13-14). It would be chosen only because of its
promise of eternal life, and there is no other reason for the
journey Christians have taken on as life. Matthew's readers

know why they chose Christianity as part of their Jewish orientation. Now they should ask themselves if they could give up that choice to live without the promise that drove the original decision.

A closing warning is given about false prophets (7:15-20) who oppose Matthew's writing. Some within the Christian community must have been urging a retention of Judaism and relinquishing the acceptance of Jesus as Messiah. This warning could not apply to Jews who had no Christian connection. Judge them by their fruits is a repeated statement. If their advice leads away from the choice of following a Messiah judged as one sent from God, can it be good advice?

Those who say "Yes, Lord" (7:21-27), when such a choice was simply adding a Messiah belief to a Jewish religious life, would not gain life from those mere words. The disciples must have the relationship to make it their own, otherwise it remains only words. Tying one's life to this new relationship with God is the tie that would be stable for an eternity. It is the tie that would overcome even the difficulties faced in this world and specifically in Matthew's community. The hard decision which must be made is like the strong anchor in times of difficulty and should be retained.

Mark's comment on the teaching of Jesus which made a deep impression (7:28-29) closes the sermon. Mark did not give much of that teaching, but Matthew has shown some of it in his great sermon. It drives his readers to make a choice and live it just as it did for many of those who heard these same teachings directly from Jesus in different circumstances in Galilee. Now the sermon asks the same question of a different generation of people in Matthew's community.

Chapter 8
Mark is used for providing material for the next two chapters, but Matthew either makes some minor changes in the stories or has the same material with slight differences, which are substituted for Mark's accounts. In the cure of the

leper (8:1-4), a change is made from Mark as Jesus now is addressed as "Lord" by the leper who accepted him completely. Likewise, one called a disciple (8:21-22) uses the term "Lord" which has a basic meaning of one who is in charge of a person's life. The followers accept a living relationship with Jesus. A scribe (8:18-20) and a group of Pharisees (9:10-13) who are not followers of Jesus call him "teacher," one who might bring revelation as additional teaching or a better understanding, but who is not in control of their lives.

An addition by Matthew to Mark's Gospel is the account of the centurion (8:5-13) who accepted Jesus completely and did not need a special visit to live out his faith. Accepting Jesus completely as one who can control his life is all that is required by him. The closing words of Jesus praise the centurion and state that many will follow that same course and be blessed, which is Matthew's point in the writing. The remaining material of chapters eight and nine is from Mark.

Chapter 10

In chapter ten, Matthew continues to rely on Mark, but rearranges some of the material. A section on warnings of persecution (10:17-25) was included in the last-days account in chapter thirteen of Mark. The warning to Matthew's community relates to such events now closer at hand and even occurring in their midst to some extent. Rather than a remote possibility, the separation occurring within families might be commonplace as each person makes the choice of remaining Christian or ceasing to witness as they accept the new rules of Judaism condemning Christianity.

The directive from Jesus (10:26-42) is added material from Matthew about doing the opposite of those who would accept silence about Jesus to remain within Judaism. Accepting Jesus as Messiah must be shouted from the housetops (10:26-33) and only that witness on earth would assure Jesus' witness for disciples in heaven. There could be no quiet or hidden disciples. Such decisions to remain Christian could result in separation of families as must have been occurring already in Antioch and other places where Christians were excluded from the synagogues (10:34-39).

A condemnation of Christians was included in synagogue prayers, calling down a curse on those who deviate from very restrictive Jewish teaching. The resulting separation would be described, in the limited Aramaic language used by Jesus, as hating. Accepting a prophet or holy man (10:40-42) may obtain their type of reward, but living the life of Christ in even a simple fashion will receive the real promise of the kingdom.

Chapter 11

John the Baptist seemed to have questioned Jesus (11:1-19) about his teachings as if they did not follow Jewish interpretations of the Law. John must have been a lively preacher who warned of fire and brimstone coming down on those who did not return fully to the Law. Yet, as he sat in prison, the accounts of this Messiah's teachings seemed to be less strict than John supposed they would be. Jesus was merciful to an extreme to those judged as sinners, and he dined with them and with tax collectors.

In this account John asked if Jesus really was the Messiah. The fulfillment of prophecies by Jesus was shown in quoting from Isaiah about the conditions that would occur when the Messiah arrived (Is 35:5-6). That provided an Old Testament answer to a prophet who expected an Old Testament messiah. However, Jesus went beyond the teachings of the Law just as his signs went beyond anything expected in the Law by John or by any other prophet.

The real Gospel is so different that it could not even be recognized by the prophet who came to announce the Messiah. The faith statement is not just accepting signs, but being willing to accept a separation from the past as Matthew's community is being asked to do. John may have been the greatest of Judaism (11:11), however, the least of those living in the Christian relationship with God would be greater. It is not a putdown of John but a comparison of the two ways -- staying with Christ or returning to only Judaism -- proposed in Matthew's time. The generation of Jesus' time must have ridiculed both the asceticism of John and the openness of Jesus (11:16-19). Yet, it is this same rejection of signs that those in Matthew's community would have to agree with if they return to Judaism.

In the lament over the towns of Galilee (11:20-24), Jesus proclaimed that Gentile cities, or even the worst cities of the Old Testament, would have responded better to the signs introducing the Messiah than the people of his own generation. Yet, the conclusion (11:25-30) is that a real knowing of God, or having a true living relationship, only can come in accepting the revelation of God, which comes in the Messiah. The rejection of the Messiah would not be a retaining of an existing covenant in the Law but a rejection of the fulfillment of that covenant made in a revealed living with Yahweh. To accept a yoke that required separation from family and culture seems hard (11:28-30), but its reward in a new closeness with Yahweh will make it light.

Chapter 12

A parable from Mark is used to open chapter twelve but with one important change. Jesus indicated that the Messiah is something "greater than the Temple" (12:6) which was the place where the Jewish people would meet God on earth. Then an addition of a prophecy quotation from Isaiah (12:15-21) tells that the Messiah would proclaim the faith to the nations and in him they will put their hope. Nations is a reference to those living outside of Judaism and the word is usually translated as Gentiles.

Matthew's additions start again with the familiar theme of being known by one's fruit (12:33-37). If rejection of the Messiah, which was required for anyone remaining with Judaism, did not produce an evident good, it would say much about the nature of that decision. Then, in response to the request of the Pharisees for a sign (12:38-42), Jesus states the meaning of going beyond Judaism. A comparison is made between Jonah and the Messiah as being entombed for three days, as a way of saying the Jonah story should be examined again after the Resurrection. Those Gentiles who responded to Jonah, as a prophet of the Old Testament, would condemn a present generation for not responding to the Messiah who is even greater than a prophet. Likewise, the Gentile Queen of Sheba could condemn a present generation because she responded to the wisdom of Solomon and the Messiah is greater than Solomon. These two comparisons complete a series of comparisons between the Messiah and the essentials of Judaism, their Scripture and the Temple.

The comparisons started in chapter five, in the Sermon on the Mount, when Jesus gave the teachings of the Law from the Old Testament. Then in six antitheses he responded with a "but I say" to introduce a teaching that went beyond the Law. In this section he is shown doing the same with the Prophets, represented by Jonah, and the Wisdom writings, represented by Solomon. The Law, Prophets and Wisdom are the three sections of the Old Testament. Jesus has placed himself above the whole Old Testament writing or above the revelation given to the Jews.

In the picking of corn on the Sabbath account (12:6), Jesus stated that he was greater than the Temple, the basis of all Jewish worship. At the very time of Matthew's writing, the Jews, who had lost the Temple when it was destroyed by the Romans in 70, were changing their religious practices to continue Judaism without a temple. In doing so, they were not fulfilling those parts of the Law related to temple worship. The comparison to Matthew's readers is that staying with the Messiah is going beyond the revelation given to the Jews in terms of their temple worship.

The celebration of the Eucharist fulfills the sacrificial aspect of worshipping God in a way that is totally acceptable to God. A return to Judaism would not even respond completely to the revelation given to the Jews in terms of their temple worship. Matthew's use of the sayings of Jesus focused directly on a problem which did not exist for Judaism during Jesus' public life when the Temple was still in place.

Concluding this comparison is the teaching on the return of the unclean spirit (12:43-45). The message of Jesus can drive out evil. However, just accepting that message only as a teaching will not create any permanent change. The evil spirit could return at any time that a teaching passes from one's mind. Only if the place of the expelled spirit was filled with the life of the Lord would the evil spirit be permanently evicted. It is not enough to say "I believe." The living of a different life is required. Likewise, it is not how people are born and raised that is important (12:46-50), but that the Messiah's revelation of a life relationship with God is lived out by a disciple.

Chapter 13

Using Mark's chapter on parables, Matthew selects some additional ones in chapter thirteen to produce a different understanding of kingdom. The parable of the weeds (13:24-30) involves a weed known as darnel which, when it sprouts and starts to grow, resembles wheat. Only as it matures does its presence become known since the wheat produces a stalk with grain while the darnel produces no fruit. It restates Matthew's theme of knowing what is true by its fruit. This was not a condemnation of Jesus' opponents, but a statement to those who have accepted Jesus in a "Yes, Lord" statement, and now would remain quiet about that choice by returning to the synagogue. In that situation, they could produce no fruit by their witness.

This concept was then carried further with the parable of the yeast (13:33). Unlike even the small mustard seed (13:31-32), yeast once mixed into flour could not even be identified. One would not see a new plant arise, as with the mustard seed, but would expect that the whole mass of flour would rise and change in volume from the yeast. If no change occurred, then clearly there was no life in the yeast. The so-called Christian who wished to retreat into Judaism and not witness would cause no change to occur in that whole community. Such a situation must mean the Christian life is dead for that person. The explanation of the parable of the weeds (13:36-43) continues this theme since the Messiah is the sower of the good seed and only those who produce fruit would have any value in the kingdom.

A final question is then raised about how the readers would respond to anything of value that they find in life. A treasure in a field or a fine pearl (13:44-46) would produce an obvious change in how they lived since anyone would attempt to acquire such value. Yet, that value is limited only to this life and only to one's remaining years. The dedication of everything one owns for a temporary ownership of a pearl or buried treasure is a pale imitation of a dedication for an eternal treasure as in baptism.

The parable of the dragnet (13:47-50) makes the point clear that those who call themselves Christians, yet do not live that life, would receive the punishment. The net is the kingdom, so the outsiders remain in the sea. Those in the kingdom will be separated between the good and the wicked. Just being in the kingdom is not the guarantee of reward, but how that life is lived.

Matthew's conclusion (13:51-52) is that just knowing is not enough for discipleship. To be a disciple means producing something new; it means producing a new fruit. This section causes commentators to speculate that perhaps the Evangelist doing the writing was a scribe who became a disciple. In his additions, he is only recording the teachings of Jesus, teachings that are "old" and known, and yet, in compiling the Gospel for his community, new understandings emerge. Therefore, the speculation points toward the real meaning of the Gospel writing rather than the identity of the Evangelist.

Chapter 16

After another section from Mark, the opening of chapter sixteen gives a means of predicting the weather (16:1-4).

Perhaps Matthew is suggesting that if a little experience with something as unpredictable as weather can produce valid foresight, surely the same must be true of one's religious life if only a person would look for it.

Peter's confession sequence (16:13-20) received major additions from the simple text of Mark. Jesus stated that flesh and blood, the human argument or reasoning of people at that time or from the history of Israel, were not the deciding factor in Peter's believing and faith witness. Yet, the community of Antioch, where Peter's name was revered, may appear to be listening only to human reasons regarding a decision to remain within Judaism and making no faith witness about the Messiah. That would not be what comes from God. Peter is then declared to be the rock because he would not change his witness regardless of what came to him. Clearly he was remembered that way in the early Church after accepting martyrdom in Rome, rather than denying Jesus during Nero's persecution.

Even the gates of Hades, the place of the dead, or death itself, will have no control over those who choose to live the life of Christ in this world. Instead, a life of unchanging witness makes Peter the one who has the keys to enter the kingdom for himself and all who follow his example of always witnessing. This section, which has been used as a statement on the establishment of the papacy, carries a broader message in the context of Matthew's writing, even though it does establish Peter's position of primacy as understood by the early Church.

JOURNEY TO JERUSALEM

Chapter 17

A temple tax question (17:24-27) asked if Jesus was a Rabbi since that class was exempt from the temple tax. Peter's answer that Jesus will pay the tax is to say Jesus is not a Rabbi, certainly not in the concept of being only a teacher of Judaism. In fact, Jesus is a teacher who chooses to hide the title because it would be misunderstood during his public life. Matthew included this story to say that calling Jesus only a teacher in this writing, one who brought only new teachings rather than a new relationship with God, would cause a misunderstanding in the time of the writing as well.

Chapter 18

Life in the Church as a disciple (18:1-35) uses some of Mark's work and then Matthew adds some teachings related to the fracturing of the Antioch Church which was occurring in his time. Disciples in the Church community should be open to saving all of their own (18:12-14), no matter how they stray. That is the primary purpose of Matthew's Gospel.

When disagreements arise (18:15-18), as Matthew's community had experienced, individual and group corrections should be tried. Only the one who refuses to respond should be separated from the believers. Prayer together (18:19-20) is necessary since the same union with God that results from a prayer life is the union that exists between members of the Church itself.

Finally, in a community subject to internal divisions, there is never an end to forgiveness (18:21-35). The gift of life from God is eternally open to all of humanity. There can be no witness to Christ which does not contain the constant invitation to enter the kingdom. Those who reject that concept of kingdom reject the kingdom for themselves and are not in the kingdom of God. The unforgiving debtor could never overcome his own debt without the mercy of the master, so such mercy must always be included in the kingdom presented here on earth by disciples reflecting the life of Christ.

Chapter 20

The decision to enter the vineyard (20:1-16) is a parable that acts as a model of the kingdom which brings the reward. The reward does not come from the amount of work that could be done by an individual. If the reward could be earned, it would only be proportional to human value. The Law does not promise salvation, so it does not promise a resurrection beyond a human life. That is not so with the kingdom which is an entry to life with God starting in this world and, therefore, far beyond what could be earned by human activity. First and last, in this world goods have no meaning in relation to an eternal reward.

JERUSALEM MINISTRY

Chapter 21

Matthew made a change in the Palm Sunday entrance to Jerusalem (21:1-11), which is often viewed as a misunderstanding by him of how Scripture was written. It is more likely just another statement against those who might attempt to inwardly accept the Messiah and outwardly remain within Judaism without witnessing. A repetition of statements with the same meaning is very common in poetic writing in the Old Testament. The quote from a prophet (21:5) is about the Messiah "riding on a donkey, on a colt, the foal of a donkey" (Zec 9:9). This repetition of donkey and colt would be interpreted as riding on a young donkey on which no one else had ridden with the second phrase modifying the first one. It may have a meaning that there is something special or unique about such a rider that is now lost in modern understanding. Matthew made the quotation say that Jesus rode "on a donkey and on a colt" as if he actually had sat on two animals at the same time. The disciples are said to have laid their cloaks on "their backs" and Jesus sat "on them."

To assume that such a scene was actually meant by the Evangelist, because he had such a poor understanding of how the Old Testament writing should be interpreted, can hardly be taken seriously. The more reasonable assumption is that Christians in Antioch were questioning if it were possible to remain Jewish and Christian at the same time when one required silence about the Messiah and the other demanded a

witness. Matthew seems to ask if such a dual religious decision would be any more comfortable, or even serious, than
Jesus trying to ride two animals at the same time as he presented himself on Palm Sunday. The picture presented was
meant to be humorous and would have been read that way by
those early Christians familiar with the text. However, the
question addressed was very serious for the community of
Matthew and that is shown clearly.

Matthew added three parables into Mark's Jerusalem
ministry that address the Antioch decision to respond to the
Messiah. The parable of the two sons (21:28-32) is very
direct since it involves those who say one thing and live
another. The one saved is the one who lives out the request
of the father. The parable clearly relates to those who had
been baptized as Christians but then contemplated living
only as Jewish. They hoped that their acceptance of Christ
would be valid when the Second Coming occurred. Accepting the Messiah by name, yet not witnessing to the relationship with the Lord in one's life, is not living out the Christian
responsibility.

Chapter 22

The second and third parables involve a wedding feast
(22:1-14). In Jesus' time, the key to the wedding feast was
the attitude of people living in small remote villages. Life
there would have been dull, incredibly dull by today's standards, with an occasional wedding feast being a major social
event. The wedding feast of a well-to-do landowner might be
the social event of a decade and no one would ever consider
missing it. Yet, as Jesus tells the parable, the people are more
interested in everyday farming or business than in this very
special event. Jesus' listeners originally would have been
shocked at the conclusion of the parable which proposed such
a foolish choice.

Matthew may have adjusted the parable slightly to make
it fit the big city conditions of his readers. Thus it becomes
the wedding feast given by a king which would be a

once-in-a-lifetime event even in Antioch. Instead of just ignoring the invitations, these people also attack the king's servants who are delivering the invitations. They are guaranteeing that their response would not be simply a neutral missing out of a great party. Rather, those who did not choose to come to the banquet were actually inviting death. Those who rejected the Messiah who is the son of an Almighty Father would reject everything. With reflection, humor would come from the fact that no one could ever make such a choice in real life. However, the serious side would be in the decision of real life with God who invited everyone to life. That was the choice being considered in Antioch.

An addition by Matthew to the parable of the wedding feast involves a guest without a wedding garment (22:8-14). This is another parable since it carries a separate meaning pointing toward a common conclusion. Anyone familiar with Middle Eastern hospitality even today would recognize that conflict and opposition would remain outside and not enter a celebration. The guest to a meal within a home is made to feel like an important member of the family. To simply admire something within another's house is to have it immediately given as a gift. There is practically no request by a guest that could be refused. At an important feast, such hospitality would be carried to an extreme degree. What is described as a host deliberately rejecting a guest would be beyond the belief of anyone.

The story in Matthew's time was related to the disciple invited into the kingdom who wanted to remain in Judaism without showing through discipleship that the invitation has been accepted in baptism. The garment is the life of Christ which was not being worn by the one who wanted to live within the kingdom. Yet, if that life of Christ were not worn, if that life were not lived out, the person would have no life within the kingdom. Rejecting Christ is as unbelievable as ignoring the wedding feast invitation, and not living the life of Christ is as final as an action which could never occur at a wedding feast.

Chapter 23

A sermon on the woes (23:1-32) counterbalances the Sermon on the Mount earlier in Matthew's Gospel. It starts with Jesus addressing the people (23:1-12), those open to being his disciples in Antioch as well as those with him in Palestine. Jesus calls on the people to accept the interpretation of the Jewish religious authorities about Scripture, since that is revelation from God. He cautions them not to follow the example or the life of these authorities since they stop at following rules related to the Law rather than living the revelation completely.

Matthew then seems to add a second set of prohibitions about following the lifestyles of Jewish leaders. The Pharisees would certainly have been called Rabbi, meaning teacher, and were probably addressed by devoted students as father and master or leader. While these titles would apply to how the disciples are to live, they were not used by the early Church because only the Lord is the Christian example of living the relationship. Were Matthew free to change Jesus' words, the explanation might be made more clearly. Paul used the term Body of Christ when explaining how to live the relationship that brings salvation. That term would fit the meaning that Matthew seems to express as the teacher, father, and master which the disciples are to find only in the heavenly Father and in the Messiah.

A list of "woes" (23:13-39) against the scribes and Pharisees could have been developed from isolated sayings of Jesus against Jewish interpretations of the Law. It would have been a common expression relating to an action which did not make a person "blessed." The term hypocrite could have had two possible meanings in Matthew's time, but neither would carry the same negative connotation at that time, as it does today.[23] The first meaning refers to the mask that is worn by an actor to designate a character in a play. The actor can change roles simply by substituting a different mask, since the remainder of the costume is the same for each actor. The criticism meant by referring to this practice is of one playing a role, rather than actually living a life. However, for Matthew's purpose, just playing the role would be the same as accepting baptism but not living the life of Christ.

The second meaning of the term hypocrite would be "nitpicker" which fits the Pharisee's interest in minor rules and resulted in criticism from Jesus earlier (Mk 7:1-8). That meaning would fit almost perfectly with what Jesus is saying in some of the woes listed below, but it would be a less clear warning to the early Church. Matthew writes the Gospel for the Church, not just to tell disciples what Jesus thought of Jewish leaders. Here, either meaning could be used, but someone acting like a Christian but not living the relationship would be the stronger message.

The first woe (23:13) is against those satisfied with the rules and not actually entering the kingdom. Nothing would strike a familiar chord so quickly in Antioch. This would be the opposite from living the kingdom completely. The second woe (23:15) is against the Jewish practice of not being open to outsiders even though Judaism itself had been admired by Gentiles in parts of the Middle East. In Matthew's situation, Judaism would not be open even to those of Jewish background if they accepted the Messiah. That attitude could hardly be kingdom-oriented.

The obsession with rules and insignificant interpretations (23:16-22) would be criticized by Jesus as an indication that his opponents could not even agree on the presence of God. Not wanting to speak the Divine Name of Yahweh, Jewish practice was to shy away from even using the term God. Temple, the place of God, or altar, a place where God accepted a gift, could be used as substitutes in common oaths as a way of calling on God as witness without using the word God. The insistence that the gold of the Temple, a reflection of God's beauty, or the altar gift, something actually accepted by God, be used as substitutes for Temple or altar was an example of adding minute regulations to no end. Such meaningless practices could hardly be a source of blessing. Yet, for a Christian to not witness to the living of a shared life with God would be a denial of revelation itself.

Making a show of giving tithes on the smallest of assets (23:23-24) or being concerned with insignificant cases of ritual impurity might have been a common criticism of Pharisees (23:25-26). However, to do that while ignoring a witness to the Messiah of God would be a difficult criticism to accept for those of Matthew's community contemplating a return to Judaism. Being worried about a loss of ritual purity by stepping on the marking stone of a grave (23:27-28) while not being worried about losing the life that gained the kingdom also carried a grave message to any wavering disciples. Judaism had built monuments and decorated tombs for prophets sent from God (23:29-32) but had a history of ignoring their messages. Now some members of Matthew's community are considering ignoring the message of salvation that goes beyond all previous revelation. They would have to see this as a repeat of earlier failures.

The condemnation by Jesus (23:33-36) of such practices found in Palestine was repeated in Antioch for Matthew's readers who were considering the choice of going down that same path. Jerusalem and Judaism would be left desolate unless the inhabitants called the Messiah of God blessed, one truly from Yahweh (23:37-39). That was something that would no longer be allowed in the synagogue when the Gospel was written. Matthew's readers should not wonder about what Jesus might say to them if they refused to witness that Jesus is the one from God. That would be another woe, but this time directed at themselves rather than scribes and Pharisees.

Chapter 24

After a section of Mark's comments on the last days, Matthew introduced a Second Coming and judgment teaching (24:37-44), which started with a warning to live the awareness of the last days even before they came. Warnings of the need for change had been recorded in the Old

Testament and the results for those who ignored such warnings were known. Judgment after the coming of Christ would be similar, so why would anyone risk living differently than required for salvation. A disciple who was assured of salvation would be the one who was always conscientious (24:45-51). Even if there was an unexpected delay, as with the original view of a Second Coming, to abandon discipleship in the interim was to court disaster.

Chapter 25

Disciples who did not adjust to the changed conditions of a delayed Second Coming (25:1-13) would likewise fail. A quick Second Coming had seemed to make the choice of being a disciple of the Messiah quite easy. That choice required some adjustment over time to remain loyal to the calling since the expected Second Coming had not occurred, while the conditions with regard to Judaism had changed dramatically. An adjustment was what would be required in Antioch also and the adjustment period would be a time to use one's gifts to expand the kingdom (25:14-30). The one who used the period as a time to hide their position as disciple, to bury their relationship with Christ so deep in the synagogue or otherwise that it could not be seen by others, would lose even the little reward they had earlier accepted.

Then, in what might be the most terrible words in the New Testament, Matthew includes a description of the reality of the last judgment (25:31-46). There would be no easy rules to being a disciple; it would require living the life of Christ in whatever situations arise. This scene was not presented as good versus bad, Christians versus Jews, or church versus unbelievers. Both groups were to be Christian and the difference in judgment is based on how they lived out the Christian life.

Neither of the two groups in the judgment scene were sure of the results of their actions and neither remembered seeing the Messiah specifically. Those who fail do not seem to know where they failed, and those who succeed do not remember which described actions had been done by them as disciples. Those who lived as Christ did, by acting as a result of love rather than rules and in being open to all the opportunities to do the work of the kingdom, became members of the kingdom. The others did not.

Suddenly, in very specific ways, Christian morality and the heart of discipleship are shown to be active love, the same love as shown by the Messiah. How would that be expressed if no indication of a relationship with the Messiah could be expressed? The words of Christ are teachings of how to live the kingdom. In this Gospel, they became teachings to Antioch, and to every other Church community, with a clarity which cannot be avoided.

PASSION AND RESURRECTION

Chapter 26
The Passion and death narrative as a fixed narrative from an earlier time meant Matthew could make few changes to it just as Mark had to accept it in his Gospel. A number of minor changes may only reflect differences between the original narratives used by Mark as known in the Church of Rome and Matthew from the narrative known in Antioch. The formation of the plot to accuse Jesus of sedition before Pilate so as to obtain his crucifixion is retained as in Mark (26:1-5).

In the institution of the Eucharist (26:26-29), instead of Mark's simple "Take it" when the bread is distributed, Matthew has "Take it and eat." In the passing of the cup, Matthew adds, "Drink all of you from this." Such changes may only represent Eucharistic traditions at Antioch, but it could be a reminder that every disciple must be part of the new covenant, not just know about it. They must actually participate in the Eucharistic meal not just the Service of the Word in the morning synagogue meeting. What feeds their lives as disciples is the Body and Life of Christ.

A significant addition is the information given about Judas in this Gospel. The amount of payment made to Judas is given as thirty pieces of silver (26:14-16). That was the price of a slave's life according to the Law (Ex 21:32). When the disciples were told that one of them would betray Jesus, they answered "Not I Lord, surely?" except Judas (26:20-25). He calls Jesus Rabbi, or teacher, the term used by Jesus' opponents.

Chapter 27

Finally, the Gospel tells in detail of the death of Judas (27:3-10), which could produce a somewhat better picture of him. However, the end of the account is often given a confusing interpretation because Matthew mentions Jeremiah as the prophet being fulfilled by the actions, yet the actual words of the prophet being quoted are from Zechariah (Zec 27:9-10).

Some background to the Judas story (27:3-10) is helpful. It was a practice among Jews to allow certain purchase agreements to be rescinded if the money was returned to the purchaser within a certain period of time. For certain property purchases, the period for backing out of a sale was one year, after which the sale was permanent. Occasionally a purchaser would hear, just prior to the one-year period, that a deal might be rescinded. He might then take a leave of absence so as to make return of the purchase price impossible. The seller could prevent this ruse from being successful by depositing the money in the temple treasury for the absent purchaser and the deal was considered cancelled.

The importance of Judas returning the thirty pieces of silver to the religious authority is that it indicates a desire by him to rescind his involvement in the plot. When the money was not accepted back by religious authorities to rescind the deal, Judas flung it into the temple sanctuary as if to cancel his involvement in the plot in accordance with the Law. Yet, Judas died after opposing Jesus, while Peter gained forgiveness through repentance for denying the Lord. The conclusion is that following the Law as Judas did resulted in death, while going beyond it in faith and being forgiven resulted in life. That conclusion could not be missed by Matthew's readers in Antioch.

The second point of the Judas text involves the Jeremiah prophecy (27:9) which is said to be fulfilled, but is not quoted. At the time of the fall of Jerusalem to the Babylonians in 587 BC, Jeremiah was asked to give a good prophecy about the result. However, Jeremiah received a message from Yahweh to buy a field from a relative (Jer 32:1-44) and he did so. Then he seemed to question the order to buy a field at the very time when Jerusalem's walls were being breached. He extolled all of the great works of Yahweh on behalf of the Jewish people and asked if, at this desperate time, all the help that would be given to Yahweh's people was advice to buy a field. The response from Yahweh was that Jerusalem would fall and the Israelites would go into exile. However, owning part of the promised land would mean that the people would have a place to which they could return and have their fortunes restored at some future time.

The fulfilling of this prophecy of Jeremiah, by purchasing the potter's field through money involved in the death of Jesus, seems to be that a right is purchased for Gentiles to be in the promised land. It is a way of saying that what is actually fulfilled is that the kingdom is opened to Gentiles and to the world. The promise of God through the Messiah goes far beyond just a right to live in Jewish Palestine. The fulfillment, while adding Zechariah's words about the purchase of the field, is understood in Jeremiah's context in that the sacrifice of Jesus opened the kingdom to everyone, just as Matthew has written.

Another minor change is the addition of Pilate washing "his hands" of responsibility for the crucifixion and the response of the crowd. Pilate's washing of his hands shifts blame more directly to the Jewish leaders even though his innocence isn't much different from that of Judas. In response, the people present before Pilate declare, "His blood be on us and our children" (27:25) as if they were accepting the guilt of having Jesus crucified. However, that language reflects Moses sealing the covenant at the base of Mt. Sinai by pouring half of the blood of the covenant sacrifice on the altar and casting the other half on the Israelites (Ex 24:6-8). It is the language of accepting a new covenant through a sacrifice to Yahweh. For Matthew, the words are the proper acceptance of a new covenant regardless of how those present with Jesus may have understood the meaning.

At Jesus' death (27:51-54) an earthquake and the rising of the dead are recorded. Such language was intended to convey the earth-shaking nature of what has occurred and its meaning for everyone, that death in this world is not final for disciples. The mention of a Roman guard at the tomb (27:62-66) was to counter the explanation from Judaism that somehow the disciples removed the body from the tomb rather than admit that a Resurrection had occurred. Jews would have had to claim a human removal, yet there was clear evidence that such a removal could not have taken place.

Chapter 28

The Resurrection scene (28:1-8) was changed little from Mark except that the women, who were the original witnesses, "ran to tell the disciples," rather than running away in fear. In an appearance of Jesus to the women (28:9-10), the disciples are to be told to leave Jerusalem for Galilee. Matthew's readers would see in this an instruction not to be afraid to leave Judaism for an area of both Gentiles and Jews. A plot to explain away the Resurrection (28:11-15) was recorded as the basis for Jewish non-acceptance of that event which declares Jesus to be beyond the Law. Matthew probably was warning his readers that, as obvious as the plot would be to anyone who had become a disciple, this type of deception is what would have to be accepted by anyone returning to Judaism and remaining silent about the Messiah.

A last appearance of Jesus to the disciples (28:16-20) occurred in Galilee where he gave a concluding command to all disciples. They fell down before Jesus indicating their certainty that he is the risen Messiah, with the comment that "some hesitated." Surely those who hesitated would be the ones in Antioch who were still undecided about the decision they were facing. However, it is to the disciples who accept Jesus as the resurrected Messiah that all authority in heaven and earth is given. They are the ones sent to the whole world. Their baptism will be in the name of the Father, Son and Holy Spirit. There can be no baptism given, no salvation opened, without proclaiming the conclusions that Jesus is the Messiah and that he came from God with God's own Spirit

The silence of a Christian trying to live within Judaism would be impossible if salvation was desired. The promised relationship is of the Messiah with the Church always. It is a living relationship not merely the revelation of some additional teachings. The Gospel ends with the proclamation that Jesus remains with Christianity forever since they share the same life.

THE GOSPEL OF LUKE

CONTEXT OF LUKE AND ACTS

The context proposed in the introduction for the Gospel of Luke and for Acts, Volume II of Luke's work with the same context, to a great extent is as follows:

- Written in a city of Greece or Macedonia in 80-90
- After the separation of Christianity from Judaism
- By Luke, a disciple of Paul

Subjects addressed are:

- Does the lack of an expected Second Coming indicate failure?
- Does the lack of a connection to Judaism indicate a failure?
- Did Jesus intend to include Gentiles in the kingdom?

Luke's responses:

- The kingdom was always meant for the whole world
  - in the Gospel of Jesus (Luke's Gospel)
  - in the Gospel of the Holy Spirit (Acts)
- Live discipleship as a means of bringing the kingdom to all people

The additions that Luke makes to Mark's Gospel emphasize that the kingdom is open to everyone including the Gentiles who may constitute a majority in Luke's community. Living discipleship means making the Body of Christ, which is present in the Church, reflect the way Jesus lived in his public life. A major section of the additions are included in the journey to Jerusalem which, in the early Church and in Mark's Gospel, was called the Way of the Lord. The sections of the Gospel that are additions are shown in Appendix A.

A second major addition by Luke is the document known as the Acts of the Apostles. In reality, it is simply an extension of the Gospel itself. As Jesus brought the message of revelation to those in Palestine who knew the One True God, Acts describes how that message was brought from Palestine to the Church community of Luke. That was the work of the Holy Spirit even though carried out with some initial hesitance, in the acceptance of Gentiles, before the Council of Jerusalem. While the view Luke presents from the teachings of Jesus and the work of the early Church differs from the earliest expectations of the Church, there is no indication of failure. The plan of God from the start was to open the gift of a relationship with God to everyone, and at the time of the writing that plan was being implemented.

The recipients of each Gospel should recognize all of the stories told about Jesus. They would see the response to their situations in what they already knew about Jesus. In the same way, the stories that are stitched together in Acts would have been entirely known by Luke's readers. Like the Gospel, Acts is not new information but a new view produced from a selection and arrangement of existing information. There could be no indication of failure if Luke's community had known all the stories at an earlier time and now saw it collected together to answer their questions.

THE BIRTH NARRATIVE

Chapter 1

Luke's great additions to Mark's Gospel spell out how to live as disciples by looking at how Jesus lived. The introduction (1:1-4) seems to dedicate the account to a disciple named Theophilus who is addressed as someone important in Luke's part of the Church. Since Theophilus means "Friend of God," the dedication could be to all disciples rather than a single individual. Luke knows of accounts written by others, which include Mark's Gospel for sure, but he calls his own writing an "ordered account." It is not clear what that statement means since the order of Mark's account in terms of events is kept intact with few changes. Apart from the birth and Resurrection narratives, Luke's additions are primarily teachings, rather than a change in the order of events. The ordered account could be one prepared especially for the community of Luke to address their specific questions and so be ordered for them. The comment that Theophilus will know how "well founded" his earlier teaching was means that from reading this account we have evidence that all, or nearly all, of the stories must have been known to him from before the time of the Gospel.

The opening of the text itself is through a series of parallel accounts of the annunciations and births of John the Baptist and Jesus. It seems to have major differences from the birth narrative of Matthew, yet they share a number of important concepts as shown:[24]

1. Jesus' birth is related to the reign of Herod.
2. Mary is a virgin, betrothed to Joseph, but not yet living with him.
3. Joseph is of the house of David.
4. An angel announces the birth of Jesus.
5. Jesus is to be recognized as a son of David.
6. Jesus' conception takes place through the Holy Spirit.
7. Joseph is not involved in the conception.
8. The name of Jesus is imposed from heaven prior to his birth.
9. The angel identifies Jesus as Savior.
10. Jesus is born after Mary and Joseph live together.
11. Jesus is born at Bethlehem.
12. The Holy Family settles in Nazareth in Galilee.

Even though there is a distinct variation in how these points are described in the two birth narratives, it seems obvious that some common tradition must have existed very early. The variation in the explanation must have occurred in the half century between the Resurrection and the writings of Matthew and Luke. It seems unlikely that two different ways of expressing the birth events could have come from the Holy Family or relatives of Jesus. On the other hand, independent compositions by the two Evangelists would require their readers to suddenly accept an unknown story from disciples who may have been known in their communities for a long period of time. That hardly fits with the pattern of using known traditions and stories to construct a narrative as seems so obvious in all of the Gospels. However, it should be noted that any attempt to present the twelve points in a narrative form would require some explanatory writing to describe the scene. The birth narrative is little more than the list of concepts converted into such a narrative. Such explanatory notes could have developed over time or been established by the Evangelist. The variation in setting does not detract from the essential points. Only the Magi story is really different.

The birth narrative could have been an addition after the remainder of the Gospel had been written, at least in a preliminary form. If the birth narrative was removed from the Gospel account, there would be no hint in the remainder of the Gospel that it had been left out. However, these birth narrative stories only resemble an addition because Mark, for his own purposes, started his Gospel with the opening of the public life of Jesus. The major parables found in this Gospel are not seen as a later addition just because they do not occur elsewhere, yet the situation is the same.

The public life of Jesus is introduced (3:1-2) with a dating in the reign of Tiberius Caesar which introduces the concept of an initial starting point. However, the composition of the Gospel out of stories known to the early Church argues against that concept. It is unlikely that the stories of Jesus' public life would include birth details unless they were mentioned by Jesus at the time. If the Evangelist had added little to these stories collected by the early Church, the lack of birth narrative connections would be the likely result. The repetition of dating new sections of the Gospel seems to be a technique of Luke, rather than an indication of an earlier starting point, since the birth of Jesus also has a separate dating introduction.

An annunciation to Zechariah, the father of John the Baptist (1:3-25), starts the parallel annunciation accounts. This is a Jewish event so the dating is only in connection with King Herod. The annunciation account includes Old Testament imagery with both Zechariah and Elizabeth being old and childless, like Abraham and Sarah. The annunciation is only to Zechariah and he is shown to be lacking in faith, but will become God's agent anyway. However, Zechariah's response of "How can I be sure of this?" is the same as Abraham's response (Gen 15:6-8) which God "counted as making him justified." So Zechariah's doubting must be considered worse than Abraham's because so much more revelation had become available to him through Judaism. The meaning of the annunciation is not just as a birth, but as a sign to Israel which confirms John as a prophet.

A parallel annunciation to Mary (1:26-38) introduces Jesus' parents and the fact that they also were not expecting a child. Here the annunciation is to Mary only and her response is an act of faith in the Christian tradition. What is asked of Mary, to have a child, is not considered to be a difficult task, but something commonplace which a young woman would want and expect from marriage. Mary's response is one of complete faith because of the divine nature of the request, rather than because the request is difficult or that she fully understands what outcome will result from the request. Her single question concerns how she will accomplish this, since at this time she is not living with Joseph and doesn't know when that will occur. The answer is that it will be accomplished by God's will, which means that her part is to have faith in God's plan. She is the first of the new kingdom to say "Yes, Lord" and is, therefore, the first and model disciple for Luke's readers.

Mary had no knowledge of the relationship of this promised birth to salvation for all people. She didn't respond out of knowledge but out of the trust she would have in anything coming from God. All disciples are called to review their own response in trust of God. What has been accepted as a message of revelation is sufficient for Christians to change their lives, or in times of extreme difficulty to give up this life. In that trust there is an imitation of the acceptance of Mary. In her acceptance of God's will in her life, Mary makes a statement equal to the baptism promise which is to put on a new life. Her acceptance of the role of disciple, especially letting the Spirit control her life, is the same as the meaning of confirmation. The result of the acceptance of a living relationship with God is to receive the physical body of Jesus Christ within her, which is what the disciple receives in Eucharist. The basis for understanding sacraments may be more clearly seen in sections like this than in hunting for isolated proof texts from the sayings of Jesus. Luke's readers would grasp this meaning.

In the two annunciation accounts, there is the closing of the Old Testament relationship in John and the opening of a New Testament relationship in Jesus. What occurs should be understandable within Judaism because God's method of speaking to them through prophets or messengers as signs is utilized. The annunciation to Mary is a model of the Christian relationship where a faith response was made even though the future results of such an act of faith were never completely known. This structure of understanding the annunciation would be recognized by Luke's readers, who originally made an act of faith based on an expected Second Coming and an earthly kingdom. Later they saw conditions change from what they had expected as a result of their faith, but now are asked to live the faith response as outlined by Luke in this Gospel.

The two annunciations are brought together in the visitation scene of Mary going to Elizabeth (1:39-56). It is not just a three-month visit to assist Elizabeth, but the explosion of recognition and joy of the true fulfillment of Judaism's relationship with God after centuries of waiting. Only Luke could have two women knowing, yet hiding, the news that was so important to Judaism and, of course, to the whole rest of the world.

Elizabeth's cry of "Blessed are you among women" might have been more shocking for Mary than for us. It is about the same as Uzziah's praise of Judith (Jud 12:23) when she returns with the head of the Assyrian general, Holofernes, resulting in the defeat of the Assyrians. Mary may well recognize that she will be involved in something beyond what she could have expected. Her response in the Magnificat probably comes from a Jewish hymn which Luke has used to conclude the scene. The Magnificat is Israel's own statement, yet many of the Jewish people will fail to recognize the meaning when it is fulfilled in their own lives.

The birth of John the Baptist (1:57-58) is minor compared to the birth of Jesus. However, John's special selection by God (1:57-80) and his importance as a prophet, as proclaimed in the Benedictus by Zechariah, show how he must have been seen within Judaism. Judaism knew he was from God and should have responded in faith, but many failed to do so. This tradition could have come from disciples of John the Baptist. Luke, as the companion of Paul and perhaps involved in Paul's mission to Ephesus (Acts 19:1-7), could have had a continuing contact with such disciples and their traditions.

Chapter 2

Jesus' birth account (2:1-20) starts with a new historical introduction, not in a Jewish setting but in the history of the whole world. It produces an emphasis that the meaning of the Messiah is a change affecting the world rather than only Judaism. The mention of the census while Quirinius was governor of Syria provides the only questionable date in the entire New Testament dating of events. The birth of Jesus is tied to the reign of Herod in Matthew and also in Luke through John the Baptist's birth. Herod died in 4 BC while Quirinius did not become governor in Syria until 6, ten years later. A census would occur when there was a change in the rulership situation to gain an understanding of both population and the resources of an area. A census could have occurred when Herod was followed by his son Archelaus in 4 BC, but was essential ten years later when a Roman governor was put in power. Therefore, what is known about the political situation in the Middle East from Roman history does not support Luke's dating of a census near the end of Herod's reign. Many attempts have been made to justify Luke's report, but all require rather extreme assumptions.

A change in addressing this problem by challenging the death dates of Herod and of his son Philip could reopen this question of the census. Herod's death occurred after an eclipse of the moon and before Passover according to Josephus. A partial eclipse on March 13 in 4 BC is the basis for using that year for Herod's death. A total lunar eclipse in 1 BC would meet the same criteria and, to some scholars, might fit the situation more easily. Were that used, then 1 BC would be the "0" year for establishing the AD dating. Jesus would have had to be born before April of 1 BC or, if the December birth date were used, just before the beginning of 1 BC. That change would make the present calendars correct in representing present years as actual years after Jesus' birth.

An argument which has been used against the 1 BC eclipse date is that it doesn't fit with the date of Philip's death, another son of Herod, which occurred in the twentieth year of Emperor Tiberius' reign, or 34, after a reign of 38 years. However, unlike present copies of Josephus' work, the oldest copies of his writings do not say Philip died in the twentieth year of the reign of Tiberius. Most of the oldest copies say it occurred in the twenty-second year. That would fit with a 2 BC death date for Herod, or even an early 1 BC date. Like so many details from Scripture that were declared "false" by scholars and later found to be correct, Luke too could be proven correct.

Luke's purpose in mentioning the census may be no more than to explain why Joseph and Mary, who lived in Nazareth, journeyed to Bethlehem at the time of Jesus' birth. The connection between the census and the place of birth may have already been present in the material Luke used rather than a connection written into the text by him. Even though the normal view of Joseph is that he only operated a small carpentry shop in the village of Nazareth, his real position might have been quite different.

A person called a carpenter, or tekton in Greek, would be someone involved in the construction of larger buildings and providing roof beams. That type of position might involve moving from project to project. Joseph could have found work at Sepphoris which was being built as a major city only four miles from Nazareth. Therefore, his need to return to Bethlehem for the registration could be due to that being his permanent residence, especially if he owned property there.

The return from Egypt in Matthew's Gospel indicates he intended to settle in Bethlehem, but decided instead on Nazareth because Archelaus was then ruler of Judea. These details of place and time have no meaning in reading Scripture, but are still used on occasion to call Scripture into question. The use of an unsuitable date has no effect on the faith statement made in the narrative.

The birth of Jesus is normally thought to have occurred in a stable which may have been in a nearby cave (2:6-7). What is stated in the text is only that the baby Jesus was laid in a manger. Mangers most likely would have been available at an inn, in that part of the courtyard where the animals of travelers were sheltered and fed overnight. Most of such guests would have camped elsewhere in the courtyard rather than having private rooms inside, as modern-day travelers would expect. All Luke may have intended in the "no room in the inn" statement is that there was no room for the Messiah among his people, since that could have been a question in Luke's community.

The shepherds were similar to outsiders in Judaism even though the King David image as shepherd is not the image of an outsider. Shepherds would take their flocks away from settled areas during the winter time when forage was available

on the hillsides and the fields near villages were under culti-
vation. Only after crops had been harvested in the spring
would the fields be used as pasture areas. The shepherds
would be away from Jewish religious life for much of the year
and would have to tend their flocks even on the Sabbath.
Therefore, they could appear to be closer to resident Gentiles
than faithful Jews. In that way, they were both outsiders and
the ones from Judaism who accepted the sign that the
Messiah had come. It is easy to see Luke's purpose if his readers would look like "resident Gentiles" by being excluded
from synagogues after the separation of Christians from
Judaism. The statement that puts the shepherds in the fields
(2:8) suggests a birth in the May to October period after the
harvest, rather than the popular December date used today.

The circumcision and naming of Jesus (2:21) requires
no comment. However, the purification rite is combined
with a redemption payment in a presentation of the child in
the Temple (2:22-24). The purification ritual was due to the
shedding of blood in the birth and required the sacrifice of a
pair of turtle doves or pigeons. A redemption payment
involved first-born males who originally in Judaism were con-
secrated to God for duty in the Temple. Once the tribe of
Levi had been dedicated to Temple duty, the first-born sons
could be freed from that requirement by the payment of a
small tax. Luke does not mention that payment, and it is
often assumed that he did not understand the rules connected
with these rites. However, it might be Luke's deliberate way
of saying that Jesus retained the dedication of his life to God.

Two representatives of Judaism who recognized the
Messiah in the Temple were Simeon and Anna (2:25-38).
They are portrayed as faithful Jews who lived their whole
lives in anticipation of seeing the Messiah and were rewarded
for their dedication and loyalty. The lesson would be clear to
Luke's readers that those who were faithful to Jewish traditions could find and recognize the Messiah. The lack of a
Jewish connection to Christianity would not be a failure if
the reason for separation could be found in Judaism choosing

not to accept the Messiah who was heralded by a prophet and signs from his birth.

The early life events are then introduced (2:39-52) to present some conclusions about the Holy Family prior to Jesus' public life. He grew up quietly in Nazareth. However, he recognized his ministry from little on and, quite certainly, at the time of coming of age as an adult. There was no surprise for him when he embarked on this public ministry. Mary became aware of the meaning of the signs as they unfolded and that was acceptable to this perfect disciple. She knew God's will was involved and that was adequate for her faith without understanding ahead of time where it would take her son or what it would mean to her.

JESUS' PUBLIC MINISTRY IN GALILEE

Chapter 3

Luke opened the public life of Jesus with a new historical introduction of both political and religious leadership (3:1-2). As at Jesus' birth, the meaning of his public life affected the world but with special emphasis on Palestine and the surrounding area. The final inclusion of high priests expresses the Jewish religious meaning, of course, but has the look of an afterthought.

The introductory quotation (3:3-5) from Isaiah has an addition (3:6) to show that, even in the Old Testament, the Messiah would bring a message to the whole world, including Luke's community. Then Luke introduced much of the John the Baptist material Matthew also had added, and to be so similar indicates that it must have come from a written source. However, a section of teaching on how individuals are to respond is an addition found only in Luke (3:10-14). The starting point of Luke's Gospel message was that hearers must respond with a change in their lives which makes the world better for everyone. The role of discipleship in the kingdom, which Luke will stress, exists from the very beginning, even from John the Baptist.

After the baptism scene, Luke provided a genealogy quite different from the one provided by Matthew (3:23-38). The genealogy starts with Jesus as an adopted son of Joseph and then proceeds to David through a different series of descendants than given by Matthew. Such a second lineage cannot occur in a list of descendants so both genealogies cannot be authentic. Luke's version would be the more difficult to obtain because the latest name that could be know from Scripture would be David's son, Nathan, from the tenth century BC. Having different names for Joseph's father causes problems in accepting either list. However, the real meaning behind Luke's genealogy is probably shown in being traced back to Adam and creation rather than in the details of Joseph's descent from Abraham and David. The meaning of the Messiah for Luke is never found only in Jesus' position within Judaism, or from Abraham, but in what was meant for all creation. The plan of God from the start is a Messiah who comes for all peoples not just those of the nation that was prepared to recognize him.

Chapter 4

Luke changes the order of the temptations (4:1-10) from Matthew's by reversing the second and third temptation. While there isn't much agreement from scholars on the reason for the change, it may indicate the devil's interest in determining what type of Messiah had come. In that case, the production of bread in the desert may mean a test to see if the Messiah would be greater than Moses, who was associated with manna. The second temptation would be the test to determine if the Messiah would be greater than David who was associated with political power. The last temptation would be a test to see if the Messiah was greater than the temple religion. The devil's temptations do not produce an answer since that will come only "at the appointed time" (4:13). However, for Luke's community with some questions about a kingdom to be established in a Second Coming, the real answer would be beyond any of the three possibilities.

The divinity answer would be given in the final form in John's Gospel, but the Messiah, as one who is filled with the Spirit of God, had already come to the readers in the teachings of Paul and, therefore, is a Lukan view.

The Galilean ministry of Jesus opened in the synagogue in Nazareth (4:14-30), rather than making that a later visit as in Mark. Jesus proclaimed a reading about the coming of a promised one who is anointed and then declared that it is "fulfilled today." There should be no doubt among the Jewish people that just in knowing the Messiah, by being a relative or someone who grew up with him, is not what determines who is a disciple. The prophet Elijah had been sent to outsiders (4:26) and that condition was present with Jesus, not due to a failure among Judaism, but because it was the plan of God from the start.

Chapter 5

The first disciples were then introduced by Luke in a situation that supports their decision (5:1-11). Unlike in Mark, where the first four drop their nets and follow because Jesus bids them to do so, the first four in Luke follow him in response to a teaching and a sign. To the community of Luke, the disciples were those who changed their lives in response to the signs, rather than in requiring a personal invitation.

Chapter 6

The next break in Mark's sequence of the unfolding of the Galilean ministry is Luke's version of the Sermon on the Mount (6:17-49). Luke tells of Jesus coming down from the mountain to a level place, so it is sometimes called the Sermon on the Plain. It is given where people are waiting, even as occurred at Mount Sinai for the Israelites, rather than only to a select group on a mount as in Matthew.

Luke's beatitudes are shorter and a more stark version than Matthew had given. Now the blessed are those who are actually "poor" and "hungry," rather than the more easily accepted "poor in spirit" or "hungry for justice" that Matthew recorded. Luke's version probably reflects a more literal translation of the Aramaic spoken by Jesus, yet the meaning of the two versions is about the same. If people are fully satisfied with the world as it is, they are less likely to search for the kingdom. It is not in accepting difficulties in life that salvation comes, but in recognizing that the real gift of God goes far beyond creation. When persecution comes (6:22-23), it proves that a person has decided to follow the Lord. The disciple is the one who will accept the kingdom while in this world and reflect it to others, rather than one who only reflects worldly goods. Those who have made worldly goods the meaning of their entire lives (6:24-26) will have those goods while they are in this world, but will be without anything in the next.

A series of teachings that sound difficult to keep, and would prove to be so (6:27-35), provide a different format from the antitheses of Matthew. Normally, decisions are made on the basis of right and wrong. People try to do what is right and avoid what is wrong. In Luke's view, Jesus does not ask about what is right or wrong, since Christians clearly know they should not do what is wrong. The Christian choice in Luke's situation is between what is right in terms of the regulations of the Jewish Law and what is good. Even the kingdom of evil can do what is legally right, but only the kingdom of God is good. To be a disciple is to go beyond right, which in the time of Jesus was to go beyond the Law.

In the question of loving enemies (6:27-28), it is easy to conclude that to designate others as enemies, rather than as opponents, would be to accept hatred since that is the meaning of enemies. A person who accepts someone as an enemy brings hatred into life and in doing so expands the kingdom of evil. It is only in bringing love into a situation that the kingdom of God is expanded (6:29-35). However, that expansion can never be seen by the world if it only happens in situations where the world itself would exhibit love, such as to friends and some relatives. The kingdom of God can only be seen to expand when a disciple brings love into a situation where the world could never exhibit love, such as in a situation with someone whom the world would classify as an enemy. The witness to God is only visible when it replaces a natural reaction.

The same situation exists with regard to compassion (6:36-38), because compassion is an attribute of God's character. Therefore, it must be made present by disciples for the kingdom of God to be seen. Jewish teaching would be to judge leniently, never requiring the full payment. However, the disciple is called to go so far beyond the Law that the disciple would never judge at all.

The parable of the blind guide (6:39-45) carries the concept one step further. Regardless of how great a fault may exist in someone else, people can only change their own lives. Therefore, it does not matter greatly what faults are seen in others; the kingdom of God becomes more present through disciples when they correct their own faults. The fruit produced in that endeavor (6:43-45) shows the world a disciple. Attempts to change others would only reflect the world's own ways. Finally, the definition of disciple is clarified (6:46-49) from the one who says "Lord Lord" to the one who "acts" on the teachings of the Lord. To anchor one's life to a living of the teachings of Christ is to set it on a firm foundation that weathers storms and continues beyond this life.

Chapter 7

This sermon is simpler and more straightforward than the way it was presented in Matthew's Gospel. However, it does not end at this point even though the text says the teaching was over (7:1). The events of chapter seven are a continuation of the additions made in this section to Mark's Gospel. Jesus must move to different scenes to take part in the following events, but the reader should recognize that Luke has inserted them to explain the kingdom teachings, and that is how they should be interpreted.

The cure of the centurion's servant (7:1-10) shows an outsider, the Gentile centurion, and one classified as poor, a servant or slave, since the same Greek word was used for both. The relative positions of the two matter little, since the centurion reacted in concern to the servant's illness. The centurion did not separate his religious experience from his professional experience. In addition, the centurion did not need special visits by the Lord to believe. He resembled Luke's readers in that he would never be visited by Jesus in person. The centurion story has a significant difference from the same story in Matthew. In Luke, the centurion does not meet Jesus but is represented by the Jewish elders, those who are in charge of the synagogues. He may represent Luke's community more clearly because they met Jesus only through the stories brought from Palestine by pilgrims from the Jewish synagogue. Judaism played an initial role in their conversion.

In curing the widow's son (7:11-17) Jesus responded by healing without being asked to intervene. She had lost both her husband and her only son and, therefore, had no one to rely upon for support. Jesus reaches out to her immediately because of her obvious need. Where goodness can be accomplished, a disciple should never need to be asked. Searching out opportunities for doing good should be the way of a disciple.

The section on John the Baptist's questions (7:18-35) is the same as in Matthew. In Luke's time, there could be no second guessing of the decision to follow Jesus. The signs were clear just as they were to John the Baptist and no additional signs were necessary for disciples or for John. Luke's readers may have misunderstood the early Church's expectation of a Second Coming and questioned why the Messiah was not accepted by Judaism. That would be corrected in looking back at the actual teachings of Jesus just as John's disciples were asked to reexamine the prophecies of Isaiah that John originally accepted.

The woman who was a sinner (7:36-50) would have been someone who seemingly had the least claim on the kingdom of God. As a woman, she had little standing in the Middle Eastern culture. Being unmarried she had no real standing in the community. Finally, being a sinner deprived her of any standing in the Jewish religion. She is the true outsider who had no claim on anything. Yet, in her exhibition of love and faith, the attributes of a true disciple, she gains what is needed to enter the kingdom of heaven.

Position in the world, so important in Judaism and often to Christians, counts for nothing, while the signs of poverty, a life of no standing, or even evidence of previous sinfulness are not barriers to the one who accepts discipleship, as Luke's readers are called to do. Jesus sees her love and concludes her sins must have been forgiven. It is a declaration that she must have gained a relationship with God. In her, the Gentile Christians for whom Luke is writing would see their own fears of a separation from a relationship with God disappear in their living discipleship.

Chapter 8

How disciples are defined is shown in the short section (8:1-3) that ends this Lukan insertion. The Twelve, who were known throughout Christianity as disciples, were with Jesus on his journey. Important also were three women named and several others unnamed who assisted in the journey in their own ministry to the Church. Historically in the Church, Mary Magdalene has been equated with the woman in the previous story. However, here she is described as someone possessed "by seven demons." Possession by demons would more likely represent a severe mental condition (8:27) rather than someone involved in sexual sins. Joanna could be a Jewish wife of a non-Jewish steward of a non-Jewish king and, therefore, somewhat of an outcast from Judaism.

The common view of both of them and the meaning of disciples is changed by this short section. These women provided out of their own resources. They gave of themselves and, more clearly, they took on the life of Christ completely. These women had subjected themselves to some danger by traveling around with a group of men to whom they were not married. Even today in parts of the Middle East that situation means they could be punished severely for such actions. They are true disciples.

JOURNEY OF DISCIPLESHIP

Chapter 9

Luke's second insertion is a much greater one which starts as Jesus begins his journey to Jerusalem (9:51). After nearly two chapters of Luke using Mark's writing on the closing of the Galilean ministry, a major teaching on discipleship is given in this journey to Jerusalem. Discipleship had already been called the journey with Jesus, or the Way of the Lord, by the time of Luke's writing (Acts 18:25). Therefore, there could be no better place to insert discipleship teachings than in this journey to Jerusalem and the cross, where Jesus was presented as being involved in fewer events and had more time with the disciples. If Luke's community must now carry out the spreading of the kingdom, which they assumed would be done by Jesus upon his return in the Second Coming, how was that to be accomplished?

Luke's reply is that it would be accomplished by disciples who imitated Jesus in his public life. Luke showed his readers a large number of situations where Jesus taught or responded to problems as they arose. By giving a long list of examples, ten chapters of them, the pattern of Jesus' actions would become known. The disciples of Luke's day may not face the same events as Jesus, yet in being familiar with how Jesus responded elsewhere, they could determine how he would have acted in the situations they faced. Knowing Jesus and responding in his way was the meaning of discipleship. Being Christ to others is all the kingdom instruction a disciple would ever need.

The first few chapters of this addition stress the meaning of discipleship in a way that would seem like new teachings to Luke's community even though they had already heard all of the stories. The initial lesson, perhaps the most basic for any Christian, occurred as they approached a Samaritan village at the start of the journey (9:51-56). The Samaritans, as opponents to Judaism, were less than friendly, and Jesus and the disciples were turned away to start the journey through a different village. James and John suggest that the inhospitable Samaritans should be punished. Jesus rebukes them for treating historical opponents as enemies.

The story takes on a different meaning for Luke's community as they recognize that as Gentiles they were much more clearly enemies of Judaism than the Samaritans. The first lesson becomes: The reign of God is never forced upon anyone. If love is to be a sign of the kingdom, it should be most obvious in how it is spread.

Three potential disciples (9:57-62) met Jesus, but had other concerns. Jesus' message accepts that it is right to have a home, bury the dead, and show friendship in saying farewell. However, in the choice between legally right and good, or close to God, the call of the kingdom is good and must be first. The question of how one's time is spent, as a means of determining what they thought was important, could be asked of all disciples.

Chapter 10

The mission of the disciples (10:1-20) was not just a sending out of the Twelve that Luke had included from Mark's Gospel (9:1-6). Here it is an account of the sending out of the seventy-two, a reference to the seventy-two nations in chapter ten of Genesis. Rather than in seeing ministry only in reference to the twelve tribes representing Judaism, this account reflects evangelizing of the world. We can't tell if this story having seventy-two disciples comes directly from Jesus. However, the Christians of Luke's Church would know of at least Paul, Luke, Timothy, Titus, and Silas as additional disciples sent beyond Palestine to them, so the change in numbers is warranted by their experience. The command to not delay the mission for preparations and lengthy greetings or moving about for comfort, emphasized the need to start the kingdom immediately.

A second conclusion relates to the early Church's insistence on taking the message only to Judaism. That was a decision about being right, or in accordance with the Law, rather than fulfilling the real intent of Jesus. The change to include Gentiles in the kingdom, far from being a result of failure in evangelizing the Jews, was the good decision. That conclusion was substantiated in the response of Jesus as the seventy-two disciples returned (10:21-24). The change could be seen as inspiration from the Father coming through to the Church at some time after the teaching of Jesus was heard. The messengers of the Old Testament revelation and the prophets would rejoice at knowing that the message was now proclaimed everywhere rather than being restricted to Judaism, as it had been in the early understanding.

The acid test of discipleship was shown in the parable of the Good Samaritan (10:25-37) even though the original meaning in the teaching of Jesus carried little of the social gospel message later associated with that parable. The questioner was called a lawyer rather than a temple scribe, since the term scribe would carry the designation of a stenographer among Luke's Gentile audience while a Jewish scribe was an expert in the Old Testament text or the Law. The scribe would have believed that any opportunity for eternal life must come from the Law as expected by any dedicated Jew. Jesus had him recite the pertinent section of the Law to show that the answer is really from love rather than details of the Law. The lawyer was shown to question the designation of neighbor only because Jewish practice would be to interpret neighbor very narrowly. Luke then shows Jesus as interpreting the meaning very broadly so as to include Luke's readers.

A major point in the parable understanding is that the injured traveler was left "half dead," obviously beaten and unconscious. To determine if the traveler were dead or alive, a passer-by would have to touch him and see if he had a heart beat, pulse, or any reaction. The priest and Levite were not included to give an anticlerical cast to the story, but because of their need to retain ritual purity. Touching a body would bring ritual impurity on any person and, for a priest or Levite who worked in the Temple, this ritual impurity might temporarily prevent them from fulfilling their temple duties to God and their nation. Their caution was seen as a decision which is legally right under the Law. However, the most basic reading of the Law would say that a response in love would be a good response, especially at a time when special love was demanded. The Samaritan was an outsider, and even though he accepted the first five books of the Old Testament that make up the Law, he made a choice based on fulfilling the Law most perfectly, rather than being tied to a temple response. Moving beyond the Law was necessary for discipleship rather than an indication of failure.

Martha and Mary (10:38-42) faced a similar choice between right and good. However, this story had a meaning that carried over more directly to those disciples living outside of Judaism. Martha's duties were essential to living and to do them and request assistance from others was indeed right. However, for a disciple, being with the Lord is first in importance because that relationship was always related to God's work and, therefore, to doing good. It is related to the life put on at baptism rather than only to activities related to normal everyday life and comfort.

Chapter 11

Prayer was emphasized by Jesus as part of a personal relationship with God (11:1-13) rather than as a legal requirement. Luke would include this teaching because prayer among Gentiles would be much less developed than among Christians of a Jewish background who would have started with a more developed prayer life. The version of the Lord's prayer used by Luke probably reflects a rather literal translation to Greek from the very crude Aramaic language spoken by Jesus. That it had not been polished into a liturgical form, as in the version used by Matthew, probably indicates that it was not used as regularly in a Gentile community. Yet, the prayer brings out the daily personal relationship with God necessary for a disciple, shown by asking for bread, an every-day necessity. Kingdom comes in everyday events and in for-giveness, or, as it would be seen in Judaism, in eliminating any separation from God's relationship. That would apply to Gentiles as well. The starkness of the language seems to emphasize the important points in the way Jesus actually taught it to the original disciples.

That theme is continued in the story of the person com-ing at night for bread (11:5-8). If even under extreme condi-tions someone on earth would respond to a request made in need, wouldn't God, who gives all things, be expected to pro-vide for the necessities of the kingdom? The need for trust in prayer is also stated in the account of how prayers are answered (11:9-13). Even if prayers are not answered in our own words of petition, they certainly would be answered in a way which is good, since every act of God must be good.

Mark's account of arguments related to casting out dev-ils (11:14-22) was retained, with a slightly different meaning in the addition at the end (11:23-28). Jesus' acts may have been questioned originally as perhaps being the work of evil since he was not keeping all the rules of the Law. Now in Luke's Gospel, where Jesus' conflicts with the Law were more distant, the account provides an introduction to opponents of discipleship. They may have questioned differences which existed within the Christian communities.

The traditions of the earliest Christian communities came from a strong Jewish understanding of the new relation-ship with God. Luke was writing to a community with either stronger Gentile traditions from the start or, more likely, one which had become more Gentile over time. Some of Luke's readers may have proposed a wide range of different interpre-tations in keeping the teachings. Luke cannot ask Jesus a new question about such interpretations. However, by adding a conclusion from Jesus' public life (11:23), he can show that moving away from the teachings constituted a moving away from Christ. The disciple is one who is filled with the life of Christ (11:24-26), rather than being open to what might be unacceptable. The relationship from family or a personal connection with Jesus was not what brought discipleship, but by living the whole message (11:27-28).

The problem of opposition continues to be addressed throughout the remainder of the chapter. The Jews had been selected as the people who could recognize the revelation brought by the Messiah. Their failure was not in direct opposition to Jesus so much as in not seeing the direction in which God was leading them in the Old Testament revelation. The section about the sign of Jonah (11:29-32) is one of not understanding the later additions to the Old Testament, such as the book of Jonah, that would have made Judaism more open to a developing revelation. That is followed by a second version of the parable of the lamp (11:33-36) which implied Judaism tried to hide the light.

Judaism did not believe the revelation to them was meant for Gentiles, so they did not allow it to shine to the world. In the process, they did not allow it to fully shine even in their own culture. In a sense, revelation would fail within Judaism when they did not allow it to go beyond Judaism, because that was a failure to see the whole message. No one could have light separate from how one lives, since just knowing something is not sufficient for salvation.

The attack on the Pharisees (11:37-54), a scene unlikely to occur while dining as a guest with them, continues this theme by showing why the Pharisees opposed the Messiah. Rather than direct opposition, they only looked for what was included in the rules associated with the Law. The Pharisees tried to narrow the plan of God to what they already knew, so in effect, there would have been no additional revelation from Jesus. Jesus accused them of judging based on the narrowness of their own viewpoint (11:37-44). They were fully conscious of minute purity rules and tithing on insignificant herbs, yet are accused of overlooking justice and love which are at the heart of the covenant with Yahweh.

The judgment of Judaism against Jesus as Messiah, which was questioned by Gentiles of Luke's time, was shown to be a failure of Jewish leaders rather than a failure of Christianity to gain acceptance within Judaism. Christians also may have had the same failure. Surely they waited for the Second Coming, which was looking for the least response in discipleship. The separation from Judaism in Luke's time brings his Church face to face with a need for a more complete response.

At this point a lawyer, actually a scribe, included his group of interpreters of Scripture into the discussion (11:45-54). If they thought Jesus' words were equally critical of them, they surely received the same condemnation. Scribes were not teachers in the same sense as the Pharisees, but provided the interpretations that Pharisees would use to buttress their approach to religious practices. The scribes are shown to be the ones who knew how the prophets tried to bring change to religious practices, but they did not include that as part of their interpretation of Scripture. They would have recognized that the Wisdom literature promoted a reevaluation of the Law in response to the great change in understanding of God which occurred after the time of the Exile. Therefore, they had the "key of knowledge" (11:52) but did not use it to unlock revelation and, in not doing so, prevented others from accepting revelation.

For Luke's readers, Christianity had provided the key, which Judaism knew and had available, in recognizing that God's plan would be open to the world. Had Judaism done as much, there would have been greater acceptance of Gentiles, and the Messiah would have been accepted by Judaism. The complete separation of Christianity from Judaism was triggered by the destruction of the temple in 70. However, in Acts, it is clear that the practical separation started earlier as Christianity accepted Gentiles without requiring them to become Jewish at the same time.

Even though this section gives the impression of being anti-Jewish, it is used by Luke to lead his readers past the question of why Judaism had not accepted the Messiah. At the same time, it may be addressing a tendency in Christian communities to see a keeping of rules as the basis for religion rather than the full living of the life of Christ in all that it entails. In the New Testament, criticism by Jesus of religious practices had to be of Jews, since they represent the only religion involved. Yet such criticism often is repeated in these Gospel writings and may be directed at Christians because of similar failures in Christianity.

Chapter 12

Jesus then is shown as directing warnings to his disciples (12:1-12) not to be caught up in the same yeast of the Pharisees. They should not allow the doing of established religious practices to be the only life in their community. Instead, they must be the opposite, witnessing from the housetops to the new relationship they have heard from the Lord and the need to live that relationship. If the revelation of God is important, it should be broadcast fearlessly, since the repayment for doing God's work is greater than any repayment for doing what might be desired on earth. The list of places where charges might be filed against Christians (12:11) includes both the synagogues and before political authorities. That would have been true of Jesus and the initial disciples in Judea, but now it should also be something remembered by Luke's community as Christianity and Judaism split apart.

Treasures for a Christian (12:13-21) should always be seen as rewards that occur in the afterlife, since the taking on of Christ's life has its greatest meaning in the sphere of eternity. Jesus' advice, in this case from his own time, was not to consider him a judge of cases brought for judgment in this world since other means could accomplish that. However, to give one's attention to only treasures in this world could result in being free of any treasure at the end of life here (12:21). Far better to put industry and effort in what could be gained for eternity.

When coveting goods (12:22-32), a disciple should look for the most generous source of what has been given to people and put all one's trust in that source. If what has come from God is greater than what could be accomplished by any personal action in this life, why change and make the goods of this life primary? The wise disciple is one who trades any gain from this world (12:33-34) for what can be acquired from it in the next. Possessions in this world most certainly must be lost, while those in the next are forever. Accepting the life of a disciple, which provides the means of accumulating wealth in the world beyond, is the great gift of God.

A significant change in the understanding of discipleship for Luke's readers is the shift from a diligent waiting for the Second Coming to productive activity in the time of waiting (12:35-48). The real test would be how the time before the final judgment is actually used to expand the kingdom. Peter's question (12:42) seems to be a Lukan addition to the teaching section which focused the discussion into the future for Luke's readers. Were Jesus' words only for the disciples with him in his public life or were they intended for disciples who may come much later, as did Luke's readers? Jesus' response shifts the discussion from those waiting for the master's return to faithful stewards who use the time of waiting by being productive. One who is always vigilant in carrying out the stewardship need not worry about the Second Coming. The living out of discipleship, therefore, answered both questions: how to be ready for the Second Coming and what to do while waiting. Finally, those who have been given the clearest understanding of discipleship will be expected to be the most faithful (12:47-48). That was true for the original Twelve, and as Luke's readers see the teachings of Jesus clarified, they would recognize it was expected of them as well.

Jesus used Old Testament imagery to describe the decision as called for by God (12:49-53). What comes from God is actually the opportunity for disciples to make individual decisions which could result in conflicts even between people who made up a single household. If that were so, Luke's readers need not be concerned that many Jewish people had decided against accepting the Messiah, any more than the fact that some Gentiles would do the same. Such rejection was not a sign of failure of Christianity, but a prophesied result of everyone's free choice to enter the kingdom or not.

Everyone should recognize the signs (12:54-59), and then respond individually and wisely just as they would to problem situations that arose in the everyday world. The Jewish people had waited a thousand years for the coming of the Messiah, and many seemed to have missed it. Yet, if they had been involved in a business decision going against them, they would have adjusted from a set position. Surely any disciple should do as well in choosing the kingdom. To reject the Messiah is to put oneself in the impossible situation of the insolvent debtor, without funds to pay the debt and, while in prison, with no means to earn.

Chapter 13

The second part of the journey additions relates to the personal response to the kingdom which starts in chapter thirteen. Jewish belief was that if a person were rewarded in life it was a blessing resulting from one's own obedience to the covenant, while ill fortune surely indicated that one had sinned against God. Jesus opposed making such a connection between what comes in life and how a person was responding to God, since his own experience would be coming to the cross while carrying out God's plan explicitly. The events mentioned to open this subject (13:1-5) are known only from this text but the lesson was clear, worldly blessings or difficulties mean nothing, each person must repent to be saved.

That point is made more strongly in the following parable of a barren fig tree (13:6-9). This tree was about to be destroyed but gained a reprieve of a year and some special care. A casual observer would assume that the tree must be the best in the vineyard, based on the special care it was receiving. Such care has the appearance of worldly blessings, but it was a last effort to make the tree measure up to expectations before all was lost for the tree. Only if it changed from a worthless life to a fruitful one would it survive in the vineyard or in the kingdom in the Christian life situation. Good fortune, far from being a sign of blessing, was in this case a sign of certain doom if no change was made. Therefore, disciples should take no special joy from what appears to be rewards in this life.

A woman healed in a synagogue (13:10-17) is a teaching more than a miracle and proclaims that, for those in the kingdom, evil must always be opposed. Normally, the woman would be in a separate part of the synagogue and a man would not touch a woman while in a synagogue. Jesus related the cure to untying the woman from an infirmity since untying on the Sabbath was allowed in the Law. However, the clearer lesson was that if a person suffered because of an evil spirit, the spirit must be opposed under any circumstances. The sign of evil being allowed to continue would be a sign of successful opposition to the kingdom and must be rejected. The importance of each individual is made clear by the mustard seed and yeast (13:18-21), even though Luke's readers may not have recognized their own importance in the kingdom.

A notation that Jesus was still on the journey introduced a teaching that past relationships were not as important in the kingdom as a present response (13:22-30). This appears to be a warning to Jews in the time of Jesus that their past covenant relationship would not be adequate. However, the journey notation indicates this occurred after Jesus left Galilee, so it seems to say it is applied after his public life. That concept is reinforced with a warning that it was after the master has "got up" (13:25), a statement indicating it was after the Resurrection. Surely the basic message was that those under the old covenant could not count on that past relationship to save them. However, Luke's readers could see that the change after the Resurrection would affect them as well. They were disciples who had "ate and drank" (13:27) in the Eucharist and so, perhaps, that alone would not be a guarantee of salvation. Any failure in Judaism and the resultant loss of their favored position in line for salvation could be repeated by Christians who judged they would be saved entirely by an early decision for Christ. The living out of the relationship is the essential element of salvation.

Even though Jesus could have struck down Herod Antipas, the ruler of Galilee and Perea (13:31-35) who threatened him, he stayed with the journey which fulfilled the plan of God. Striking out against opponents, especially those with political power to punish and execute, always is alluring for one trying to promote the kingdom. Yet, it produces no real gain because that is not the means of promoting the kingdom. Going to Jerusalem with its risk was the necessary step for disciples who would be blessed because they too came "in the name of the Lord."

Chapter 14

The healing of a man on the Sabbath (14:1-6) is similar to the healing of the man with the withered hand in Mark and almost a duplication of the cure of the woman on the Sabbath (13:10-17) except it did not occur in a synagogue. The result of that second cure was that the Pharisees were forced to respond to the actual situation without hiding behind synagogue rules. When questioned in this case, they remained quiet, and in doing so failed to respond in love. Luke's readers were asked to respond to the meaning of discipleship outside of Judaism, so the event asks Christians to face the same reality as Jesus asked of the Pharisees.

Choosing places at the table (14:7-11) would be a common sense situation that the Jews hearing Jesus would understand. Luke's use of it in his teaching on discipleship might refer to practices at the Eucharist in his time. To be a servant, one who sat at the most distant tables, and also to occupy the place of honor, were difficult to reconcile. Jesus' advice is to go where the opportunity to serve, or to be disciples, was the greatest. Knowing that Paul had to correct early Christians about Eucharistic practices (1 Cor 11:17-34) makes it likely that Luke added this for the same purpose.

Little did he know that Christians would take this advice to heart so completely that even today the last pews are always filled first. However, the invitation to go up higher comes at a later banquet, one celebrated in heaven. We shouldn't look for honors on earth.

A choice of guests (14:12-14) carries a dramatically different meaning, which must have brought confusion among the listeners of Jesus, since the Pharisees had restricted social contact with any but their own. Even Christians must have found some difficulty with the advice. Only in weighing a future reward versus a present one would the meaning become clear. Every disciple should want the results of good actions done in this life to be credited to the next life. The last thing anyone would want would be to have repayment with no net gain in this life and also gaining nothing as a future reward. Far better to be selfish about a future payment and avoid any chance of being repaid with only similar value in this life.

The parable of the great banquet (14:15-24) continues the choice between right and good. It is not the banquet of a king's son, as in Matthew, nor are any actions taken against servants bringing the invitations or the guests who declined them. It simply has the illogical choosing of the everyday events instead of a very special event. However, in Luke's time this represents the same choice as the previous pericope. Are the important parts of life related to the normal events, which in themselves are classified as right, or to the special invitation to a heavenly banquet, which because of God's presence would be good? Those who have nothing in this world could make the choice more quickly than those with much. Yet, the choice is the same because the reality of earthly possessions is that at some point they have no value whatsoever. In the banquet described by Luke, even though some rejected the invitation, as some Jewish people rejected the Messiah, the banquet is not cancelled as a result. The rejection of Jesus by Judaism should have no meaning to Gentiles who are invited and can accept the invitation.

Following the great banquet parable, Luke adds that the kingdom choice is not to be determined by personal relationships (14:25-27). There are no relationships on earth more important than those that relate to eternal life. When making a choice about eternity, all human relationships that draw us away from God have no more value than where individuals hate each other. Likewise, the kingdom choice should not be determined by possessions (14:28-33). As much value as possessions may seem to have, people would part with them even for long-term gain here on earth. How could earthly possessions possibly be a choice for us when the alternative is eternal gain? Giving up possessions is the final result of life, so only one who looks beyond life would even be asking to become a disciple.

The final comment on salt (14:34-35) is a note of encouragement. It says to keep the message alive in the heart so the meaning remains clear. In the world of science, salt is viewed as sodium chloride and the combination of those two elements can never lose their flavor. In Palestine, where salt may come from the Dead Sea, the salt would also include calcium and magnesium, carbonates and sulfates. Exposed to moisture, the more soluble sodium chloride would leach out and leave only the remaining elements which have a very flat or even disagreeable taste. The result is that the leached salt has no value at all. Judaism was the salt that made life flavorful. By this time, with the Temple gone and a much greater gift from God available, the only real choice is Christianity.

Chapter 15

Chapter fifteen introduces the opposite side of everything that has been said since it gives God's view of the relationship. Nowhere does Jesus discuss a view so different from Judaism. The surprise ending of the parable is more of a shock than a surprise and only in going past that shock of understanding could there be any meaning to the new covenant. If the normal use Jesus makes of a parable is to overcome the deficiencies of the Aramaic language, these parables are the perfect ones. They open a subject and point to a conclusion that cannot be expressed in word-rich English any easier than in word-poor Aramaic. The full meaning of God's love for humanity simply cannot be expressed in any language. Today, as well as 2000 years ago, a parable can point in the direction of understanding God's love, but never bring the hearer there completely.

The starting point is in two parables about the lost: the lost sheep and the lost coins (15:4-10). The seriousness of God in bringing back the lost or of searching out the poor could be understood by the Jews from their history. They were chosen as slaves and led out of Egypt. Certainly, that was Yahweh taking special pains to find them and bring them to freedom. Yet the record of that action shows that it was not understood by the early Israelites. The Israelites worried in the desert after the Exodus and they feared trying to take possession of the promised land.

The Old Testament often records their history in terms of failing. Even in the written record of what occurred at the Exodus, God's choice was introduced by the early patriarch stories. They seem to say, only because Yahweh had promised the land to Abraham earlier was it necessary for Yahweh to bring the Israelites out of bondage and return them to that land. To propose that the action of Yahweh was the divine approach to a relationship with everyone in creation was hardly even considered until Jesus introduced the subject. It was no easier to accept by the Gentile readers of Luke's composition.

It is quite normal to start a commentary or homily on the parable of the prodigal son or the loving father (15:11-32) by presenting the wayward son in the worst possible light. Such an approach leads to a forgiveness emphasis rather than Jesus' explanation of God's love. In reality, the wayward son is about average, rather than excessively evil. He may get into more trouble than most people would admit to, however, to be given an inheritance while still a teenager is not the experience of most people. A small amount of wealth allows

a young person to get into trouble which, under other circumstances, wouldn't be available. Furthermore, it is common for
anyone inexperienced to get deeply involved in a problem
before realizing their predicament and, once into trouble, it is
never easy to back out. This is the situation of the wayward
son, and it is one in which everyone has some familiarity.

The elder son is presented as somewhat of an ideal son
who never seems to disobey or even express an opposing
opinion. His complaint at the end seems justified to most
who hear the parable. However, the parable is not about the
two sons that every person knows to some extent from personal experience. Rather, the parable is about the Father
who is known less from experience and more from revelation
and whom we may often misunderstand.

The start of the story (15:1-3) is where Jesus is eating
with sinners and, thereby, having a relationship with them.
This would be seen by the Pharisees and scribes as turning
away from Yahweh and the Law and choosing a relationship
outside of the Law. Jesus' point in the parable is that the
Father's love is open to both sons, to all people, and would
not be withdrawn. The response of the sons would determine
if that love were accepted in their lives.

In the time of Jesus, the elder son would be seen as
Israel while the wayward son would represent the Gentiles.
Jesus would be cautioning his opponents that to remain only
with the rules of the Law rather than accepting the real gift of
God in the message of the Messiah would be a rejection of
the gift and a separation from God, even by those who wanted to preserve a union. To not accept the full revelation is to
reject it in part and that which is rejected (in not being
accepted) is the fullness of revelation. In Luke's time, and
today, the parable questions if humanity can ever understand
God's love. Does anyone recognize how loveable they are to
God? The willingness of Jesus to die on the cross was an
attempt to show the depth of this love in a human way even
though that message is often read in a more limited way even
by Christians.

The wayward son reaches a point of despair (15:17) and recognizes that he must return to his father's house even though he can never understand what response may occur. His best guess is that he could be forgiven for the evil in his life but with no expectation of being loved after his misdeeds. His plan is to compose a quick confession with a request for a job rather than acceptance as a son. He seems to think that if he can disarm his father and present his limited request before being ordered off the land, the father may give him employment. His carefully thought out plea (15:18-19) is only half pronounced (15:21) before being cut off by the father's orders to bring the robe, the ring, the sandals, and the fattened calf for reestablishing the son as a member of the family. The father's response to the wayward son will always be love and, since the father is the image of God, this is the response that disciples should see in their relationship with God.

The elder son represents the best human response to serving the Father, but that gains nothing by itself. He can only be in relationship by accepting the Father's love for himself. The gift of the Father is love and only in accepting that gift can a relationship be established. In this way the parable can only point to God's love, never fully explaining it, since it is so different from human understanding. This is true in the Jewish situation of Jesus' teaching and the Gentile Church of Luke. Yet the questions remain: Can the wayward son believe that God doesn't love him? Can the Jews believe that it was other than love that brought their relationship with God? Why would anyone question a God of love, and, yet, how many do, even among Christians? Luke's readers can easily see their problems, as proposed in the context at the start of this commentary, swept away, and they can understand that in following Christ's teachings, which were added by Luke, they would put on the life, or Body, of Christ. Accepting the reality of God is the necessary element in going beyond rules and the Law.

Chapter 16

The parable of the dishonest steward (16:1-8) opens a third section of the journey related to understanding the kingdom and builds on what has been given earlier. A difficulty in understanding the parable arises from the use of the term Lord or master for both the rich man in the parable and for Jesus. That makes it difficult to tell who is praising the dishonest steward at the end of the parable.

Basic to any understanding is an awareness that acceptance of interest on a loan was forbidden as usury under the Law. The steward was in charge of arranging loans of surplus grain and oil, or other products, and their later repayment. The cost of such services was not borne by the rich man but by commissions paid by those gaining short-term use of the products. These commissions were made part of the loan agreement and were taken by the steward upon repayment.

The steward was dismissed because of unexplained wastefulness. To gain the goodwill of others, who might provide a similar position in the future, the steward apparently had those who were loaned products rewrite the agreements and exclude the commissions. The debtors gain a benefit from a reduction in payment, while the rich man receives the same repayment as before, since he is not allowed to receive any interest or additional payment. The key element is that it only seems as if the dishonest steward is giving up something to attain a future position. In fact, he gives up nothing, since he would not be around to receive the commission if it were paid, rather than having been excused in the rewriting of the agreements. The replacement steward would receive the commission paid even though he had done nothing to deserve such payment. For disciples, who can take nothing they gain in this world over to the kingdom in the next life, giving up worldly possessions should not be seen as a loss. So the praise must come from Jesus for the steward who saw the real condition of this life and the values of the future.

A concluding section (16:9-13) does not hit the mark completely. However, it does carry the meaning that using resources for gaining the kingdom is trading benefits of this world for benefits in the next. That trade, which in the long run costs nothing, should be the goal of disciples. The following section (16:14-17) seems to continue the same idea even though the Pharisees should not be seen as interested in money so much as rigidity in following rules associated with the Law. Keeping the Law would seem wise but going beyond it to the kingdom should be the real goal.

The Lazarus story (16:19-31) would be part of this same discussion heard by the Pharisees and would serve to balance the parable of the dishonest steward. A reversal of roles would be a common element in Middle Eastern stories, yet, here it would seem that this rich man followed the Law with regard to Lazarus. Open skin sores would tend to be treated in the same way as leprosy under the Law (Lev 13:1-46), and so, the rich man might seem justified in remaining distant from Lazarus. Yet, in fact, this lack of love is a missing of the meaning of the Law altogether and gains the rich man eternal punishment. In contrast with the dishonest steward who broke the rules to gain a reward, a rigid keeping of rules may produce no gain at all. The last verse (16:31) probably carries an explanation of why the Jews did not accept the Messiah and what it could mean in the next life.

Chapter 17

For disciples there are always responsibilities to others (17:1-10), rather than the emphasis of separation inherent in interpretation of the Law. This list includes responsibilities to the innocent, or those who come from outside Judaism (17:1-3), for others in the community (17:4), and for those governed by faith (17:5-6). Real charity (17:7-10) does not keep score, but must be there for any situation without regard to position.

The parable of the ten lepers (17:11-19) has the appearance of a gratitude lesson. Yet, placed next to the comparison between the responsibilities of disciples and those under the Law, it takes on a different meaning. All ten are told by Jesus to show themselves to the priests as required by the Law. The healing, which occurred while carrying out those instructions, was a sign that went beyond the Law. Nine of them continued on as before, ignoring the sign itself and giving full attention to the Law. The one who recognized the sign left the rules of the Law for something beyond the Law. That is the response of a disciple rather than only a response to show gratitude. These disciples are the ones who have left the Law and are part of Luke's community as the Gospel was read.

Some Pharisees question Jesus about the kingdom (17:20-21), however, they only reveal that the true meanings of the signs have escaped them. Unless one is willing to see signs as pointing beyond present conditions, there is no means to recognize that the kingdom has arrived (17:22-37). Even in the time of Noah and Lot, Scripture teaches there were many who disregarded actual signs and warnings to their own destruction. The Second Coming could be expected to produce similar results. For Luke's readers the question will be: Do they look only for the religion they want or are they open to the real relationship promised through Christianity? Some would make the proper decision while others in the same families and communities would fail to do so. Living discipleship everyday is the only guarantee of always being ready.

Chapter 18

Prayer life must follow and reflect a real faith (18:1-8). Perseverance that keeps disciples always open to God even in difficulties and injustice is part of being ready. The Gentiles of Luke's community must persist in gaining their reward even if the "Law" seems to be against it. Likewise, holiness is accepting God (18:9-14) as things change, rather than following rules which may no longer be suitable. It is not the right of the Pharisee that makes prayer good but the tax collector's openness to God. This section ends with Mark's journey of discipleship (18:15-43) being attached to the end of Luke's extended journey.

Chapter 19

Two short sections summarize the journey: Zacchaeus and the parable of the pounds. The Zacchaeus story gives the call and response of disciples (19:1-10). As a tax collector Zacchaeus is a traitor and a thief who seems to seek out Jesus more because he has heard of him than as an act of faith. Jesus calls Zacchaeus by name and tells him he will be a guest in his home, both great honors. Luke's readers recognize that this is the same as the call in baptism, naming and indwelling, so Zacchaeus was called to be a disciple. Zacchaeus responded to that call with a complete change of character. He is compared with Abraham who made the same type of unquestioning change. The story can be read as if Zacchaeus is already giving justice to others. However, that interpretation doesn't fit the Abraham remark or anything in this section of the journey. Surely the changing of Zacchaeus is the correct meaning.

The parable of the pounds (19:11-21) may have carried some different meanings in Jesus' time since it has allusions to a Jewish protest to Rome about making Herod's son, Archelaus, the new king. However, in Luke's time, the parable concerns how disciples respond to the kingdom while Jesus is gone for a time. Each servant is given the same amount, but accomplishment is different according to their abilities. The disciple who fails is the one who doesn't use his gift to make Christ present in life, rather than any judgment on the level of accomplishment or abilities. Disciples must make their gifts useful or they lose the kingdom. They must make the journey with the Lord successful even though they do not know the end. The magnitude of the reward is far beyond anything they accomplish with the original gifts given to them in life. The control of ten cities is the same as being a small king, rather than something equivalent to the earnings. Heaven is like that.

PASSION AND RESURRECTION

Luke includes Mark's Jerusalem ministry and end times sequence with only minor changes and little indication that he intends to derive a separate meaning (19:28-21:38). Likewise, the Passion and death narrative starting with the Eucharist (chapters 22-23) retains its character as an early composition that cannot be changed significantly by any of the Evangelists.

Chapter 22

A change made in the Last Supper commandment, to take part in the Eucharist, is more clear than what was used by Mark or Matthew. Mark's terse "Take it" was changed to "Take it and eat" by Matthew, with a similar change regarding the cup. Luke uses sacrificial language. "This is my body which will be given for you" suggests the sacrifice, and "Do this as a memorial of me" stresses the need to repeat the Eucharist. However, the repeating of the Eucharist was never as an annual celebration as was Passover. It was a weekly event from the earliest times, indicating that while the Eucharist is related to a Passover understanding, it is a memorial of living Christ's life rather than an annual remembrance. The language of offering the cup relates the blood to a new covenant in addition to the sacrificial language of being "poured out for you." That, too, is a sharing of Christ's sacrifice, with a reflection back to the Passover sacrifice. The covenant connection to blood of a sacrifice is also a reflection to the establishment of the covenant in the blood of a sacrifice at Sinai (Ex 24:3-11).

A minor addition (22:35-38) indicates that a time has arrived when disciples will have difficulties and even face danger. If Luke's community has experienced such a change, these words would erase any thought that such problems were any indication of a failure in how the Church expanded.

Chapter 23

A significant addition to the trial scene is to involve Herod Antipas in the crucifixion (23:8-12). In this text, it was Herod's soldiers who seemed responsible for the mocking of Jesus, rather than only the Roman soldiers. This change is often seen as an attempt to shift the blame for the crucifixion away from Roman authorities to some extent. It is just as easy to see the change as spreading the responsibility to everyone. The question of good and evil is not determined by assessing blame on a single group or nation. The way all authority in the world is exercised is as something legally right, while the kingdom of God alone is good. God's kingdom is not established through blaming some individual or group, but by being lived throughout the world in discipleship. What happened to Jesus was an example of how the world judges and such judging must be replaced rather than used to condemn on an individual basis.

On the way to Calvary, the women lament what has happened to Jesus (23:26-32). The disciples who seemed chosen as leaders were absent, while the women, who are portrayed in Luke's Gospel as living discipleship throughout the life of Jesus, were faithful. Jesus started the crucifixion by forgiving everyone (23:34), a reminder that every disciple is called to live forgiveness.

A scene was added with Jesus responding to the good thief on the cross (23:39-43). The thief was seemingly beyond forgiveness. Since he had been condemned to death, he could expect no help here on earth. Because he was being crucified, he was seen as cursed by God under the Law (Dt 21:22-23) and, therefore, beyond help from heaven. He was the complete outcast who was beyond any help. Yet, he pleaded for salvation from the Lord who was under the same sentence and seemingly also beyond help. The plea could be only an act of faith since there was no reason to believe assistance would be forthcoming. Yet, the faith response was all that was required for salvation and the thief succeeded.

The opening words from Psalm 22 included by Mark were omitted by Luke and other sayings substituted which present Jesus as being more in control of the crucifixion. Jesus committed his life to the "Father" (23:46) expressing the real meaning of discipleship. When Jesus died, the centurion noted that Jesus was "good" or "innocent."[25] That would be the mark of a disciple, rather than using the "Son of God" formula relating to a King David concept of messiah, as in Mark's Gospel.

Chapter 24

In Luke's Resurrection account the women, who were the first witnesses to the Resurrection, were not believed (24:9-11). Peter examined the tomb and binding cloths and was described as "amazed" rather than believing. The meaning of the death and Resurrection was not immediately understood even though it was clearly good news. The failure of Luke's community to understand is similar to what occurred in much of the early Church when faced with the new situations.

The story of the appearance to the disciples returning home to Emmaus is a major account concerning the Resurrection (24:13-35). They are a couple who might have been witnesses to Jesus' ministry only in Jerusalem and who wanted to see the time of salvation, but did not recognize it in the crucifixion. They are often presented as two men in art, yet, since Passover is celebrated in a family setting, it seems clear that the most normal interpretation is that it would be a husband and wife. They represent those in Luke's community who are attracted to discipleship and respond in faith.

The story is often explained in terms of journey and meal, the two expressions of ministry and unity among disciples. The explanation of Scripture on the road is associated with a Liturgy of the Word in worship. The meal together with the Lord is the Liturgy of the Eucharist which came after the closing of the Sabbath and the gathering for the evening meal in the early Church. It comes after the Liturgy of the Word even at the present time.

A point less emphasized is the response of the disciples (24:33-35) after coming to recognize the meaning of the Lord. They start to witness to others immediately. There can be no delay in telling others of what has come into their lives, as should be true for all disciples. This final example of living discipleship could hardly be missed by disciples of Luke's community who have had this conclusion driven home to them throughout this Gospel writing.

The final teaching (24:36-53) is to recognize that the Lord indeed lives among disciples after the Resurrection. When disciples come together in the Eucharist, this should be evident in anyone with faith. The instructions to disciples include the message of revelation given in Scripture (24:44-49) which points toward the true Messiah and the complete message. Every disciple should be a true witness to all that has been revealed. The period after the Ascension was not only a time to wait until the Holy Spirit came upon them even though that was an instruction. It also was a time to use in witnessing. The Gospel ends back in the Temple where it had begun, opening the meaning of the Messiah all over again.

The Second Coming as the start of the kingdom was an early Church understanding. Here in Luke's Gospel and in Acts, the receiving of the Holy Spirit is given as the start of the kingdom. That change is consistent with Mark and Matthew and provides the emphasis that has been carried out in history. Luke's great teaching on discipleship became the message of everyday living for those who have come to the Lord after these events which Luke has used to describe the teaching.

THE ACTS OF THE APOSTLES

CONTEXT OF ACTS

The context used for the Gospel of Luke continues in Acts, which is sometimes referred to as the second volume of the Gospel of Luke. The understanding of what takes place in Acts is that events are directed by the Holy Spirit acting through the Church. Acts should not be considered an addition to the Gospels, but almost certainly part of the same inspiration received by Luke. The full response to the questions of Luke's community required both writings at the same time. The repetition of the prologue should be seen as making clear the integration of the two.

Questions of dating Acts have arisen from time to time because Acts ends in 61 with an epilogue that knows about the succeeding two years. Since Paul is executed during Nero's persecution of 64-68, it may seem strange that Acts would not include recognition of such an important event. The thinking behind such an approach to the writing is that it is a history of the early Church and all the events should be recorded. Acts should never be seen as a historical writing even though, like all Scripture, its religious message is recorded in a historical framework.

The purpose and message of Acts is to tell a small Christian community in the first century, and all people for all time, how the plan of God was to unfold in creation. The very direct action of the Holy Spirit is shown in that early expansion beyond Jerusalem (1:8) and beyond Judaism. When Paul arrives in Rome, the capital of the Mediterranean world, and, in a sense, the whole world for that time, the message is given and the writing ends. Acts is not about Peter or Paul, even though both are important; it is about the Holy Spirit. When we examine what is revealed about God's plan, we open ourselves to the real meaning of revelation.

INITIAL DEVELOPMENT OF THE CHURCH

Chapter 1

Luke opens Acts with the same type of introduction (1:1-5) as in his Gospel writing. Just as the Gospel introduced Jesus in his birth, Acts introduced the Church in its beginning. The Spirit of God was the essential element in both events. The disciples were to remain within Jerusalem, perhaps with the meaning of remaining within Judaism, until called forth from there to witness to the world. However, the question of the disciples to Jesus about restoring "the kingdom to Israel" indicates they still have an Old Testament view of the kingdom. Jesus' call was defined in his statement (1:6-11) telling what would occur when the Spirit came upon the disciples. The witness would spread beyond Jerusalem and Judaism outward to Samaria and the world. This ended the instructions and gave the plan of the writing. The disciples as a total group (1:12-14), rather than the Twelve, waited in prayer in the upper room. This may constitute the actual Last Supper group.

The election of Matthias (1:15-26) reestablished the Twelve as in the plan of Jesus in his public life. While the Church was in Judaism, in the same way as in Jesus' public life, the Twelve would be retained as an institution. However, the community included 120 people, the minimum number that would constitute a new legal community in Judaism. Therefore, the very completion of the Twelve was also the starting point of something independent and new, rather than a continuation of the limited group learning directly from Jesus.

The Church may have thought about having that same group ready for the return of Jesus just as he had risen. However, the action of the Spirit would send the Church far beyond such a limited view. Only in chapter six will the Twelve ever be mentioned again and the expansion will never be limited by human expectations.

Chapter 2

Pentecost as an event (2:1-13) was a meeting with the Divine and was indescribable, as would be all such meetings. There was no wind or fire, but a sound like a wind from heaven and something that seemed like tongues of fire. There was a strange reaction among the disciples, unplanned and unexpected, because they were filled with the Holy Spirit. They started speaking to all the nations rather than carrying out their own plans to evangelize only within Judaism. The ability to witness to others was never subject to their own limitations, but was shown as immediately open to the entire world. Just as Moses could not explain the presence of God on Mt. Sinai, neither could these disciples at Pentecost.

Peter spoke for the early Church in terms of what the event meant in relation to their Jewish roots (2:14-36). It is a speech that is repeated to some degree in chapters three, four, five and ten. In a basic way, the speech seems to proclaim a meaning of the Messiah to Judaism. Perhaps in the first two decades after the Resurrection, this was the message for the Jewish audience in Church preaching. Luke will show in Acts that the Spirit finally led the Church beyond this message and beyond Judaism rather than that being a change that occurred due to human planning.

A prophecy of Joel (2:17-21) starts the speech after Peter had removed natural explanations for the public action of the disciples. The prophecy, related to the coming of the Day of the Lord, contains Second Coming language which must have been the early Church teaching. It seems to stress that there was a need to call on the name of the Lord before the "great Day" of the Second Coming in order to be saved (2:20-21).

The witness of Jesus to a new revelation should have been obvious from his works (2:22), and the crucifixion and Resurrection should have overwhelmed the Jews (2:23-24). That Jesus was crucified meant he should have been cursed by God under the Law (Dt 21:22-23), but he was blessed instead by being raised. This meant Jesus was not subject to the Law but was above the Law. Therefore, Jesus' revelation also was above the Law. This meaning is repeated in each account of Peter's speech. "This Jesus whom you crucified" (2:36), God has made both Messiah, anointed one from God, and also Lord. He is the one who should control the lives of disciples.

Those who heard this message (2:37-41) knew there was no escape from its conclusion and wanted to accept Jesus even after he had been rejected by Jewish leaders. The answer of Peter is very clear; through public baptism, simply accept Jesus as the one who controls life and salvation would be theirs automatically. Since the Gift of the Holy Spirit is a relationship in life with God, the acceptance of that life relationship must be in living it. From 120 who met in the upper room, another 3,000 were added to their number. The result of the coming of the Spirit was immediate and overwhelming.

A summary statement (2:42-47) tells what occurred in the early Church following Pentecost and previews what was to come in the next few chapters of Luke's writing. The membership was faithful to Church teaching, to the common relationship in life (Body of Christ), to the celebration of the Eucharist, and to the praise and petitions to God.

Chapter 3

Peter was involved in the cure of a crippled man in a repetition of the cures worked by Jesus during his public ministry (3:1-10). The cure was worked in the name of Jesus Christ at the entrance to the Temple. Judaism had no control over the place of God, while in Christianity the presence occurs in disciples who live out a revelation beyond Judaism.

Peter addressed the astonished crowd (3:11-26) using about the same arguments as his earlier speech. Central to his argument is the repeated charge that the Jewish leaders were responsible for killing the Messiah, but God has raised him from the dead (3:14-16). Judaism also does not control the one who fulfills the prophecies of the Old Testament revelation. The event has an appearance of Peter accusing Judaism and condemning the leaders. But in fact, the speech is an interpretation of the Divine action and of the Old

Testament revelation. Jesus is called Holy One, a title used for God at the time of this event (3:14), but it also is applied to one who was especially close to God.

Chapter 4

The event portrays the Christian message as continuing the growth of the Church (4:1-22). Its confirmation, in a sign worked in Jesus' name, brought retaliation by temple officials. In an interrogation by the officials, Peter repeated his speech for the third time. The theme of "this Jesus you crucified, God has raised from the dead" (4:10) restated the charge to the very people who would understand its meaning most clearly. The disciples also had gone beyond Jewish authority, under the Law, by proclaiming a message beyond the Law (4:11-12). The officials were taken aback by the meaning that removed their own authority and responded only by cautioning the disciples to cease witnessing. Peter and John could not agree to shut up the Spirit within them by refusing to do as the Spirit directed them.

The Church agreed with the decision of Peter and John not to be silenced about what had happened (4:23-31). Those opposed to the inspiration of the Holy Spirit, given here in a quotation as including both the Jewish and pagan leaders (4:25-26), would be in opposition to the Messiah. However, the disciples prayed for assistance to continue the witness (4:27-31). They seemed to understand that the Church would expand beyond the message of Judaism. A second summary statement (4:32-37) describes the Church living together in the Spirit by dedicating all of their possessions to the community. The gift by Barnabas introduces two disciples who only partially gave their lives to the Spirit while pretending to be fully devoted.

Chapter 5

Ananias and Sapphira (5:1-11) asked to live in common while secretly retaining part of their own property. There was no requirement for them to give up all they owned, but to publicly pretend to do so was a sin against the Spirit. Yet, if salvation came by accepting the Spirit, and they did not, the lesson was that they did not accept the life of the Spirit either. It is a story which is not enjoyable, but must have been retold often. There could be no halfway acceptance of the common life and no deception before the Holy Spirit. The final comment (5:11) appears to be completely unnecessary. At the later time of Luke's writing, Christians faced a requirement to offer sacrifice annually in Roman temples, perhaps more as a ritual acceptance of Roman rule than a religious observance. This story of not allowing only a partial commitment to the Spirit may have been repeated to warn later disciples to resist halfway acceptance in their own time.

The scene shifts back to Peter and others being involved with signs in the temple area and in disputes with officials (5:12-33). The Apostles were arrested and after a miraculous release from jail were found witnessing in the Temple and brought to the officials. The earlier threat of punishment had failed to stop Christian witness and it failed here again. Once more the speech of Peter was repeated, stating that Jesus is above the Law, in the clearest possible understanding to Judaism (5:30-31). The Apostles faced death from the infuriated officials who recognized the importance of the charge, but who refused to accept the conclusion even though it could not be denied. If Jesus were above the Law, by the Law's own criteria, then anyone accepting the Law should be the first to accept the Messiah.

A Pharisee named Gamaliel proposed a compromise (5:34-41). Judaism would have to consider the statement made by Christians if acceptance continued to grow throughout the countryside. If the movement succeeded, then God was indeed speaking to all Jews. If it was not from God, then it could have no lasting meaning for Judaism. The Christian sect would disappear on its own, as had support for others who had been proposed as messiahs in the past. The Apostles were flogged and released as the Jewish leaders took a wait-and-see attitude toward the result of Christian witness.

The question of Judaism accepting Christ was put on hold, yet, for anyone reading the remainder of Acts, the conclusion would be clear that the Spirit of God supported this new kingdom. Had the Jewish leaders followed their own decision as proposed by Gamaliel, they too would have become disciples. Instead, the leaders would slowly separate themselves from Christianity until, in the end, they neither accepted Jesus Christ nor understood sufficiently to reject the message.

OPENING BEYOND JUDAISM

Chapter 6

Chapter six describes a change in direction for Christian witness which became the starting point for a witness outside of Judaism. It was not apparent at first, since it was not in the mind of the disciples themselves, but came from the action of the Spirit within the Church. With a change in how the kingdom was expanded would come a change in characters involved in the expansion. There were no limitations on the direction in which the Spirit moved nor were there limitations on how the disciples responded in new directions.

A conflict arose between Greek-speaking Jewish Christians and those Jewish Christians who were native to Palestine and, therefore, Aramaic speaking (6:1-7). The Twelve, in their last official role recorded in Acts, appointed Greek-speaking leaders to assist them. The seven are shown as being put in charge of the Greek-speaking Hellenist community and of exercising an evangelical ministry, especially to Greek-speaking Jews before Stephen's death, and also to Gentiles afterward. Therefore, the interpretation seems to be that the seven were not appointed only because of the need for more help, but as part of the Spirit-directed process of expansion beyond Palestine. The other part of the story is that growth continued in the Christian community within Judaism (6:1) and, especially in Jerusalem, even among temple authorities (6:7). The compromise of Gamaliel had a positive effect on those who were open to the message of God which was revealed to them.

One of the seven, Stephen, carried the message of Christ to Greek-speaking Jews, who originally were most likely Roman slaves who had come to Palestine after being freed. Stephen was charged (6:8-15) with what is called false and blasphemous language about the Temple and the Law, at least to Jewish ears. Such charges surely would seem justified to Judaism as a result of Stephen's speech.

Chapter 7

Stephen's speech (7:1-54) was a commentary on events of God and Israel outside of Palestine. Since he was charged with speaking against the Temple and the Law, his response could be to show that God is not limited to a presence in the Temple. That is easily seen in the history of Israel before the Temple, which is the totality of the speech.[26] He described the building of the Temple in Jerusalem as not desired by God and, therefore, a mistake. This would be the position of Samaritans who accepted only the Pentateuch or Torah as Scripture, with the speech focusing on the giving of the Law before the Israelites came to Palestine. Samaritans were opposed to the Temple which was constructed after the period described in the Pentateuch.

In the speech, Abraham was said to have left Haran after his father died (7:4). This is not in agreement with the Old Testament (Gen 11:26, 32 and 12:4) used by Jews (and Christians), but is consistent with the Samaritan traditions. This could indicate that Stephen may have come from a Samaritan background, and perhaps Philip as well, since he ministered in Samaria after the death of Stephen.

The result of the long homily was that the listeners were infuriated but Stephen seemed safe. However, at that point Stephen was filled with the Holy Spirit (7:55-60) and repeated the statement of Jesus when being questioned before the Sanhedrin. The response was the same and Stephen was executed. Stephen gave up his spirit to the Lord Jesus which was a change from Jesus' words on the cross and could be an expression of divinity (Lk 23:46).

Judaism was a wall around revelation. The meaning of Christianity was that the wall was broken and revelation was becoming available to the world in a process started by the Holy Spirit through Stephen's death. Saul (8:1-3) was involved in the stoning of Stephen and was a factor in the persecution that followed.

Chapter 8

Philip, another one of the seven, worked the same type of signs in Samaria as Jesus worked in Galilee (8:4-8), but now the signs were outside of Judaism. The Samaritans were open to the Spirit and even the magician Simon became a believer because he recognized that the signs were beyond magic (8:9-25). Peter and John were sent to Samaria to lay hands on the Samaritan converts who received the Spirit as the first group outside of Judaism. Yet, there is a rejection of any idea that such signs were worked through personal power in Peter's repulse of Simon. It was an initial contact of Peter and John with those in opposition to the Temple that represented the first official action of the Apostolic Church outside of Judaism.

The baptism of the Ethiopian eunuch (8:26-40) would be a further step away from the concept that Christianity existed only as a group within Judaism. The Ethiopian was at least a God-fearer, one who practiced Judaism. He could have been Jewish since he was on pilgrimage to Jerusalem, even though his eunuch status tends to oppose that conclusion. He was from outside of Palestine and possibly outside of official Judaism. The meaning of the account is expressed in his question: What prevents his baptism? That question was asked of the Church by the celebrant at a baptism, but here it must be asked by the candidate. Since Philip was completely open to the Spirit and under the influence of the Spirit when meeting the Ethiopian, the Spirit answered in Philip's baptizing of the outsider. Another step had been taken to open Christianity to the wider world.

Chapter 9

Paul's conversion (9:1-19) is the great event of Acts and the account will be repeated twice more in later sections. It was the change of one opposed to the revision of Judaism by making it open to Christianity, to one becoming a disciple who was open to changing Christianity. It was a response to a calling from God rather than a calling that came through Church. If Luke's readers wondered if Christianity was meant for them, Paul's conversion, in conjunction with his later missions among the Gentiles, brought an affirmative answer.

The conversion experience is described as an illumination, a term for baptism. The light was blinding and yet, when his sight returned, Saul, as he was known then, saw the meaning of Jesus as the Messiah. Not only did Saul know the meaning of Jesus, but he acted on that understanding as a disciple, as one who responded fully to the Spirit. He preached immediately in Damascus (9:20-25) because he was not required to go to Jerusalem and be authorized as a disciple. When Saul finally went to Jerusalem (9:26-30), the Church was afraid of him. While the Spirit had clearly called Saul, those who remained in Jerusalem were not open to that action of the Spirit. Some of those same disciples later would represent opposition to the message being open to Gentiles.

A mission by Peter to Lydda and Jaffa (9:31-10:48) provided the first clear opening of Christianity to Gentiles. Even that opening by Peter was not made very early nor was the lesson fully understood afterward. The Church was still growing, but there was no indication they understood this to mean a change in mission. Yet that opening would start an outgrowth to the full plan of God. It was not a Peter and Paul decision that caused the change to a Gentile mission. Both of these Apostles required action by the Spirit. Paul required a change from his course of opposition to the message, and Peter required a change from being an opponent of opening the kingdom to Gentiles.

The starting point of Peter's journey was the cure of Aeneas (9:32-35) by invoking the name of Jesus Christ in an account similar to Mark's description of a cure. Raising Dorcus to life (9:36-43) was a major miracle of Acts. Both events were part of the normal progression of events in expanding the kingdom and both produced a strong response from those witnessing the cures.

Chapter 10

Cornelius, the Roman centurion in Caesarea, was a Gentile who was a God-fearer (10:1-36). He had clearly accepted the relationship with God defined by Judaism, but had not been circumcised and so remained a believing Gentile or God-fearer. His call was not due to Christian witness, but as a direct revelation from God even though he did not fully understand it. Likewise, the involvement by Peter was unrelated to a human decision, but was also a direct call from God. Peter even resisted the obvious interpretation of his vision. Both Peter and Cornelius moved toward an involvement, not of their own decision nor due to full understanding.

When Peter met Cornelius, he was far more concerned about regulations related to keeping the Law and the fact that coming to Cornelius' house was an exception to those regulations. Cornelius, on the other hand, seemed to have no expectation related to Peter's coming and awaited whatever message would be delivered. Both had an explicit calling but failed to understand the meaning of their callings.

Peter started his important speech for the fifth time in Acts (10:34-43) as if he intended to proclaim a different conclusion. However, it quickly became the same speech as if no Gentiles were present or no new instructions had been given to him. The important line, that Jesus was killed by hanging him on a tree and then raised to life by God, would have been the important message to Judaism, and even to a God-fearer who understood Judaism in general, but should not have been so meaningful to Gentiles. Peter seems not to have recognized that the message should be enhanced. When he came to the final line (10:43), no clue is given that the phrase "all who believe in Jesus will have their sins forgiven" was going to mean including Gentiles in the Church. The Holy Spirit interrupted the speech (10:44-48) by coming upon the Gentiles present to give the revised conclusion. The Jewish Christians recognized the presence of the Spirit and were astonished, while Peter finally gave the order to accept the obvious in baptizing them after the Spirit had come, rather than bringing the Spirit about after baptism.

Chapter 11

Once back in Jerusalem (11:1-18), Peter was required to explain the occurrence to a group of Jews who seemed to be Jewish Christians but could easily have included any Jewish person. Peter claimed not to have taken any liberties with the Law in terms of associations with Gentiles. He gave the complete details of the story and admitted that it was only the coming of the Spirit in the house of Cornelius (11:15-18) that gave him any idea of what was to occur. There is little indication that any of the disciples anticipated taking the Gospel message to the Gentiles in the five to ten years since the Resurrection. There would not be much of an indication in what followed that the lesson was accepted as a course change in Christianity. Rather, it was seen as a special exception to the normal mission within Judaism.

In this account it is easy to see the difficulties Jews had with opening the ministry to Gentiles. Since Christianity was a sect within Judaism at the time, those same difficulties existed in the early Church as well. As Christianity became more accepting of Gentiles being baptized, it became progressively more separate from Judaism, as a source of new converts.

MISSION TO THE GENTILES

At this point, the writing shifts beyond Palestine as the plan given at the start of Acts, "and indeed to the ends of the earth" (1:8), continued to unfold. A remnant of Stephen's group, driven by the results of his persecution and death, went to Antioch (11:19-24). Some of them preached the Gospels to "Greeks," which would indicate God-fearers, who believed and were converted. Even though no mention is made of their being baptized, that would be inferred. However, they must have become Jews at the same time since the baptizing of Gentiles who were not Jewish converts would become a major issue later in Acts. It would be a great problem for Paul throughout his ministry. It is not likely to have happened here without raising any questions and then being a problem for Paul later. Paul is reintroduced at this time as Barnabas went to seek him out in Tarsus (11:25-30), where Paul had been for the past decade or so since his ministry at Damascus. His mission became active as the Church became more oriented toward Gentile lands even though the focus was still on the synagogue in those areas.

Chapter 12

At that same time, the situation of proclaiming the Gospel among Jews in Palestine seems to have been reduced by growing Jewish opposition (12:1-19). For a few years (41-44), the Jewish ruler, Herod Agrippa I, who was king of the lands originally controlled by Herod Antipas and Phillip (Lk 3:1), became the ruler of all of Palestine. With that change Christians in Samaria were threatened by Jewish regulations. The execution of James, the son of Zebedee and the brother of John (12:2), may have come from a decision by Jewish leaders that non-Jewish Christianity would not be tolerated. It may be an indication that John, and James with him, had maintained a tie with anti-temple Christians.

Peter also was threatened (12:3-19) and, in a miraculous escape from Herod's prison, left Palestine and, for the most part, the Palestinian scene. He had exercised a role of leader in the Jewish Christian Church and that would continue outside of Palestine. However, the focus of Acts would now center on a Gentile mission and Paul's role would be recorded, especially since Paul must have been directly involved in the community to whom Luke was writing.

Chapter 13

The Spirit had to intervene once more to produce an outward expansion of the kingdom to Cyprus and Asia Minor (13:1-3). Whatever had occurred earlier with regard to preaching the Gospel to Gentiles was not interpreted automatically by the Apostles as a change in mission. In Cyprus, the preaching was done exclusively "in the synagogues of the Jews" (13:4-12). Only in a conflict with a Jewish magician, who acted as an advisor to the Roman proconsul, does a Gentile become involved in their teaching. The proconsul became a believer through his astonishment at Paul's power and the message from the Lord.

The next part of Paul's first journey (13:13-16) was into the country now called Turkey. He landed at Perga (near modern Antalya) and proceeded inland to Antioch in Pisidia (modern Yalvac). There Paul started by going to the Jewish synagogue and preaching to a crowd of Jews and God-fearers. The speech (13:17-43) is a summary of the revelation to the Israelites starting with the Exodus event. The message was meant for both Jews and God-fearers (13:17 and 26), yet it was witnessed by disciples only among "our people" (13:31), who seemed to be the Jews. Certainly the promise was to Judaism (13:32-37) while justification was offered "to every believer" (13:39).

As the group broke up, those who followed Paul to continue the discussion were Jews and "worshipping proselytes" or converts to Judaism (13:42-43). The next week (13:44-52) when Gentiles also were present (13:48) some Jews rejected the message, or opposed giving it to Gentiles, and Paul left their city.

Chapter 14

At Iconium (modern Konya) (14:1-7) Paul again started at the synagogue but there the crowd included both Jews and God-fearing Gentiles. Many Jews and God-fearing Gentiles became believers, but opponents among the Jews made sufficient trouble that Paul continued his journey to

Lystra. There the situation was quite different (14:8-20) as Paul, through the healing of a crippled man, became involved with a crowd that was entirely pagan with no God-fearer or synagogue connection. The crowd had no acceptance of Christianity, but saw the teaching as if it were from pagan gods.

The necessity of preaching the Christian message within Judaism is quite obvious from this account. Converts first had to accept the Jewish understanding of God and only then could they be introduced to the Christian relationship with God that went beyond the Law. A Gentile could not understand a relationship with God without first being introduced to the One True God for all of creation. Paul would continue the synagogue association as the starting point for his mission. Jews from Antioch and Iconium interfered and caused Paul to leave for Derbe after nearly being killed by stoning. The text does not identify those who accepted the message in Derbe, so it might be assumed that both Jews and Gentiles were converted.

Paul then retraced his steps back to Perga (14:21-28), setting up a Christian organization in each town in which he had preached. He then returned to Antioch in Syria where the journey had begun. Since the Christian organizations required the appointment of elders, the normal leaders of synagogues, we could assume that separate synagogues were established for Christians both here and in places evangelized in later journeys.

Chapter 15

The question of how a non-Jew would become a Christian (15:1-4) was raised at Antioch by Jewish Christians who stated that a person first would have to become Jewish. This was the opposite of Paul's experience with Gentiles on his journey. It was decided that a meeting should be called in Jerusalem to settle the matter, however, many of those who heard that "pagans" had been converted were pleased (15:3). Certainly there was no indication that the Church had previously been open to baptizing Gentiles, unless they also had been converted to Judaism, except for the Cornelius episode by Peter.

The meeting in Jerusalem (15:5-29), sometimes referred to as the Council of Jerusalem, settled the question through a statement by Peter and acceptance by James, the head of the Jerusalem Church. Those at Antioch who held that only a Jew could be saved by becoming Christian (15:1) were from Jerusalem and under the authority of James, a cousin of Jesus (Mk 6:3). Therefore, it would be necessary for James to overrule their teachings.

Peter opened the subject at the Council by referring back to the early days when the Spirit revealed the will of God in the conversion of Cornelius. His statement silenced the assembly and gave Paul the opportunity to describe his own experience with Gentile converts. However, it appears as if Cornelius' conversion and Paul's central Turkey experiences were the only places where non-Jews had become Christians.

James agreed with the conclusion that baptism should be open to non-Jews (15:13-21) but added some rules. The additions, concerning worship of idols, keeping Kosher food laws, and accepting Jewish moral codes, might be seen as requiring acceptance of some Jewish practices. Since Jews would be required to follow the rules under the Law, some common standards were needed for Jews and Gentiles to worship and share meals together. Seen in that light, baptism would be fully open to Gentiles, but to include them in a mixed community with Jewish Christians, and even Jews, would require that they refrain from practices unacceptable to those practicing Jewish customs.

A letter (15:22-29) was prepared to overrule what had been said by members of the Jerusalem Church and to make the decision binding everywhere the Christian message was preached. Paul and his group returned to Antioch (15:30-37) with the letter condoning the great change in how the Gospel would be taught.

Chapter 16

Paul's second journey opened in a conflict with Barnabas (15:36-40) and then a return to central Turkey to consolidate and support the Churches founded earlier (16:1-5). After passing through Turkey (16:6-10), the Holy Spirit again intervened in how the Church would expand and Paul was called to cross over to the Greek peninsula. In the crossing, the narrative shifts from the third person to the second as if the author of Acts was now part of the group traveling to Greece.

At Philippi (16:11-24) where no synagogue existed, Paul went to the place along the river where Jews prayed on the Sabbath. Again, the primary mission was to take the Gospel to Jews with no indication of direct preaching to Gentiles. Later an incident occurred with a fortune teller that caused Paul and Silas to be put into jail. After an earthquake provided Paul and Silas a release from prison, the jailer and his family (16:25-40), who must have been pagan, were baptized. While earthquakes happen in that area, Luke's readers would see the hand of God in that event or, as they might say, the activity of the Holy Spirit. As Paul left Philippi, the description of the account shifts back to the third person as if the writer had remained behind.

Chapter 17

At Thessalonika (17:1-9), the preaching process started once more in the synagogue where some Jews became converts. There also were converts among worshipping Greeks and prominent women. While these might have been Jewish converts to Judaism, it is more likely to mean God-fearers who had not become Jews. The mission in Thessalonika came to an end when Jewish resentment built among those who did not accept Paul's teaching and trouble was stirred up throughout the city. Their opponents took some of those who accepted Christianity before the "magistrates and authorities" in the words of warning used by Jesus to tell what was to come (Lk 12:11). The charge was that Paul was breaking Roman law, but that would be the case only with Gentiles becoming Christians.

Going on to Beroea (17:10-15), the scene was repeated in a mission starting with Jews at the synagogue and then extending to those who seem to be clearly identified as non-Jewish God-fearers. Opposition seemed to start with Jews who came from Thessalonika after such God-fearers were converted.

In Athens (17:16-22), the mission started at the synagogue and was open to God-fearers. However, Paul also spoke to pagans in the market place. This is the first clear evidence in the second journey that Paul had a direct mission to pagans. The approach failed when Paul attempted to convince pagans using their own form of arguments rather than with the Gospel message.

Greek pagans would understand humans to have a soul and a body. The soul was seen as the person and the body as a temporary situation for the soul to gain knowledge through the senses of the body. However, the goal of the soul was to become free of the body, which was like a prison for the soul. When Paul told of Jesus dying and then being raised back to life as a reward, the Greeks laughed since going back to prison was not a reward to them.

So Paul could only leave and remember not to use philosophy as a means to evangelize. Paul seems to have left Athens after establishing only a minor Church. However, the mission approach of going directly to pagans, rather than to Gentiles with some synagogue background, may have suffered a setback.

Chapter 18

Corinth was the site of a major mission lasting about 18 months (18:1-17) and requiring later visits and correspondence to resolve problems. However, Paul's approach was the same as his earlier ministry. The synagogue was a starting point and both Jews and God-fearers were the focus of the evangelizing mission. Opposition from some Jews resulted in

Paul not being able to continue preaching in the synagogue, but this did not stop his preaching to the Jews.

The account does not define the Church community either in size or composition. However, Paul's first letter to the Corinthians, written later from Ephesus, seemed to describe a Church that was primarily Jewish Christian and converted God-fearers with at least a few baptized pagans. These baptized pagans could have been spouses of converted God-fearers. Their lack of understanding of Jewish traditions caused problems in how they lived and acted in the mixed Church community. Yet, it is quite possible that some pagans heard the message and responded on their own once Paul started preaching outside of the synagogue. Their different backgrounds also would have been a source of problems in a community oriented strongly toward Jewish Christians.

The Jews attempted to use the Roman courts to silence Paul (18:12-17) in the same way as the Jewish authorities in Jerusalem did against Peter and John earlier. This is an indication that such efforts may have been more common than recorded events indicate. At the time of Luke's writings, it seems possible that Jewish authorities throughout the Roman Empire were denying that Christians were Jewish. That would mean Christians would not be excused from offering sacrifice in Roman temples under the exemption given to Jews.

When Paul left Corinth (18:18), Priscilla and Aquila accompanied him to Ephesus. Both had been expelled from Rome by an edict of Emperor Claudius after a conflict most likely between Jews and Christians. They were part of the Ephesus ministry of Paul and could have been his contact with the Church at Rome at a later date if they had returned to Rome after the Emperor died. As Paul was leaving Greece at the port of Cenchreae, he cut his hair, ending a period in which he was under a Nazarite vow. The vow indicated that he sincerely lived out his Jewish religion in opposition to the charges that would be made against him in Jerusalem at a later date.

Paul stopped in Ephesus on his trip back to Jerusalem and Antioch, promising the synagogue community that he would return again on his next journey (18:22-23). This stop was used by Luke to introduce Apollos who came to Ephesus (18:24-28). Apollos provides a very different view of Christian missionary efforts than is popularly accepted, yet he may represent a common situation in the Church. At the same time, Apollos' preaching caused problems for Paul and the early Church. Apollos understood the Old Testament background of the Messiah and the common stories about Jesus later used in the Gospel accounts, but he seemed to be unconnected with the Apostolic Church.

This incident indicates the existence of an audience of Jews who had some understanding of Christianity and some acceptance of Jesus as Messiah prior to the coming of Paul and Apollos, but not as a separate Christian community. Priscilla and Aquila gave Apollos instruction not just on Jesus as the Jewish Messiah, but on how to live the Way of the Lord, the living of discipleship.

Chapter 19

A second incident involved Paul with some disciples of John the Baptist (19:1-7) as he returned to Ephesus after visiting the Galatian cities of his first journey. These disciples were another group of Jews who accepted the concept of a Messiah. They must have been familiar with the stories about Jesus since they are described as disciples. However, they appear to have had little or no contact with the Apostolic Church. They may have been baptized by John the Baptist while on a visit to Palestine at the time of a feast. It is another indication of Jews with a knowledge of Jesus as Messiah which had been obtained from sources outside of any evangelization effort by the early Church.

Paul started his ministry at the synagogue (19:8-10), as in earlier efforts, and continued for three months before being barred from the synagogue. He continued his preaching to both Jews and Gentiles, who were most probably God-fearers, at a public hall in Ephesus. This work attracted people from the major towns near Ephesus. We could suppose that such listeners who journeyed to Ephesus to hear Paul had no previous background in Christian teaching. However, it seems far more reasonable to assume that such people would be Jews who had some familiarity with stories about Jesus. They would have gained such knowledge while on their own visits to Jerusalem or from pilgrims who returned from Jerusalem with such stories. They probably knew the stories about Jesus used by the Evangelists to compose the Gospels. Having been told of Paul's preaching, their previous exposure to Christian teaching would have promoted their interest in hearing Paul.

Paul's ministry included the working of miracles just as in Jesus' own ministry (19:11-20). When Jewish exorcists attempted to duplicate such feats, they were totally unsuccessful. Some believers admitted to the same type of actions, again indicating that many people had a crude association with Christian teaching outside of the Apostolic Church. Such groups must have been significantly numerous, and may have been involved for a considerable time, in order to collect books worth 50,000 silver pieces. Since this group is described as believers, the comment provides a tie between Christian teaching and spells and magic which Paul would have to correct. The picture from Ephesus is of a rather extensive association of Jews with Christianity, in places distant from Jerusalem, and with very little connection with the Apostolic Church. Much of Paul's work could have been to clarify the meaning of Christianity rather than only introducing it.

Paul's ministry in Ephesus ended (19:21-41) when people, who earned their living in making images of the pagan goddess Diana, saw Christian beliefs as threatening their livelihood. A group of Jews present at an uprising pushed a disciple named Alexander to the front to head off the trouble (19:33). The attempt failed, but using the term Jews to describe Alexander's supporters points to a church strongly Jewish rather than strongly Gentile at that time.

Chapter 20

Paul's journey back to the cities of Macedonia and Greece (20:1-6) gives an indication that churches had been established in the places he had visited earlier. This was about the time when Paul wrote his second letter to the Corinthians and his great letter to Rome preparing for a visit there later. The author again seems to join Paul in his travels as they leave Philippi (20:6), where the description of the journey shifts back to the second person.

At Troas, where Paul had passed through earlier, a significant Church must have existed even though no real ministry has been described in that city. The description of a Sunday liturgy there (20:7-12) is given as taking place on Saturday evening corresponding to the Jewish definition of how a day started at the previous sundown. It also gives a warning of the dangers of preaching too long.

CONFLICTS IN JERUSALEM AND JOURNEY TO ROME

On Paul's return to Jerusalem, he stopped at Miletus (20:13-38), a port city near Ephesus, where he met with Church elders from Ephesus. Paul's speech is thought to have been composed by Luke rather than being a presentation of a message recorded from Paul. However, the language and way of speaking sound very much like Paul in his letters, so it reflects Paul quite well and tends to confirm the writing of Acts by a close disciple of Paul. The speech has a note of fear about what will occur in Jerusalem that serves as an introduction to the remainder of the book (20:23).

Chapter 21

The journey to Jerusalem (21:1-14) included warnings for Paul from disciples in other cities about trouble that would come in Jerusalem. However, Paul had the collection of alms and, perhaps, temple offerings and would not consider stopping his journey short of Jerusalem. The responsibility for delivering offerings to the Temple was established by the Roman government in addition to being a religious require-ment. Some of these funds may have been collected to have sacrifices offered for the Roman empire. All the people in the empire were required to offer such sacrifices but Jews could offer them for sacrifices at their own Temple rather than at pagan temples.

'The Spirit spoke through others telling Paul not to go to Jerusalem (21:4-5) just as earlier he seemed warned himself quite directly (20:23). The message of the Holy Spirit seemed to be a clear warning to those receiving the prophecy, and they tried to convince Paul not to return to Jerusalem and instead to go to the ends of the world and to everyone. Yet, Paul was determined to respond first to his obligations to the Jewish Temple and to his mission (24:17), and he suffered as a result. The picture is one showing the difficulties of Jewish Christians as they move away from Judaism.

While passing through Caesaria, Paul met Philip, one of the seven from chapter six who had remained in the area of Samaria. Philip had survived the persecution that brought the death of James, the son of Zebedee. It is easy to see such a meeting as a source of information for Luke's description of the early Church in Palestine even though Luke was probably from Antioch.

Paul's arrival in Jerusalem (21:15-26) provides a differ-ent view of the early Church. Christianity had been accepted by thousands of Jews who remained very faithful to Jewish practices. The Jerusalem Church would have had no Gentile Christians except those who had become Jews at the same time. The changes that had been described in communities visited by Paul were not the same picture as seen in Jerusalem. A charge made against Paul that he instructed Jewish Christians living with Gentile Christians to break from faithfully practicing the Law was sufficient for Jewish Christians in Jerusalem to turn against him.

To assure this group, James advised Paul to take part in a ritual shaving of those under a Nazarite vow, which would signal Paul's continued acceptance of important Jewish religious practices. Paul did this, but a group of his Jewish opponents from Asia later found him at the Temple and caused an outcry against him (21:27-40). Their understanding or at least their charge was that Paul had brought a Gentile into the restricted area of the Temple Mount. Even though this had not occurred, the outcry at Pentecost, when many outsiders were present, would be sufficient to nearly cause Paul's execution. The resulting riot brought Roman soldiers who assumed Paul was a revolutionary and, in arresting Paul, saved him from the crowd.

Chapter 22

Paul used this intervention to give a speech to the crowd introducing himself and recounting how he was converted (22:1-30). Paul is presented as a believing and practicing Jew, and his mission to Gentiles was the result of a revelation from God rather than disobedience to the Law. However, the mention of God reaching out to the Gentiles was unacceptable to the crowd, and they nearly succeeded in turning Roman power against Paul once more. Paul's Roman citizenship saved him, but the next day he was required to answer Jewish charges.

Chapter 23

Paul answered the charges before the Jewish authorities (23:1-11) and then attempted to create a diversion between the Sadducees who had no belief in an afterlife and his fellow Pharisees who did. The device worked and Paul received some support for his position. However, the uproar that accompanied the disagreement frightened the Roman guards to the point that they took Paul away and kept him in custody. It is difficult to see the work of the Holy Spirit in the diversion attempted by Paul in bringing up the subject of an afterlife as he did. As with his disregard of the warnings not to go to Jerusalem, one could wonder if this represents a lack of following the words of Jesus and advice from the Holy Spirit.

Roman authorities became an obstacle to further anti-Christian action by official Judaism in this case. Even then, the Jews developed a plot to kill Paul (23:12-22). The Romans found out about it and transferred Paul back to Caesarea (23:23-35). In making the transfer the judgment of the Roman tribune Lysais in Jerusalem was that Paul was not guilty, yet Paul was forced to stay in Roman control for the following two years.

Chapter 24

At this point, the Roman and Jewish bureaucracies became involved in the case. Neither the Jewish authorities, who had no love for Paul, nor Felix, the Roman Governor, who was only interested in having no public unrest, had first-hand knowledge of the actual situation that caused the trouble (24:1-10). They could not come to a decision since the Jewish authorities would rather have had Paul dead, and the Roman Governor did not want to provoke trouble.

Paul's defense speech at a hearing (24:11-21) could never convince the Jewish authorities to change their charges nor could it be so understandable to Felix that he could rule in Paul's favor. The plan of the Holy Spirit can never be understandable to opponents or the world. Felix even brought his Jewish wife to hear Paul (24:22-27) but to no avail. Instead Paul was held for two years and at that point should have been judged or set free according to Roman law. This, however, was the time when Felix was succeeded by the new Governor, Festus, who was given the case with no background.

Chapter 25

Festus heard the request of the Jewish leaders to have Paul judged by them according to the Law (25:1-6). He also listened to Paul's defense that he had broken neither Jewish nor Roman law (25:6-12). Festus' easy way out would be to accept the fact of a Jewish charge, since there was no Roman charge, and transfer Paul to Jerusalem for judgment. To this

Paul appealed to Caesar and went to Rome not according to his own plan but in the way the Holy Spirit seemed to have called him there.

Chapter 26

After the decision had been made, Festus had Paul's case presented before the Jewish ruler, Herod Agrippa II (25:13-26:32). The presentation is a summary discussion by Luke of the whole episode, but done outside of an atmosphere of religious dispute. It includes Paul's third description of his conversion with the small differences that Luke found acceptable between separate accounts of the same event. The conclusion of these two political leaders was that Paul was not guilty of any political or civil crime. Christianity was not in opposition to governments of the world. Paul's problem was related to the resistance people had to the coming of the Holy Spirit in their lives. Even though the Holy Spirit came only with the great gift of God, people could be so involved in tidy religious systems that the gift was rejected.

Chapter 27

The journey to Rome (27:1-44) returns to the "we" sections as the author seems to travel with Paul again. The journey was dangerous and the boat sank in a storm. Paul knew that it was the Holy Spirit's plan for him to reach Rome so he appeared to be fearless. There were no natural forces which could interrupt this journey.

Chapter 28

Coming ashore in Malta (28:1-16) after the shipwreck, Paul continued his mission among the people he met there. On his arrival in Italy, disciples who must have known him from some earlier time came from Rome to meet him. These were people open to the Holy Spirit, and the government officials in Rome did very little to interfere with Paul's work.

As in his earlier journeys, Paul's first task was to meet with Jewish leaders in Rome (28:17-28). They were not in

opposition to Paul's work even though they were not support-
ive of Christianity, of which they knew little. The meeting
indicated that the Christian mission was not opposed everywhere by Judaism. The uproar in Jerusalem was primarily a
result of some individuals who opposed Paul's mission to the
Gentiles. They stirred up trouble among Jewish officials and
raised concerns among Roman officials. Judaism, for the most
part, was not open to an expanded revelation even though
much of it had been proclaimed earlier by the prophets and
should have been accepted. Such non-acceptance could not
interfere with the Holy Spirit working through disciples.

Acts ends as Paul waited another two years for his freedom, but carried on his work during that period (28:30-31).
The writing does not tell us what Paul did afterward, not does
it give an account of his death, perhaps only two years after
he gained his freedom.

Acts is not a story of Peter and Paul. It is an account of
the plan of the Holy Spirit that moved Christianity beyond
Judaism and beyond Palestine. Christianity had become a
religion for the whole world. The first generation of
Christian disciples had started that process by taking it to the
very center of their Mediterranean world.

To Luke's readers, the account adds an answer to any
questions of how they became involved in a Messiah who
came to Palestine. God had sent the message of life with
God to humanity and God had provided the means to spread
the message throughout the world. Some steps in that double
mission may not have been perfect in implementing the plan
and there was opposition. However, the message will succeed
in being spread so that everyone has the opportunity to
accept the reward. Everyone will not understand the message
fully and some will even reject it. Luke's Gospel, including
the second half of his writings, tells the Church to be part of
making God's work successful, and in doing so, to gain the
reward ourselves.

THE GOSPEL OF JOHN

CONTEXT OF JOHN

The message of this Gospel is that Jesus is Divine. However, a second part of the message seems to say that knowing Jesus as the Messiah, but not understanding his full nature is to hardly know him at all. Historical Judaism had expected a human messiah as one chosen by God to rule God's kingdom. The concept of a Divine Messiah is such an extension beyond the historical expectation that to not grasp the extension is to know very little.

The context of John's Gospel is known primarily from the writing itself, with some historical traditions from outside of the writing. Each Gospel is written directly to a portion of the Church, but becomes very important to the whole Church. Mark wrote to the Roman Church, but the message becomes a Gospel for every Christian, especially in times of difficulty. Matthew in the same way wrote to a local church separating from Judaism, an issue which affected all of Christianity. Luke reassured his local church that Christ intended a universal church to offer everyone salvation, yet everyone must live the discipleship outlined in the Gospel.

The problem with John's Gospel is that, while the purpose seems clear, there is no identifiable group within the Church to which it is initially directed. John's community, as it is called, seems to have been separated from Judaism earlier than the rest of the Apostolic Church. There are strong indications that it split internally, which is a subject of the Letters of John. Yet, the separatists seem to have accepted the message of the Gospel, but drew a gnostic conclusion from it that is addressed in the First Letter of John. So it would be difficult to conclude that the Gospel was written to heal that split.

Since the Synoptic Gospels are directed to groups within the Apostolic Church, John could be writing to such a group as well. If the Gospel is written in 90 or later, as is often suggested by scholars, the group would be a second generation of disciples. There is no use of the term Apostles in this Gospel and the Twelve are mentioned by name less often than in the Synoptics. In many cases they are referred to as "his disciples." The first chapter, the Multiplication of Loaves, and the Passion section use names in a way similar to the Synoptics. In that part of the Last Supper Discourse in chapter 14, some members of the Twelve ask questions in which they seem to fail to understand what Jesus is saying. However, the Twelve are not described as understanding Jesus' message any more clearly before the Resurrection in the Synoptic Gospels than in chapter 14 of John's Gospel.

Another group that could be considered are those referred to in the statement, "many of his disciples left him and stopped going with him" (6:66). The group that left may be all or only part of the group that found the meaning of the Eucharistic language ending Jesus' discourse in chapter six as including "intolerable language" (6:60). The Twelve are asked if they would also leave and, without much enthusiasm, Peter responds that they would stay (6:67-69). The other groups are unidentified except as disciples. These others could constitute groups from the Church at the time the Gospel was written who found some teachings that were unacceptable to them. John, as perhaps the last Apostle, may have responded to that situation to gain the return of such a group to the Apostolic Church or to prevent further dissension. The Eucharist question doesn't seem to be a major subject of this Gospel, so the real problem may be some understanding of Jesus' Divinity. If so, those groups, or that issue, would be the object of the Gospel.

A last group to consider would be Judaism itself which walked away from their Messiah. They would consider any close connection of a human with God as an insult to God and, therefore, blasphemy. While there is no indication of a major problem arising from that subject in the New Testament writings prior to the Gospels, it is reasonable to expect that when the Divinity of Jesus was initially discussed between Jews and Christians, a great separation would occur. Even Jewish Christians who had followed the Christian teachings for a reasonably long time might consider that language "intolerable." All of the Gospels are responses to later Church problems through the direct use of Jesus' words and acts, and that would be a possible situation.

The Gospel makes use of the term "Jews" very often even when everyone in a scene is Jewish. Such terminology probably results from a time when there is a separation from Judaism and the term is convenient in identifying those listening to Jesus. However, it would not be a very convenient term if the group that is being addressed by the Gospel is even strongly Jewish Christian.

Therefore, the group being addressed directly by the Gospel cannot be clearly identified. It would seem to be a significant group or the effects of the group's objections to a belief which might raise doubts in the minds of a larger audience so as to require this magnitude of response. Where the objecting group is referred to in this commentary, it will be designated as "opponents." Where the supporters of the Evangelist, who is the authority behind the Gospel, is referred to in this commentary, they will be designated as John's community.

The tradition about John the Evangelist is that he is John, the son of Zebedee, even though the authority behind the Gospel is called the Beloved Disciple. The tradition that the two are the same has been questioned in the last century or two, but the evidence for separating John of Zebedee and the Beloved Disciple is far less than the evidence for their unity. Therefore, in this commentary the traditional designation of John will be used where such a finding is required.

The tradition that the Gospel was composed in Ephesus may be more important for the letters of John than for the Gospel. However, that John came into an early contact with anti-temple groups within and outside of Judaism and with Gentiles is important for seeing a progression in composing the Gospel. That subject goes beyond this commentary, yet, recognizing it as a possibility may give a different view to parts of this Gospel.

PROLOGUE

Chapter 1

The Gospel of John, with its great emphasis on the Divinity of Jesus, opens with an overwhelming statement on that subject in a prologue which essentially summarizes the Gospel as it is introduced (1:1-18). The divinity issue is not a mystery which slowly unfolds in the Gospel as it appears to have done in the life of the Apostolic Church. Rather, it is presented as the clear subject of the Gospel in the prologue so the reader will recognize the subject from the start. In the prologue, "Word" is used to describe the Second Person of the Trinity, yet this prologue is the only place in the Gospel where the term is used. That fact often is used to support the proposition that the prologue is a later addition to the Gospel. However, it shows that the prologue does not present actual sayings by Jesus but only could have been developed when the community of John came to a full understanding that Jesus was Divine.

The prologue states all in the first verse that the Word existed prior to creation, is proclaimed as being with God, and that the Word is God. The Word was with God at the time of creation (1:2), and then, in a difference from what is normally thought, the Word is described as the Creator of the universe and the origin of life (1:3-4). God as the Father is the usual understanding of God who creates. However, the prologue distinction will be used consistently throughout the Gospel, showing it is the Son as God who is present to the world in creation. It is the Son who is present in revelation that followed creation. It is the Son who is named Yahweh as recorded in the Old Testament. Jesus will apply the name Yahweh to himself, in its translation as "I Am," just as it is given in the Old Testament (Ex 3:14).

The information on John the Baptist (1:6-8, 15) has been added into the prologue, perhaps from a text used to introduce him prior to the addition of the hymn material, if such an addition were the method of composition. Setting John the Baptist in his proper place as the witness may have been dictated by some of John the Baptist's disciples who, even late in the first century, saw him as the Messiah. The coming of the "Word" into the world (1:9-13) is shown as occurring after John is introduced as the witness, even though it seems to precede the Incarnation. However, if the meaning of revelation is to bring the gift of a union with God to all humanity, then the "coming into the world" would include the Old Testament period as well, since the Second Person of the Trinity is present throughout the revelation.

The Incarnation event (1:14) with its non-sexist use of "flesh," as an alternative to the less clear translation to "became man" in the English translation of the Nicene Creed, defines the "Word" as God becoming fully human, not just disguised as one. The terms grace and truth have the actual meaning of gift and revelation; that which comes from God is not earned by humanity so it must be gift and the message from God is truth, rather than how the term is used today.

Then the purpose given for the Incarnation action is to reveal the gift of God to humanity (1:16-18), something required so that all will know that salvation, through union with God, is open to all humanity. The gift is given sequentially, or as "grace in return for grace." The acceptance of an element of the gift opens humanity to being able to accept additional elements. The use of "only Son" for the Word Incarnate is a major change in meaning from "Son of God" used in the Synoptic Gospels and the Old Testament. After the Exile, Judaism came to know that Yahweh was not just the God of Judaism but the Only God of all creation. Only Son seems to provide a clarification from the Old Testament title, Son of God, which sometimes retains that earlier meaning when used in the Synoptic Gospels.

JESUS' PUBLIC MINISTRY

The appearance of John the Baptist (1:19-28) is described in the context of his rejecting existing expectations: those of his own disciples, "I am not the Messiah"; the expectations of Judaism, "I am not Elijah"; and perhaps a rejection of Church understanding with his "No" to the question about the prophet. John the Baptist did not bring a new message or interpretation, since his message of repentance was from the Old Testament. Rather, he pointed to one person as Messiah. He opened the way to the coming of life, but did not make it happen.

In describing the event of the next day (1:29-34), an addition was made to what the Apostolic Church had written about John the Baptist in the Synoptic Gospels. Here, John did not know the one he was to announce, but simply witnessed that the time had come for the Messiah and waited with the other disciples to see the event (1:31). Finally, when the signs told him that the Messiah had arrived, he become a witness to him, like every other disciple. He identified Jesus as the "Chosen One of God." The signs that the Church relied on to make a decision were all anyone had to make a decision. The Gospel's introduction to the Apostolic Church seems to say it is necessary to examine the signs rather than assuming that one knows the full meaning of the Messiah based on what had been written before his coming. Even the one who announced the Messiah had no real understanding of him, he only looked at the signs. To know Jesus is Messiah is almost nothing; to know the Messiah is Divine is to know everything.

Another day, or perhaps another stage of understanding, brings the first disciples of the Apostolic Church to a meeting with Jesus the Messiah (1:35-51). They meet him as a "teacher" (1:38) and as "Messiah" (1:41). Peter experiences a special calling beyond his identity as a Jew (1:42). The disciple Philip (1:45) sees Jesus as the one "Moses wrote about in the Law" (Dt 18:18), as the fulfillment of the Old Testament promises. At least Nathanael will wrestle with Jesus' apparent origin in Galilee (1:46) and overcome that hurdle to accept Jesus in the titles "Son of God" and "King of Israel," which most completely describe a new King David-type of messiah (1:49). Jesus adds the title "Son of Man" as he was shown as doing in the other Gospels (1:51). Even though the chapter designations are introduced into the text at a much later time, the conclusion seems to be that the titles of Jesus known to the Apostolic Church in the Synoptic Gospels can be disposed of in a single chapter. Certainly these titles do not come close to the meaning of Messiah which is put forth in the prologue.

The opponent group is asked in this Gospel account to go over the signs and sayings of Jesus once more and come to understand the full message of Jesus, rather than the identification they had before the signs. They are told to put on the attitude of John the Baptist, which could be stated as: "Even though I was sent to reveal Him, I had no real knowledge of Him until the signs occurred within creation." John the Baptist was not just the representative of the Old Testament people in pointing out Jesus, he was the representative of the New Testament people as well, by playing a part in identifying the full meaning of the Messiah.

Chapter 2

This journey of full meaning starts with the first sign given at Cana, which may have had the appearance of a magician's trick (2:1-12). This sign was not given to change the opinions of outsiders, but to describe the attitude of the true disciples. Jesus' mother is identified but the story is not about being his mother. She is called "woman," a title of respect, but not a suitable title for a Jewish man's mother. "Woman" would be a more appropriate title for a close disciple. In this account, she is identified as the perfect disciple before Jesus starts his public life with signs. Luke had identified her as the perfect disciple in the birth narrative; here the same designation is reflected at the start of Jesus' public life.

At the wedding, Jesus and his mother came to a situation where people had less than the fullness of life. She asked Jesus to enrich the new life the couple came to in a union of coming together before the Lord. Christians would recognize that as the meaning of Church. The day of the Lord in the Old Testament was characterized as a time when the mountains and valleys flowed with wine. Mary's plea, "They have no wine," would mean that the couple, and all people, need the Lord in their midst. Her words are the equivalent of "they have no salvation." It was a request that only Jesus could fulfill. There was no statement that Mary had a full understanding of what would occur, but her witness was to tell them to follow whatever they were called to do by the Lord. "Do whatever he tells you" is an instruction now used by John to the opponents.

What occurred is perhaps beyond belief by any who did not know the full story of the Messiah. It was a sign of wonderment to those who only saw the results. The "best wine," the greatest part of the salvation message, is in this later Gospel writing. In this first sign the reader is told that "his disciples believed" (2:11). The story is an introduction of the signs, and the implication seems to be that the signs will point far beyond just the satisfaction with the results. They who were present as the signs unfolded should see the complete meaning, rather than only celebrating the results. In doing so, they would become the complete disciples of a revelation that goes far beyond their expectations.

When Jesus brings the message of change to those at the heart of Judaism, in Jerusalem and at the Temple, they hear his claims but never look for the meaning (2:13-25). In this account, the expulsion of those who service the cult of temple sacrifices is a starting point for Jesus' public ministry, rather than part of its conclusion as in the Synoptic Gospels. Jesus seemed to say that Judaism should change from a religion of doing things, if they are to accept a new relationship in life with God. The Jewish officials demanded a sign to cause them to change from their relationship with God in the

Law, just as in the Synoptic account (Mk 11:27-33). Then Jesus responded with a comparison between a covenant inscribed in the Temple with its rites and a living relationship in the Resurrected Christ (2:19-22). The Jewish people could hardly be expected to understand the meaning of Jesus' statement, and we are told even the disciples only remembered and believed after the Resurrection. However, many others who saw the signs did believe, even if they did not respond with a full changing of life (2:23-25).

For those who stayed or wished to stay within Judaism and the Temple worship, this story does not commend them for their level of acceptance of the message of Jesus. Instead, it seems to say that only remembering that a saying fulfills an Old Testament prophecy is not the full acceptance of the Messiah's message (2:17). Even a belief in Jesus' title of Messiah is only half belief if the signs really point to a totally different relationship with God from the traditional view of Messiah. To destroy the Temple, as the place of God on earth, and to replace it with the Resurrected Christ, as the place of God on earth, meant something far different from remaining within Judaism and "continually praising God in the Temple" (Lk 24:53). This teaching of Jesus, about the meaning of the Temple after the Resurrection, carries an instruction to reevaluate their relationship with God when the "three days" have been fulfilled. The teaching is remembered as central to the beliefs of the disciples.

Chapter 3

Nicodemus, the Jewish official who recognized that the signs had great meaning, would try to come to a fuller understanding even if it meant risk to his position and entire career in Judaism (3:1-21). Even without a full understanding, Nicodemus recognized that the signs pointed in a new direction from Judaism and demanded a deeper understanding than might be apparent from their results.

John's Gospel includes a series of discourses which are different from any writing in the Synoptic Gospels. In many modern translations of the text of the discourses, the words of Jesus will be shown in a poetic format while the remainder of the text is in prose. The words of Jesus must be remembered from his public life and known to the Church in general. Without the words being known widely, it is unlikely that they would be convincing, especially in something so important to the Church. There is no threat to the community of John at the time of writing the Fourth Gospel, but what is being proposed is so foreign to Jewish belief that even Christians separated from Judaism would not accept it easily.

The text in prose may be related to problems and questions of John's own community, or more likely, the opponents. Certainly, the other three Gospels relate to problems and questions from a later time. The use of names, such as any of the Twelve or Nicodemus, in the section opening chapter three, would represent early views that had been accepted by the opponent group. The questions are being answered by the words of Jesus, even though Jesus never faced those same questions in his public life.

When Jesus' words are used to answer a question, they might not do so directly. The Evangelist would then raise the question in a different way, as if in a misunderstanding, and a second response from Jesus would add to the first answer. In a series of such responses, a fuller answer would be produced than could be known from a single teaching or saying of Jesus. The teaching of Jesus must be authentic, but the questions that produce the answer would be the work of the Evangelist, at least to some extent.

An emphasis that indicates Jesus' words in a discourse are directed at the opponents, rather than only those involved in the discourse, is when the words are introduced with "I tell you most solemnly," or more literally, "Amen, Amen." It indicates to the first readers of this Gospel the need to listen carefully to what Jesus is saying and change their lives and faith.

The position that Nicodemus could recognize was a concept of being "born again" even though it had no meaning within Judaism. A person originally born Jewish also would be reborn within the Law. Therefore, being born again would be only a return to the same position under the Law. The Apostolic Church recognized baptism as being reborn into a new life. However, its full meaning would remain hidden if the life of Christ was not beyond what had been proposed as the traditional view of messiah, one anointed by God as political and religious leader of Judaism.

The idea of "born from above" (3:3 and 3:7) may have had little meaning in the time of Jesus, since in Jewish thought only God and the angels would be associated with "above." Humans were born on earth, lived on earth, and after death went down to Sheol below the earth. However, Paul had described baptism as going into the water as if going into a tomb and dying to the life governed by the world and then rising out of the water to live for God in Christ Jesus (or in the Body of Christ) (Rom 6:1-11). That understanding of dying to one life and putting on another would be described as "born again." However, the introduction of Jesus as Divine produces a new meaning for baptism, which comes from the teaching of Jesus about disciples as "born from above," since the Body of Christ is changed in meaning as well.

The Evangelist inserts the question of Nicodemus (3:4) into the remembered sayings of Jesus to draw attention to the fact that the earlier description would be at variance with the full meaning of Jesus. Jesus' response (3:5-8) is that a new life comes from the baptism act and from the Spirit of God and only with that life can one enter the kingdom. A human being entering water is the action, but accepting a life with the Spirit (from above) is the result. Being "born of flesh" produces only flesh, but being born of the Spirit is the means of gaining eternal life.

An argument is often made that the same Greek word, "anothen," can be used for "from above" and for "again." However, the reality of the discourse with Nocodemus is that Jesus' words are used for correcting the "born again" understanding of the later opponent group, since Nicodemus is shown as not understanding "born again" either. It is John's way of causing the opponents, in the time when the Gospel is composed, to recognize that "born from above" is a deeper and more complete understanding. Jesus and Nicodemus never had a conversation in Greek, so the dual use of the same word never occurred in Jesus' time. The Aramaic word behind Jesus' explanation has the meaning of born "from above" as is true in most uses of "anothen" in the New Testament. The "born again" statement must have come from the Greek-speaking Church.

In John's Gospel, the meaning of kingdom is elevated beyond the concept of only a kingdom on earth that seemed to be the earlier expectation when Jesus returned to Palestine in an early Second Coming. Everyone can figure out that the wind is blowing around (3:8), even without knowing where it comes or goes, and the same should be true in recognizing the presence of the Spirit. To see the Spirit of God in those who have opened themselves to the Spirit in baptism means there has been a change in the life relationship with God and that is a kingdom change. It cannot be emphasized too often that this writing is directed at a group that seems to question a position, and is not an instruction to Nicodemus or Judaism.

Nicodemus is puzzled by the possibility of a life relationship with God (3:9) since before the Resurrection he represents a Jewish covenant understanding where not even a familiarity with God in which the Divine name is pronounced could be accepted. Jesus' surprise that a teacher in Israel could not understand closeness to God, even though open to signs, is a statement directed at the opponents at the time of writing. Unless one is open to the possibility of a relationship beyond Judaism, there can be no understanding, and that is the meaning of what will follow (3:11). However, the change to a plural subject in verse eleven must have been done by the Evangelist to emphasize the different way his community saw the teaching from how it was accepted by the opponents.

Nicodemus then disappears from the scene, and the teaching that follows is focused on the failure of the opponents to come to the full realization of revelation. If the words of Jesus concerning the relationship with God were not accepted, the opponents could not recognize the meaning of the heavenly reward where disciples lived in the presence of God (3:12). That is a description of the relationship which could hardly be breathed aloud within Judaism (Acts 7:55-58).

The sign of a Divine Messiah and a heavenly kingdom were very different from the Jewish understanding of a human messiah chosen by God to lead a kingdom here on earth. The difference is not a matter of magnitude, as much as an entirely new understanding of revelation. Yet, this would be the sign that comes from the Resurrection (3:13-15), rather than the Resurrection introducing only an interim period until a Second Coming and a King David-style messiah with a kingdom in Palestine.

As the discourse continues, it is this new understanding which is described as the fullness of God's love (3:16), God's witness in the world (3:17-18), and the fact that life or no-life are offered and what each person chooses is what will be given (3:19-21). However, what is chosen here on earth must be lived openly here on earth, or "plainly seen" as it is stated in the text, because this is where the life decision must be made (3:21). The witness requirement which seems so clear in the Synoptics is clarified by John by describing the content of the witness.

The return of John the Baptist to the scene may indicate that John's disciples had not understood the need to become disciples of Jesus, and they may have harbored the thought that John has some type of messiah position (3:22-36). More likely, there were some disciples who remembered that John the Baptist had some questions about Jesus being the Messiah (Mt 11:2-14), and such questions were now being raised against Christian teachings. The short discourse of John addresses such concerns by showing John the Baptist's complete acceptance of Jesus as Messiah and an understanding of the brief part John the Baptist plays in his coming. John the Baptist's discourse goes beyond some of the language that the opponents may be using concerning Jesus' relationship with the Father. Jesus comes from heaven (3:31), the place of God, and what he has taught is God's own message (3:33-34).

Then, in language clearly not expressed by the Apostles prior to the Resurrection, a view of kingdom is presented in which each disciple has eternal life, not just a promise for it in the future (3:36). The living of a life with God starts in this world and must be seen in this world. Being part of the Body of Christ has an extended meaning when a Messiah with an eternal life has taken on a human life. Worse for the opponents is the question raised for those not believing. Does it mean not believing Jesus is the Messiah, or does it mean not believing in the meaning of Messiah as Divine? It is not enough to say "Lord, Lord" (Mt 7:21-23); what is more necessary is to know the Lord in order to live his life.

John the Baptist is shown as the one who did not recognize Jesus initially, but had come to the more complete understanding. He had come as one who would call Judaism to move from a living of the Law to a new relationship with God. This final statement of his in this Gospel seems to call those who stayed within Judaism, or were considering a return, to take the additional steps to move beyond it. The Jewish position stopped in its tracks when it approached a divine and human union, since in their minds that seemed offensive to God. For them such closeness of a human to God was an obvious act of blasphemy (Mk 14:61-65). John the Baptist says that such an eternal life is the great step of the very journey which Judaism had been invited to take.

Chapter 4

The next part in this Gospel addresses how the message of the Messiah might be received by those on the fringes of Judaism, such as the Samaritans, who had not become dependent on a temple and its bureaucracy (4:1-42). The Samaritans were visited by Jesus before the time when John the Baptist was imprisoned, which is when the public life of Jesus seemed to start in the Synoptic Gospels (Mark 1:14).

The woman who met Jesus in public at midday is presented as one who knows Samaritan teaching but may not live it out completely. She responded quickly to a promise of "living water" which she equated with a surface stream (4:11), but which made the connection, for the reader, with John the Baptist's promise of "eternal life" (3:36). Her comparison of Jesus to Jacob raises the critical question of how far the message of the Messiah goes beyond the original revelation of the Old Testament (4:11-12). Jesus brings the subject to a conclusion by stepping away from baptismal water as something on the outside of the body, and makes it that which brings eternal life within the person (4:13-14).

The comment on the woman's husbands seems to intrude here with only the thought that Jesus' comments might suggest he could read her mind (4:16-20). Since the word for husband is "Lord," which in the Aramaic used in a conversation would be "Baal," the comments could relate to a confusion about who governs the woman's life. The "Lord" or "Baal" would be anyone who governs one's life and a woman would associate the term with her husband first, in an everyday conversation. However, the number "five" seems extreme unless she had been selected because of a life that would be considered immoral under the Law. She assumed this Baal meant husband and she responded that she had none. More likely, the Baal she was to call was her god.

The Greek text clearly states that husband is the word being discussed, but the meaning of the conversation and the entire Gospel points to divinity as the subject. Jesus' statement of "five," the number of gods worshipped by the original Samaritans brought to repopulate the region by the Assyrians (2 Kgs 17:24-34), tells her the subject being discussed is really "God." The "five" (pagan gods) were not divine while the God the Samaritans inherited from Judaism is not a "Baal" but the "Father." With that the conversation shifts back to the real subject which is God.

This conversation is not just for the woman, who clearly understands what Jesus has said and is not changing the subject, but also for the opponents. They might retain a view of God as being distant, while Jesus' message is that God is very close. The writing is not for the Samaritans but for the opponents and what follows seems to say as much.

The Jews knew the truth about there being only One God and, in such knowing, were the only ones who could be the human recipients of the message of salvation (4:21-25). However, as Jesus was speaking, the time had arrived to change to a form of worship desired by God in Spirit (the love of God) and in truth (the revelation of God). The call to change was not directed only to Samaritans, but to Judaism and the opponents as well.

The Samaritan woman knows of the promise of a Messiah who would bring a new teaching, as did Moses (Dt 18:18), rather than a messiah who would be a temporal ruler for Judaism, as was David. Jesus' answer to her was his initial self-identification as Messiah because she was open to who he is rather than what had been defined historically. The answer ended with the "I Am" name of God (4:26) revealed in Exodus 3:14. Modern translations convert the "I Am" statement to "I am he" to fit normal speech patterns, but the original Greek statement in 4:26 uses the same Greek words as in Exodus 3:14 of the Septuagint version.

The woman's response was immediate since such news should be proclaimed, but she left her water jar behind (4:28-30). Was the message too important to be slowed by everyday considerations, or does her action say she need not rely on the Old Testament view of life, the water from Jacob's well, now that a greater life has arrived?

The position of the disciples is that they seem concerned only with the rules of the Law governing contact and food from non-Jews (4:31-32). Jesus' response was to ask them to look around again to this land beyond Judaism. Are they seeing only what the words "harvest" and kingdom meant before he came, or are they recognizing that everything has a new meaning (4:34-38)? They should not be looking at the ground anymore, as if that is where the kingdom will arise, but the yield of the harvest which comes from the whole world. This language seems to be from an early position of John promoting Christianity as being open to converts outside of Judaism. It could have been from John's association with the early Church in Samaria and would be a settled matter, except for Judaizers. The Samaritans, when introduced to the real Messiah, responded completely and immediately. However, the Pharisees who searched for a living relationship with God under the Law would chase out the Messiah who brought the fullness of a life with God (4:1-3).

This section closes on a trip to Galilee with the cure of the son of a court official in Galilee (4:43-54). From the story it cannot be determined if the official was Gentile, Idumean, or Jewish. Herod Antipas was Idumean with strong Roman ties, while perhaps a majority of his subjects were Jewish. The story has similarities with the cure of the centurion's servant (Mt 8:5-18). It could be a different version of the same story where a Gentile responds in faith before seeing the results of a sign. That is not clear with the court official, but like John the Baptist and the Samaritans, the official does seem to live on the fringes of Judaism. Jesus criticized the official's need for a sign, yet his faith was placed in Jesus prior to the cure (4:49). He didn't need a sign on this account but could have been aware of earlier signs. The opponents in this Gospel would not receive a later sign, but were aware of all the signs and teachings of Jesus' public life.

The responses of Nicodemus, John the Baptist, the Samaritan woman, and what might be a non-Jewish court official were to take a strong interest in Jesus's message even with very few signs. Yet, that was sufficient to produce an opening to a change in their lives. The opponents must have known about the signs of Jesus' public life, yet not have come to the complete belief shown in this Gospel.

REPLACEMENT OF FEASTS

Chapter 5

Chapter five opens with Jesus' return to Jerusalem for an unnamed feast. If the feast was Passover, as could be assumed from the mention of the time of harvest (4:35), then with the Passovers in chapters two and six and the final Passover at the crucifixion, the ministry of Jesus would be over three years long. Commentators often note that moving chapter five events to after chapter six, which is just before Passover, would be a more logical order since chapter four ends in Galilee which is the setting for chapter six and that would eliminate one Passover.

Such types of argument assume that John the Evangelist, as an eyewitness, should have an interest in preserving the original order of events. That would be in opposition to the Synoptic Gospels in which the events were arranged to answer questions of their communities. However, there is not the slightest hint that John's order was intended to be exactly historical. Therefore, the feast being unnamed, or the interjection of chapter five in this place, could be taken as proof that the order is for theological reasons rather than any interest in giving an exact historical arrangement. The result is that it cannot be determined if there are four Passovers in the public life of Jesus just from the order of the contents. That the feast of chapter five is not named would tend to mean it was not a Passover.

Chapters three and four had a Jewish leader and a Jewish prophet interested in Jesus and the responses of a woman and a court official on the fringes of Judaism. Chapter five examines the response of Jewish leaders in facing a sign which infringed directly on the Law with regard to keeping the Sabbath. The sign in chapter five was more important than those preceding it, and since it occurred on the Sabbath, the Jewish officials in Jerusalem could not ignore the event. However, Judaism had a more difficult time seeing the meaning of this significant sign than those on the fringes of Judaism did with more limited signs. The man involved in the sign, whom we might think would be most affected, expressed almost no concern about what happened. Perhaps that description of him was used to make sure that the focus would be on the Jewish leaders, rather than on him.

The man had been so crippled for 38 years that he could not move from the side of the pool into the water by himself (5:1-18). This was a much more serious infirmity than the man with the withered hand in the Synoptic Gospels, even though similar. This healing did not require the use of the pool, but was an instantaneous response to Jesus' words. So the man was restored completely, even to the point of carrying his sleeping mat away, without the need for rehabilitation. He was so unconcerned that he could not even describe Jesus until he met him later.

The Jewish leaders, faced with the obvious sign and meaning, rejected Jesus as a sinner for doing a work on the Sabbath. They would not accept the act of a human over their interpretation of a commandment from God. Jesus' response was to clarify the meaning of the healing as an obvious action from God, rather than something sinful (5:17-18). The charge of equality with God was considered to be blasphemy and caused serious opposition to Jesus. It should have caused the disciples to consider a change in their view about Jesus.

The discourse that follows (5:19-47) was directed at the opponents who should have understood the meaning as they accepted the Messiah. The question for them may be related to the magnitude of the sign that was required to reach the Church's conclusion that Jesus was above the Law, as it governed the Sabbath. Jesus was doing divine works here on earth, and in the Synoptics the disciples accepted the works as proof that Jesus was the Messiah (Mk 8:29). In John's Gospel the question is: Do the works indicate a messiah as expected by Judaism, a new King David to establish a kingdom, or would they mean that the Messiah was greatly different from what was expected? The discourse seems to be directed at the second part of the question and the audience being asked are the opponents at the time of the writing.

The initial part of the discourse (5:19-24) describes a relationship with the Father which goes well beyond a new king who would free Palestine as a Jewish state free of pagan influences. Being able to do "whatever the Father does" or being able to give "life to anyone he chooses" are claims that Jewish leaders would never accept as the power of a messiah. Yet the Christians rehearing these claims, which they know to be true, would have to recognize that they don't just proclaim the arrival of an expected messiah. The conclusion (5:24) is that eternal life comes to the one who hears and believes without even waiting for judgment.

Judaism had rejected a further view of the Messiah that went beyond the Law, while Christianity accepted a mission that went beyond Judaism, and that also included Jesus in heaven. However, they may not have come to a conclusion about the meaning of Jesus in heaven until the early second coming expectation was dropped. Here the whole meaning of Jesus as the Messiah is given in the context of a meaning coming from that later time. Could the opponents who accept Jesus as the Messiah stop short of accepting the full description of the Messiah in the remembered sayings of Jesus?

A second section (5:25-30) carries the meaning further to the last judgment. The establishment of the kingdom was not in the return of Jesus, but in the acceptance of eternal life promised in the revelation of Jesus. How that life is lived out (5:29) produces the judgment all people bring upon themselves. Jesus is presented as the judge at the last judgment, but not as someone condemning or rewarding, since that comes from the person's life. The judgment then is in how the message of Jesus is accepted by each disciple during life, not as a surprise decision at the end of time.

A third section (5:31-43) identifies the witness they have all received, which is more than adequate for a decision in life. First, a prophet was sent to provide the witness expected under Judaism (5:33-35). That was not necessary for Jesus, but it should have removed human doubt and sparked human interest. Second, the witness of the works of Jesus (5:36-38) were not only Jesus' testimony, but also the Father's on his behalf, because they were so clearly beyond human manipulation. Third, Scripture itself, which speaks for God, identified Jesus as Messiah (5:39-43). In addition to human and divine witnesses to the disciples, their entire historical grounding of revelation points toward a conclusion which goes beyond only a life under the Law. All three witnesses are from God and point to a divine connection with the Messiah going far beyond what Judaism expected. The striking statement that not accepting these witnesses from God means they "have no love of God" (5:42) would shock the readers of this Gospel, as it would be seen as addressed to them.

Finally, a conclusion (5:44-47) forces the disciples to look beyond Judaism, which knows God but cannot accept the reality of a shared life with God. This could have been an early problem for Judaism, yet it undergoes a dramatic change when Jesus is shown to be so much more than just Messiah. To remain with the Law as relationship would have seemed to be a safe position, similar to that presented by Moses after being given the revelation (Dt 32:45-47). However, the reality of Moses is that when God called the Israelites to dramatically change the relationship with God by accepting the Law, Moses proclaimed that the change was essential and should be accepted.

The disciples of Jesus' time are not following Moses if a greater revelation is given and they will not take the step to accept it. No more than a Jew could proclaim at Passover "I will stay in Egypt as a slave," should a disciple refuse to accept this greatest step. The opponents would have to examine the teachings of Jesus again if they were to be truly open to their meaning. The ending of this section with no response from anyone indicates it had been presented for the opponents, as was the Nicodemus discussion.

Chapter 6

The multiplication of loaves (6:1-15), as the great Christian remembrance with its Eucharist connotations, is the only miracle event found in each of the four Gospels. Many of the details of the story are found only in John's account, as might be expected from an Evangelist who also was an eyewitness. Philip, who had already decided on the outcome, was tested by Jesus. There was no thought in Philip's mind that Jesus was going to present a sign of such a magnitude. This lack of understanding may be the Evangelist's way of asking the opponents if they have come to the full recognition of Jesus themselves. The response of the crowd was an attempt to make Jesus king. That would be the obvious reaction by anyone who expected a King David-style of messiah and would require no forethought. The idea of a Divine Messiah is not shown in any reaction to the event.

The walking on water account (6:16-21) follows the multiplication of loaves here just as it does in Mark and Matthew. Since John did not seem to derive a meaning from the story, it is possible that the two had been tied together earlier by the Church, if they did not actually happen together as described. However, the story even in Mark has Jesus identify himself as "I Am," the Divine Name revealed to Moses on Mt. Sinai (Ex 3:14). It is usually translated as "It is I" to fit the English text more comfortably; however, the Greek words are identical to the Greek words in the Book of Exodus account where God is identified by name (Ex 3:14). There was no awareness by the disciples in that account that Jesus was using God's name for himself. Yet, these must be authentic words of Jesus which only on reexamination show the full meaning of Jesus the Messiah. The divinity teaching was given by Jesus, but in the Jewish setting the meaning was not grasped.

The discourse that follows these two events (6:22-58) opens a discussion on the meaning of the Eucharist. This is not an area where we would expect to see a difference of opinion within Christianity because there is little discussion of it in the other Gospels or even in the other New Testament writings. If this subject had been raised at the Last Supper there would be no argument, because no discussion occurred at that time. The disciples were Jewish; it was a time close to the Passover feast and it would have been understood in that context, at least on that night. However, if the belief in the early Church about the Messiah became more clear, the meaning of Eucharist also would be clarified as well, as the Evangelist will show quite clearly. Paul shows that clarity in correcting the poor celebration habits of the Corinthians (1 Cor. 11:23-27), and here it can be addressed in the dramatic words of Jesus which must have been known within the Church.

The discourse started the following day (6:22-27) as the people found Jesus and were told their belief was inadequate. They had witnessed a great sign, but seemed to attach no meaning to it other than that they had been fed (6:26). Jesus opened the discussion by telling them that the meaning pointed to something beyond being fed, just as the survival of the Israelites in the desert after leaving Egypt gave them a very different view of Yahweh, from the normal perceptions of divinity at that time.

The response by the people in asking what "works" were required of them (6:28) was the response from the Law, asking what should be added to the Law by a new Messiah. They seemed to be willing to accept a change in the Law if it was only some additional requirements. So the answer of Jesus was that belief in the real message of the Messiah was not understood by the Jewish listeners, many of whom also were disciples. The Israelites received bread (manna) in the desert for forty years as a result of believing Moses. These people asked if Jesus was going to feed them only once, as on the previous day, or was the sign to be as great or greater than the one in the time of Moses (6:30-31).

The Evangelist continued the discourse of Jesus which was directed increasingly to the disciples, rather than Jesus talking to people on the hillside. The true bread from the

Father, which is essential to life, is the Messiah who has come
from God in heaven (6:32-40). Jesus had shown them that
he could feed them physically, however his promise was a life
beyond physical life. This eternal life is something they must
accept as their own and actually live. The request from the
crowd for "bread always" is a request for a sign greater than
the sign in the time of Moses when the Israelites were fed for
forty years. With a greater sign, they would know Jesus was
greater than Moses.   However, the real meaning of Jesus as
Messiah was not in bringing a reward or sign to this present
life, but in bringing a new life altogether.

The disciples, in reading this section, must have realized
that Jesus told them of his "coming from heaven" (6:38) and,
yet, the opponents may have taken that as meaning "one
chosen by God," as David was chosen by God to be a messiah
(1 Sam 16:1). Jewish understanding of heaven was as a place
for God and the angels. Humans were born on earth and at
death went to Sheol below the earth. If the prose section
(6:42-43) reflects the opponents view in the discourse, they
do not understand, even though Jesus must have made the
statement. It would not be understood that way as long as
the messiah was seen only in human terms. The conclusion
(6:40) may well have been understood as salvation in accepting the Messiah. Here the meaning shifts to the requirement
that they accept the real words of Jesus, not just what they
expected the Messiah to say.

The complaining of the Jews among themselves
(6:41-43) may be the creation of the Evangelist to define
more clearly the subject as something difficult to accept.
The words of Jesus say that he came from heaven, the place
of God. Jesus brings them back to the real message
(6:44-51); they must accept him as a very different Messiah.
They also must accept a relationship with God that is not
just life in an independent Palestine, but an eternal life with
God in heaven. To a nation that saw any identification of
humanity with God as blasphemy, which historically meant
bringing God down to the human level, any elevation of

humanity to a living with God was not immediately under-standable. Such a statement (6:51) would not be acceptable to them and may have been treated as a type of parable that might become more clear over time. So even though these words were familiar, they would not have been accepted at face value by the original disciples. At the time of John's writing, the opponents were faced with them again in a dis-course composition that makes the real meaning more obvi-ous.

Scripture said the teaching would come from God (6:45) and only the Messiah claims to have seen the Father, therefore, he must come from God with the message (6:46). The reward is eternal life (6:47) and is gained by accepting the life of Jesus (6:48). The Law was a life given in the desert, but it was only the normal human life directed by the Law (6:49). Now they were told about a view of life that goes beyond normal life. It is accepted by taking on (eating) the physical presence of Jesus, the flesh that is in union with God (6:51).

At this point a question about the Eucharist is raised (6:52), not in a Passover situation as at the Last Supper, but in the reality of Jesus' teachings in his public life to everyone. The question in the chapter six setting must be, what do the words of Jesus actually mean. The solemn answer (6:53-58) is that God has given a union of divine life and human life in the person sent to reveal and define the relationship of life. That is the life humans must accept as the only source of eternal life. It was not only a spiritual relationship, any more than Jesus was only spiritual, rather it is a union of divinity with actual flesh and blood. It is this actual flesh (physical being) and blood (physical life) which must be taken in by true disciples and made their own (6:53-56). The acceptance is made in physical eating and drinking and, as all life must be nourished, the taking in of the relationship must be contin-ued. This is not just the "Yes, Lord" of baptism, but the con-tinued living of the relationship. Without the physical acceptance of the life of Jesus, a person would only have the temporary human life they were originally born into and would at some point die (6:57-58). The taking on of eternal life gives them a life which continues beyond human death, and that is the great gift from God which describes salvation.

This teaching, given in a Jewish synagogue as is stated (6:59), must have been from the public life of Jesus, and would bring great difficulty in acceptance in a literal way (6:59-62). Therefore, the teaching could have been accepted as a parable, which would have some other meaning if rethought through. The language which was considered blasphemy in Jewish terms would indeed be intolerable for them as is shown by them in leaving Jesus. Here the message was given solemnly by John in writing to later disciples who were present at the Eucharist regularly.

The opponents must have accepted Jesus' Ascension into heaven, and were familiar with all of Jesus' teachings, so the time of rethinking the parable was overdue. Jesus had said that only what comes from the Spirit of God brings life, not that which comes from only a human source (6:63). This was the life "from above" that Jesus explained to Nicodemus. The words of Jesus had promised life, and if disciples looked for that, they must realize that all of the words must be accepted. The words would never point toward waiting for a Second Coming and obtaining a free land in which to live here on earth, as the only promise of a Messiah known to Judaism. The true meaning of the words must be the meaning Jesus gave to them, not just any interpretation that might seem to fit.

The result was that even some who had been disciples of Jesus would not accept all of his teachings, but returned to a life of the Law (6:64-66). Surely this had already occurred in the separation of Christianity from Judaism after the Temple was destroyed. However, the question posed by Jesus (6:67-71) and reposed by John for the opponents was: Are these second generation disciples going to accept the full message, or try to stay only in the situation of the Law? The answer of the original disciples was given with what appears to be a measure of doubt and, certainly, not a full understanding. Yet, with the realization that it was a message of eternal life, they would stay with Jesus without fully understanding everything at the time.

John was forcing the opponents to accept the fullness of the message of Jesus, perhaps even as early as when the whole church was still examining the choices of remaining within Judaism or not. However, the question that has been restated here for the opponents was one of not just retaining Christian beliefs, but, in the separation from Judaism, of reexamining the very words of Jesus. This would lead them far beyond the Jewish view of a legal covenant. It was the real Passover decision for all disciples. The words of Jesus ask disciples to go beyond Judaism in response to revelation, just as the original Israelites went beyond the covenant relationship of Abraham, and walked out of Egypt and out of that life.

What is presented is not a Passover renewal of a decision that originally had been made in Egypt centuries earlier, with all of the following results known, but of being faced with the actual decision themselves. Christianity believed the divine promise of freedom from slavery for all creation and a new life in a much different kingdom from Palestine. However, it is easy to understand that opposition groups would form. Opponents, with no real knowledge of what would be faced, now had been presented with this record from the Messiah. A second generation of Israelites at the time of Moses, while still in the desert with only the witness of an earlier generation and a retelling of stories of great signs, had said yes and moved with Joshua into an unknown land.

Now a second generation of the Christians, with the witness of the original disciples and with stories of signs which showed the message was from God, were being asked to take a step into a wholly different kingdom. The Church was not asked only to follow God's call to leave Egypt at the Last Supper Passover, but a Messiah's call to go beyond their only covenant with the God of all creation. By fleeing at

Jesus' crucifixion, the disciples had retreated from their Last Supper decision back into the Law. After the Resurrection that retreat was reversed in a faith that did go beyond the Law and in an acceptance of the guidance of the Holy Spirit leading them to the whole world. In this writing, composed of Jesus' own words and teachings, the Church would resolve the meaning of Jesus fully.

Chapter 7

A new unit is introduced in chapters seven through eleven as the previous conclusion was reached. It asks what actually remains of Judaism after reexamining the message of the Messiah more fully. The promise of Jesus was clearly something which went past any concept of a life under the Law, but was there something that must be retained?

The feast of Tabernacles was when Jewish people stepped back from what was permanent in their world and lived in temporary shelters as they had in the desert. This feast also marked the time when the whole cycle of reading the Law has been completed and when the fullness of the harvest, the gift from God, was received. The primary tabernacle in the desert was the tent of Yahweh. It was not attached to a permanent site, but went with the people of God wherever their lives carried them. The question of how God was made present to them seemed to be addressed by this feast and certainly was in the text of John related to this feast.

This replacement of feasts by Jesus could have been raised quite early as it seems to have been in the letter to the Hebrews. However, if the Temple had been destroyed only recently, this question would need to be revisited on the basis of the full identity of Jesus Christ. The replacement was then necessary and was exceedingly complete.

In the introduction to the feast of Tabernacles (7:1-13) Jesus was described as not going to the feast in Jerusalem. However, he was encouraged to go and work signs in Judea where he had disciples. This gives quite a different view of his public life from that shown in the Synoptic Gospels where a Judean mission hardly existed. However, it is more in conformance with the passion narrative where the crowds hailed and welcomed him on Palm Sunday. Jesus would not go to the feast, in a way his disciples expected, but would be there at the time of the feast to talk about the replacement for it. At the feast, the people were described as interested and, yet, divided in opinion about him (7:11-13). However, they could not be open in discussions about him for fear of "the Jews." This description may be emphasized because of the situation of his disciples at the time John was writing and could be quite different from what was expressed at the time of the event.

When Jesus started teaching (7:16-19), the Jews were astonished at his being able to read since he had not been taught by a Rabbi. If this were so significant that it would astonish anyone, it was a sign, and Jesus says the teaching is from God. What should be a sign that would encourage them to listen, instead becomes an obstacle. A message that goes beyond the Law obviously could not be found in the Law. While this may not be so evident to those hearing Jesus until the Resurrection, it should be obvious to an extreme for the opponents in reading this Gospel. Their early conclusion was that Jesus was beyond the Law, so they should be looking for a message that goes beyond the Law.

The switch back to the event of healing the crippled man on the Sabbath (5:1-14) again addresses the fact that Jesus was beyond the Law which restricted human work on the Sabbath. However, the Jewish leaders would recognize that God required circumcision on the Sabbath. Since it rained on the Sabbath and people were born and died on the Sabbath, it is clear God worked on the Sabbath. So the ability of Jesus to do God's work on the Sabbath was an obvious means of saying Jesus did God's work. Again, what should be a sign to everyone is used to condemn Jesus. The Jewish leaders are accused of wanting to destroy Jesus for a sign that says they should listen to him and even though they deny wanting to kill him, that appears to be a common understanding (7:25).

A second misunderstanding about where Jesus comes from is raised by the crowd (7:25-30). If the sign pointed toward Jesus coming from God, their question should be answered. However, they do not accept the sign and, without doing so, they cannot arrive at the full meaning of the message or his Messiahship. A reminder is given by Jesus, not to show that the Jewish leaders doubted, but to remind the disciples at the time of the writing that they cannot come to the full meaning unless they accept the sign. Only from the sign could they find the meaning of Jesus' words.

The opponents wanted to silence the messenger (7:30) and yet the confusion continues (7:31-36). Jesus' statement, "You will look for me" (7:34), and the references to the disciples not knowing where Jesus was going, reflects the expectation of the early Church that a Second Coming would occur before the kingdom was formed. That had been a misunderstanding which eroded over time and was dismissed completely in chapter 13 of Mark. However, it may have raised questions about other failures to grasp the full message. Some believed that Jesus was the Messiah but would accept him only in the context of what had been said about him in the Old Testament, not in accepting the actual message given. The "Where I am" statement (7:34) provides a "Yahweh" meaning describing who he is, rather than where he will be after a short time.

On the last day of the festival when water was poured over the temple altar as part of the prayers for rain in the coming growing season, Jesus claimed he was the replacement of the feast (7:37-39). They wanted rain for their crops in order to nourish the human life, while Jesus would satisfy their thirst for eternal life. Failure to accept Jesus, and a new message from God, was a failure to actually gain salvation. The disciples had been baptized, but if they did not accept the real gift that comes in water, it meant salvation was not understood fully and was subject to being bypassed.

When the water flowed from the rocks in the desert (Ex 17:6), the Israelites should have recognized a different relationship with God. Likewise, the promise of the prophets that a different stream of water would flow from the Temple (Zec 14:8, Ez 47:1) should have been a signal to expect further change in the relationship in the future. Finally, in Jesus' words about baptism, disciples were introduced to one more water experience. Yet it may have been accepted by the early Christians only as preparation for what had been expected, not as the changeover event to something quite different. The Church waited for a Second Coming to establish a kingdom when the words of Jesus said it would come very early (Mk 9:2).

The awareness of Jesus' role seems to grow among those hearing the discussion (7:40-44) to the point that Jesus was seen by some as a prophet. Others accepted him as someone sent with a special message or a different interpretation of Judaism. The temple police were so taken back by Jesus' words that they were afraid to arrest him (7:45-52). Likewise, Nicodemus finally starts to move from this role as a hidden disciple to one who recognized that a second look should be given to Jesus' words and signs. Only the Jewish leaders who would not go beyond the Law were prevented from moving past the pre-messiah position from the Old Testament. Yet the disciples of the early Church, perhaps some even in John's time, had not moved from a messiah as earthly ruler in Palestine (Acts 1:6) as they waited for a Second Coming (Acts 3:20-21). The chief priest was correct in claiming that prophets did not come out of Galilee in the past, but the question of Jesus being more than a prophet had not been asked.

Chapter 8

The great story of the woman caught in adultery (7:53-8:11) is an insertion which does not fit the context directly. It is not found in the oldest manuscripts, while in other early manuscripts it is found at the end of the Gospel or in Luke's Gospel. The woman had not been tried by the Jewish authorities who probably could not have ordered capital punishment in any case. The mob intended to execute her without following the Law's requirement of a hearing. They seemed to want a judgment from Jesus, probably to see if he would oppose the penalty of the Law or the power of Roman authority. It is similar to the trap of paying tribute to Caesar in the Synoptic Gospels (Mk 12:13-17). Jesus doesn't address the condoning of the sin or the condemnation of the sinner, but returned the choice to the crowd in allowing someone who has never broken the Law to initiate the action. All seem to have a transgression on their own records and walked away. However, even if some had kept the Law perfectly, they would not have broken it in this situation by condemning someone to death without having a trial.

The meaning of the adultery case shifts back to the Nicodemus comment on the requirement of the Law for a hearing (7:50-51). The Jewish leaders would never leave the Law in evaluating a Messiah beyond the Law, yet they would violate the Law if necessary to silence him. They had no case under the Law against Jesus and couldn't execute him, unless they strayed from the Law themselves.

A second part of the feast then opens with Jesus designating himself as the light to the world and, thereby, replacing the lights of the feast that only shone in Jerusalem (8:12). Normally, the light section would be at the start of the feast rather than after the water pouring on the last day. However, the real light is what comes if Jesus is interrogated and allowed to speak. With this written text the message would be given to those later disciples who read the discourse. They allow John to give Jesus' responses from words and sayings that must have come from his public life. The cramped style of the discourse may reflect the difficulty of providing a response from words spoken by Jesus during his public life to the very different situations raised in the text. If the Evangelist could compose new sayings of Jesus, the discourse would be more smooth, but only the remembered sayings of Jesus would convince the later disciples.

The discourse that followed, which seems to emphasize a lack of understanding, relates to the true identification of

Jesus in a way the Jews could not accept. Its opening (8:12-20) introduces a different concept of judging that follows from the story on adultery. Judging would not be from the Law directly, as understood by humans, but in how Jesus is accepted or rejected, or how eternal life is accepted or rejected. In continuing the discourse (8:21-30), the statements become more directly aimed at the disciples. Jesus "going away" and "you will look for me" continues to carry the meaning of the early Second Coming expectation (8:21).

Having a focus only on a kingdom within Judaism and Palestine was to not know Jesus and his message. It was a focus on remaining "from below" and "of this world" (8:23). To retain that view was to reject the real kingdom which required knowing Jesus and knowing that his life was "from above." Failure occurs in knowing Jesus if the disciples "do not believe that I Am"[27] (8:24). As before, the English translation is sometimes smoothed out to "I am he," but the literal translation of the Greek would be "I Am." There is no knowing of Jesus if his Divinity was not recognized. The crowd asks who Jesus is, but if they cannot come to accept the message of his signs and words, they would fail to understand his answers (8:27). The disciples should have recognized in his death and Resurrection the "I Am" meaning (8:28), as did John's community, but as yet they did not, even though "many came to believe" on a lesser scale (8:30).

A final section of the discourse, involving a discussion of Abraham, raised the question whether the ones hearing Jesus were even truly Jewish if they did not respond to the continued revelation (8:31-59). Only in accepting the meaning of Jesus, could a disciple move beyond the slavery to life on earth and, therefore, beyond death. The Jewish response was to see the life given through the Law or the original view of the promise to Abraham. Yet, Abraham was one who changed his life in accepting the message of revelation. He would have even sacrificed his son, who was essential in fulfilling the promise, if God so desired. Those hearing Jesus would have failed to be the children of Abraham if they did not accept a change as he did. If they were not such children of Abraham, they would not be recipients of the promise made to him (8:33-42).

Not being like Abraham was a rejection of God and the crowd would never admit to not following God (8:41-51). However, if Jesus worked signs that showed he was from God and brought a new relationship with God, the crowds and disciples could not remain as God's people and reject what came from God (8:42). The only one who rejected God completely was the devil, the one who brings no revelation or "no truth," in the Jewish usage (8:44). The charge of "the devil is your father" is literally the charge that they were living a lie or something not from revelation (truth). Those who reject God emulate the devil. The message Jesus had given here was his definition of himself as I Am. The crowd would attempt to turn the argument back on Jesus by saying that if his message were false in any way, it would prove Jesus was possessed by a devil (8:48). However, Jesus had the signs worked by the power of God to disprove such a charge and to prove his message was from God.

The climax comes as the crowd attempted to bring a statement against Jesus that everyone in history had died, even those who followed God most closely, so the argument for eternal life was false (8:52-53). Jesus' response was that, while many would receive eternal life, it would come with the fullness of revelation. That would be not just from one sent by God, but one who "knows God," and so also would have to be divine. Abraham had died on earth, but he now celebrates the fulfillment of the promises made to him (8:54-59).

The last attempt to discredit Jesus (8:57) brings the response of Jesus' identification with the Divine Name in language so clear the message cannot be misinterpreted (8:58). Jesus claimed the "I Am" name as the God of revelation and the timelessness that is appropriate. As the crowd picked up rocks to punish what they considered to be blasphemy, they clearly indicated that they had understood the message. The disciples reading this would have had to agree, that as the teachings of Jesus are put forth in this arrangement, the message was clear to them also.

The "I Am" statements are very clear in the English translations of the Bible, but they would not have been that clear in Jesus' actual speech. The people hearing Jesus would have to make a connection between Jesus' words and the text of the book of Exodus (3:14) when Moses was told the name of God as Yahweh (translated as I Am). However, Jesus was speaking in Aramaic while the Exodus text is in Hebrew. Hebrew was not spoken publicly in Jesus' time and even the reading of Scripture in Hebrew in the synagogues of Palestine would not include saying the Divine Name but would substitute the word "Lord." Therefore, the full meaning of Jesus' words would not be recognized easily even by a scribe.

In Exodus 3:14, the Divine Name is some version of "I Am." However, when it was used by the Israelites in reference to God, it would be some version of "He Is." As Jesus applied the name to himself, it would revert to "I Am," but in Aramaic. That this identification of Jesus as Yahweh was not grasped by the Church earlier is not difficult to understand. Only at a later time, when Christianity moved to Greek-speaking areas and the stories and teachings of Jesus were translated into Greek, would someone notice the same Greek words in both the Jewish Scripture and the words of Jesus. That recognition must have occurred first in the community of John the Evangelist which must have been sufficiently separated from Judaism to examine the meaning and accept the full identification of Jesus.

Chapter 9

The incident of the man born blind (9:1-41) appears as a new section but it is tied to the end of the previous chapter by comments in chapter ten. It represents the sign that Jesus is what he claimed to be, the divine light that enlightens the world. The basis for the story is that Jews saw misfortune in the world as an indication of sin in life. However, being born blind was misfortune prior to any act of the man, so what was the source of the sinful act? Jesus had taught against any identification of conditions in this world as an indication of either sin or holiness (9:2-3, Lk 13:1-5). Therefore, the miracle takes on a different meaning. The man was essentially created without sight as a decision of God. To provide sight, Jesus was not simply curing the man of something gone wrong or related to sin. He added something not present in the man's original creation. Jesus did something that only God could do, recreate part of this man. As a response to Jesus' "I Am" statement (8:58), John uses a story where Jesus provides a sign that backs up his claim of divinity very directly. The story then goes further as those who would not accept Jesus as Divine attempt to sidestep the event's conclusion. The story carries a great baptism motif, since everyone is born blind to the true light and must accept Christ to be enlightened.

The man who regained his sight was enlightened but knew nothing about Jesus (9:8-12). His understanding must come from the results of the event itself. The initial logic was that Jesus must be one sent by God (9:17). That conclusion was one accepted by the opponents as well, but it was not acceptance that Jesus was Divine. The blind man had reached the position of the opponents very quickly, yet the story goes beyond that position and the disciples hearing the story must examine themselves for a lack of seeing. The Jewish leaders would at least consider the possibility that Jesus was from God, since it was so obvious, yet they would hope to find a way out of it because of the Sabbath problem (9:18-23). However, the man's parents would not dispute the story and would rather remain separate from the Messiah decision of the Jewish leaders as did some disciples at first, such as Nicodemus.

As the Jewish leaders were forced to readdress the issue with the man, their position had hardened since they could not overlook the Law's treatment of the Sabbath observation commandment (9:24-34). The former blind man could see that the leaders were attempting to gain a denial from him of the sign which was so obvious, especially to him. His chiding

of the Jewish leaders (9:27) was directed against the opponents as well, since they could not make the final step to the
logical conclusion. The Jewish leaders would reject the sign
as they rejected the man's conclusion. They had done that
historically, however, the opponents had simply not made a
decision on the most important claim concerning the true
identity of Jesus. The man born blind would accept the logic
of the sign, if someone would point out the one responsible
for the sign (9:35-36). He believed and then, in worshipping
Jesus, it would seem that his acceptance was not just of the
Messiah, but also of his Divinity (9:38). The Pharisees
denied they were blind which was to say they saw and understood the sign (9:41). To reject a recognized sign from God
was the worst type of guilt.

Chapter 10

Speaking further with the Pharisees, Jesus gave a teaching on how religious leaders should respond (10:1-21). The
section on the sheepgate (10:7-10) was a condemnation of
Jewish leaders who had responsibility for pointing out the
Messiah and assisting the people in accepting his message (Ez
34:10). When they failed, the result was the same as being
led by a thief who allowed the flock to lose an opportunity for
eternal life, which was the equivalent of having it taken from
them. Then in the section about the Good Shepherd
(10:11-16), the criticism shifts to the opponents (Ez 34:11-12
and 34:23), who should have known the Good Shepherd
most clearly, yet until this writing they did not clearly proclaim the full message of Jesus being Divine. The early disciples ran from its fullness at the crucifixion, when Jewish leaders and secular officials opposed where the message of closeness to God would lead. If John's community had suffered
some persecution at Jewish hands as they came to the divinity
understanding, the opponent's attempt to stay close to
Judaism made plain the charge of not accepting.

The hired hand was at least the image of those fleeing
Jesus at the time of the crucifixion. Yet a true disciple would

"know" Jesus as well as Jesus and the Father know each other (10:15), as close as a sharing of life. The "others" of the Jesus fold must be a criticism of the slowness in accepting Gentiles into the early church community (10:16). The charge of not moving to the fullness of the message, or its full proclamation to the world, seems to point toward an early writing of this section. It is a section which relies on the Old Testament to a great extent. Perhaps it is a criticism from the 30s or 40s after the Cornelius family baptism produced no new understanding.

Finally, Jesus defines his power over life (10:17-18) as being able to raise himself to life, which was a big leap over Peter's speeches of "God raising" him (Acts 2:24, 3:15, 4:10, 5:31, 10:41). It was Divine Power of his own that produced the Resurrection, not just a Divine Power that would come to his assistance as the Church described the Resurrection (Rom 8:10-11). The section ends with the only two conclusions that can be considered (10:19-21). Either the claim that a human can also have divine life had no basis in logic, or the signs show that the revelation of Jesus' Divinity was the message from God. The opponents could not continue to just avoid a decision any longer. Here the question had been put before them in the clearest language. Jesus had proclaimed his Divinity, and in the I Am statement proclaims, also, that he had been the God of revelation to the Israelites from the beginning.

The feast of the Dedication of the Temple (10:22-39) celebrates its rededication after the Maccabean revolt against the Syrians was successful in 164 BC and a pagan image was removed from the Temple. However, the text continues the argument of chapters seven to ten. As the place of God on earth, temple worship occurred because of God's presence in the Temple, not that Yahweh came in response to the worship. Jesus had revealed that he was the presence of Yahweh on earth when he took the Divine Name as his own (8:58). In doing so, he fulfilled his earlier claim to replace the sanctuary with himself (2:19). So this unity with God becomes the subject of this event.

Jesus was asked to tell in plain words if he was the Messiah (10:24). Yet, he could not use the words of Judaism, since his Messiahship was different from what they expected in that term. Jesus, in being beyond the Law, means that they cannot find answers from the Law. The plain revelation was in the signs and if they did not accept them, there always would be confusion (10:25-26). Only those disciples who accepted him completely would understand the revelation and accept the eternal life offered to all (10:27-29). When Jesus gave a response in the clearest words (10:30), the Jewish reaction was to believe a blasphemy has been spoken, rather than that a plain answer had been given. The union of a plural and singular could not be misunderstood, Jesus had proclaimed his Divinity in union with God.

Jesus responded to their threat of stoning by pointing out that, even in the Scriptures, there was a unity of humans who respond faithfully to the covenant relationship and to Yahweh (10:34-35). That reopened the discussion again because it brought the historic understandings into the discussion. Yet, the answer to their request for plain words brought them back to the same conclusion (10:37-39). However the message is examined, it would lead to the conclusion of unity between the Father and Son. Here the reminder is for the disciples at the time of the writing, since the result of the confrontation left the original disciples on the side of Jesus as he moved out of Judea for protection (10:40-42).

Chapter 11

The climax of this final claim of divinity and the entire discussion with Jewish authorities, starting with the cure of the man at the pool of Bethesda (5:1-18), came in the raising of Lazarus from the dead (11:1-44). It is a carefully composed story with all of the details necessary to make it clear that Jesus was doing a divine action, not just announcing another cure. Earlier signs introduced a discourse, while here the sign is the climax of the revelation of Jesus' Divinity.

In Jewish and Middle Eastern thought, a person's spirit of life remained near the body for three days after the person died. There were always some incidents when someone seemingly dead would recover. However, in the warm climate of that area, a body would undergo clear signs of disintegration by the fourth day at the latest and recovery would be impossible. For a person to return to life after decomposition started would require the creation of an entirely new body. This event goes a step beyond the giving of sight to the man born blind, since that addition to his creation could have an element of not understanding all of the factors in the condition. However, the decomposition of the body would be widely known and easily recognized. The body would have to be recreated for life to be restored and recreation was an act of God.

Lazarus was ill and a messenger was sent to Jesus on the other side of the Jordan River, or a day's journey away, during which time Lazarus died (11:1-4). Jesus waited two days and then took the fourth day to travel to Bethany (11:5-16). The disciples who were with him did not understand at first, but the Evangelist indicates they had the situation clarified by Jesus so they would "believe" (11:14-15). Thomas' statement (10:16) also indicates the disciples recognized that Jesus' unity statements at the feast of the Dedication were being understood by the Jews as blasphemy. Therefore, they recognized, or certainly should have, that Jesus claimed to be Divine.

Jesus' arrival in Bethany (11:17) confirms the four day delay, as does Martha's later warning about opening the tomb (11:39). There could be no question that the body could simply be revived. Jesus' discussion with Martha (11:18-27), later repeated partially with Mary, brings out the conclusions that the opponents had about Jesus as the Messiah. Martha gives the confession (11:27) associated with Peter in the Synoptic Gospels (Mt 16:16). It states that the opponents would have believed Jesus could have cured Lazarus, but after four days there would be no more return to natural life, only a rising at the judgment. This confession was necessary to make it clear that what Jesus was about to do went beyond how the opponents would understand his power.

The conclusion of calling Lazarus from the tomb becomes anticlimactic to the reader because the build-up of signs had made the conclusion so obvious. The event would prove the unity of Father and Son as stated at the Dedication (10:30, 38). It would seem that even the original readers would have been forced to admit that this collection of events and teachings, which they must have all known as independent pericopes, inexorably led to the Divinity of Jesus as a conclusion. The conviction of the signs could not come from a later rewriting of the pericopes. These must be the known original stories to have any persuasive effect, as would the stories in all the Gospels. To change or add to the stories known by the Church, as a means of introducing such an important concept as Jesus' Divinity, would never have resulted in acceptance of this concept.

The conclusion to the Lazarus cure that makes the tie to the remainder of the Gospel was the reaction by the highest Jewish officials to the event (11:45-54). However good or bad these officials look to today's readers, it is clear that the officials were not eyewitnesses to either the signs given by Jesus to substantiate his teachings or the discussions with Jesus at the Jewish feasts. They understood that Jesus had performed signs that must have convinced some people. However, what seemed clear to them was that losing control of the situation could result in a public demonstration proclaiming Jesus king at Passover, when Roman soldiers would be present to prevent demonstrations. The introduction of Roman Gentiles into Jerusalem at such a feast, with a great number of outsiders present, would seem like the introduction of a torch into tinder rather than a calming influence. Since the Jewish revolt in 66-70 resulted from such an unintended incident, the inclusion of this discussion by officials points to such a sufficiently sure danger as to require some action for the safety of the country.

Prudence as seen by Jewish officials would dictate leaving revelation unproclaimed, just as preventing a later split between Jewish Christians and Judaism might require prudence in discussing the claim of Jesus' Divinity. However, John's community must have concluded that one should never be so "prudent" as to hide the real message of the Messiah, even for the purpose of preventing persecution and death. Only the chief priests and Pharisees were present at the meeting (11:47), without the Sadducees who played a major role in any of Jerusalem's actions prior to the Temple being destroyed in 70. This points to the conclusion that this discussion was directed toward the time of the writing.

Chapter 12

The anointing of Jesus at Bethany (12:1-11) carried the meaning of anointing Jesus for death beforehand, as in the Synoptic Gospels. However, it has the less understandable twist of an anointing of his feet, and then Mary wiping the ointment off with her hair. There was certainly no precedent for either action in the culture of the time. Yet it does not seem possible that this is just a mixing of traditions of the anointing in Mark (Mk 14:1-9) and the woman washing Jesus' feet with her tears and drying them with her hair in Luke (Lk 7:36-50). Since an eyewitness of the event is the authority behind this account, it is difficult to even imply that its recording could be an inadvertent mixing of traditions.

The term Messiah or Christ means anointed one. Jesus went far beyond the normal understanding of such a term, to the point that he was identified by divine signs rather than through an official public anointing as was David. Certainly, no one could anoint the head of God in the normal meaning of anointing, so the change that occurs here is in an anointing that would reflect a new meaning, as does this whole Gospel. The foot anointing seems to point toward an act which was only a shadow of the normal head anointing, in the same way that the original understanding of Messiah (even by the Apostolic Church) was only a shadow of the real meaning of Jesus as Divine Messiah. Anointing of the feet would be related to the only part of Jesus tied to the land of Palestine, while the meaning of this Messiah is that Jesus is God and is related to the whole world. The wiping away of the ointment could mean that even the traditional under-standing of Messiah was to be of short duration. Just as Martha had given the Resurrection confession at the Lazarus event, perhaps Mary, in anointing the feet, is indicating that the view of Messiah and early Second Coming was deficient to a great degree. Then her act of wiping off the ointment, which in effect transfers the anointing to her own head, would be of her being anointed in the meaning of a disciple in the Body of Christ who acts for God on earth (12:3). That meaning would reflect the sacrament of Confirmation.

For John's readers, the meaning of disciple was one unit-ed through Jesus to divinity. It was not one who accepts only the meaning of discipleship related to the original under-standing of a messiah. The foot image could hardly be a mis-understanding and, seeing how the writer has chided the opponents throughout the Gospel for missing the most important understanding of Jesus, it is reasonable to look at this event in the same way. This foot anointing prepared the readers for the Last Supper foot washing which is directed very strongly at those same disciples of the Apostolic Church.

Even a "large number of Jews" (12:9-11) were recogniz-ing that something very great had occurred in Bethany and wanted to be in on it. However, the disciples with Jesus were discussing the everyday subject of saving money for other pur-poses, by not using ointment for impractical purposes. Becoming "Christ" (anointed) by this foot "washing" with ointment reflects the meaning of disciples after the Resurrection.

The entry into Jerusalem (12:12-19) resembles the Synoptic accounts with details added, such as the branches being palms, as would be expected of an eyewitness account. However, the shouts of the crowd carry a somewhat different meaning, which is emphasized by the comment that the disciples did not fully understand the meaning until later (12:16). Blessings (12:13) were called down on the "King of Israel" rather than "on him who comes in the name of the Lord" (Ps 118:26). The Old Testament used the term King of Israel for Yahweh (Ex 15:18), while those who ruled as kings would have the designation of king only in God's name. Furthermore, the blessings called down (12:13) were on the King of Israel who comes in the name of "Yahweh" (Ps 118:26), which may refer to Jesus applying that name to himself (8:58). Finally, the quotation from Zechariah (Zec 9:9) had been changed from "rejoice heart and soul" to "do not be afraid" (12:15), which fits the situation better than "rejoice." The use of "your king" comes closer to the belief about Yahweh as king, than as a title for a Judean king. Since the disciples were only later becoming aware of the significance of what happened, it would seem that the change of titles would be noticed as the disciples from John's community addressed the divinity question.

The fear of the Jewish leaders was emphasized once more as it had been after the raising of Lazarus. A Pharisee's comment of the whole world running after Jesus (12:19) introduces a group of Greeks who want to meet the Messiah (12:20-28). For Jesus, this opening of interest beyond Palestine was a sign that the "hour" of his being known beyond Judaism had arrived. This would force the disciples to make a choice, as John's Gospel made clear to the opponents who had remained within Judaism as long as possible. Death is a requirement for life (12:24), first, in Jesus dying for the salvation of everyone and, second, for each disciple personally accepting baptism and giving up the life in this world to accept the gift of eternal life.

To love this life ends in death, while separating from it by taking on Christ's life brings an eternal life, as the image of the wheat grain explains (12:24). This eternal life is "from above" and that requires "hating" life in this world. Hating has the meaning of causing a separation, as would be necessary to accept a different life "from above." Jesus was troubled by what was occurring but, unlike the Gethsemani experience, here he would not consider asking that he be spared (12:27). The sign from heaven was a response to Jesus' acceptance of what was to come (12:29-36). The statement of Jesus, that the disciples walk in the light, seems to be quoted for those who, as yet, had not accepted the conclusion of John's community (12:35-36). The light was a revelation which goes beyond what has been accepted by Judaism.

A summary statement, which ends the Book of Signs prepared by John to show that Jesus was Divine, was intended to speak to those who as yet had not accepted the signs in their fullness (12:37-50). The quotation (12:38) from the fourth Servant Song (Is 53:1) was used for those remaining within Judaism. It acknowledged that acceptance of revelation is never easy because it required moving beyond what is known. However, to remain within Judaism required wrestling with the quotations and promises which go beyond Judaism. In this case, coming to know Jesus fully was not the end in itself. Rather, it brought a different and a truer understanding of God, an understanding only possible from revelation. Jesus' closing statement to the crowds (12:44-50) restates what was put forth in the prologue as the plan of God. Now it is made clear to the opponents, who for a generation had been disciples, but not to the same level as called for in this Gospel.

LAST SUPPER AND DISCOURSE

Chapter 13

Chapter thirteen is the start of a more common heritage of Jesus' teaching to the original disciples, rather than speaking to those who have not accepted him. In the disciple context, John includes a long discourse after the Last Supper to those Apostles. It would seem to address questions within the Apostolic Church after the Resurrection, but Jesus words are from before the Resurrection and, therefore, must be included before that event. Like all Gospel writing, the Evangelist is saying "read these sayings over again." After twelve chapters of looking at the divinity issue, look at what Jesus said and what it means, now that the divinity issue has been resolved. John's Last Supper has no identification with a Passover celebration and the Eucharist is not included in the account.

In the Synoptic Gospels the Last Supper was considered to be the Passover meal opening that feast, and the events of Good Friday occurred on the feast itself. It is difficult to see how such a feast would be interrupted by the activities of the crucifixion. John's description has the Good Friday events occurring on the day before the Passover meal. The lambs were being slaughtered in the Temple at the same time as Jesus was sacrificed on the cross. The bodies of Jesus and the two thieves would be removed from the cross and buried prior to the start of Passover at sundown, which also was the start of Sabbath. The actual Passover meal would start immediately after the burial. Since John's Gospel relies on an eyewitness, we can assume that its dating is the more correct one.

The Eucharist has always had a strong Passover connection which went far beyond just being the day on which the Eucharist was first celebrated. Certainly, it was never seen as an annual celebration, so the Eucharist meaning was not connected to Passover as a simple replacement celebration. Passover had its clearest meaning in the Israelite's decision to accept the call of a God, whom they did not know, to leave Egypt and go out into the desert. Such an action was dangerous and unlikely to succeed, yet that decision was made before the great Exodus event was made known to them.

Historically, each Jew must bring to mind at Passover every year the situation of that decision and also decide to trust Yahweh even without knowing what the next day would bring. Eucharist calls Christians to make the same decision of unity with God in the remembered setting of a meal, originally eaten prior to the Good Friday events. The Synoptic Gospels emphasize the Passover decision made at the supper and make the Passover meal connection in the process. The Passover meaning is made clear in what is being done at the Last Supper, rather than by looking at a calendar to see if the Last Supper falls on the correct day for the Passover meal.

The major event of the Last Supper in John's Gospel was the foot washing (13:1-20). Jews would wash their own feet upon entering a house. A Jew could not require a slave, who was also Jewish, to wash his master's feet. On occasion a pupil might wash or offer to wash the feet of a great Rabbi as a sign of deep respect. So when Jesus starts the washing process, Peter's protest is the great sign of his respect for Jesus. Jesus' threat, to have no relationship with Peter unless Jesus can wash his feet, brings out the other side of Peter who then asks for a more complete relationship by having his hands and head washed as well. The result is a lesson in service to the community that should go beyond anything in Jewish culture or cultures elsewhere in the world.

Often the foot washing ceremony on Holy Thursday is not examined for its full meaning. However, for these disciples to be told that Jesus will do what could only be required of a Gentile slave, especially following this long explanation that he is Divine, would have been stunning. To Jewish disciples who would have nothing to do with Gentiles, this lesson, that the disciples must take the place of a Gentile slave to serve everyone, should have been overwhelming. Yet the early Church had great difficulty in opening itself to Gentiles. John's community was more open to outsiders, surely to Samaritans quite early. So this Last Supper description was a strong reminder that the opponents did not get the full message on either divinity or on a mission to the whole world.

Judas was dismissed, and the reader is informed that night had fallen (13:21-32). This is not just a designation of time but the coming of darkness, the time of evil. The prologue talked about darkness that could not overpower the light; however, for the disciples at the Last Supper, the events of Good Friday would seem to be an overpowering by darkness. The meal is also an introduction of the Beloved

Disciple (13:24) and his closeness to Jesus, especially in relation to the position of Peter.

John, the son of Zebedee, in the Synoptic Gospels is not
described as being much different in understanding Jesus than
the other ten loyal disciples. His designation as the Beloved
Disciple is not fully accepted by many scholars, because there
seems to be little support for it. Having the designation being
applied only at the Last Supper and later, seems to make a
Jerusalem disciple the more logical candidate for the title.
However, at this point in the Gospel, the divinity argument
had been made, and the instruction had been addressed to
the disciples. For the later Church which is reading this
Gospel, it would seem reasonable that a change in describing
John might be in order.

The fullness of the meaning of Jesus as the Messiah
seems to be known only by John as one of the original Twelve
and the leader of the separate community. Beloved Disciple
could describe any disciple who carried the fullness of the
meaning of Jesus' message to the world. John had caused that
to be available and so he could be called Beloved in the early
stories being used at a later time, when he is the last of the
original Twelve. It would fit more clearly when he alone of
the Twelve remained at the foot of the cross after the rest had
fled. It could be a title that comes out of this Gospel writing
experience, more than a designation from the time of Jesus'
public life.

The discourse after the meal follows the format of chapters seven and eight where the Evangelist places questions
from his own time in the mouths of Apostles and then
responds to them in the sayings of Jesus known to the whole
Church. The opening is with Jesus addressing them as "little
children" (13:33-35). It is the relationship which they have
with the Father, but which will only be understood fully if
they recognize Jesus' own nature. The commandment given
to them is only new in that they love each other as Jesus
loves them. To just love one another would be the Jewish
understanding of the Law and was reflected in the Synoptic

Gospels as the whole commandment of the Law. Now, in reflecting Jesus' own love as the love of God, the disciples would be putting on the life from God who is love (1 Jn 4:16). That is the life which is eternal.

Peter's question (13:36-38) is based on an understanding of a King David-style messiah with the disciples as followers who would have places in the kingdom founded in Palestine. Peter asks how could they be chosen by Jesus, yet not continue with him as he comes to Jerusalem, where they anticipate he would be made king. Peter makes the Passover pledge (13:37) and is warned that he will fail (13:38), because his judgment on the crucifixion will be based on the Law, which finds that a criminal who dies by being hung on a tree is cursed (Dt 21:22-23).

Chapter 14

The "many rooms," or "dwelling places,"[28] that Jesus will prepare for the disciples (14:1-4) are the equivalent of places to stop in the evening along the major Roman roads. The disciples had been on the journey with Jesus to Jerusalem and, after the Resurrection, they would be on the journey with the Lord to the whole world. The disciples were no longer dwellers in the world, but sojourners for the kingdom. Jesus' promise to be with them has meaning only for that journey, since it is the one in which they will represent him.

Thomas opened the question further about the place where Jesus was going, stating he did not even know the way (14:5-7). Their decision must not be just in doing, as was required under the Law, but in becoming the Body of Christ. Yet, the view of Christ had been changed to a Divine person in this Gospel. If they accepted that life, everything else would have no great importance and, if they failed, nothing else had any importance.

Philip returned the discourse to the subject of the Gospel by saying that the disciples would be satisfied if they could see God (14:8). That statement is their confession that they had not yet understood the meaning of Jesus' signs and teachings. Jesus' response restates the unity between himself and God, which is Jesus' own Divine status (14:9-14). Their status would be as disciples united to the divine life, and their own actions would be like Jesus' works, in their most important aspect of building the kingdom (14:12). The acts of disciples would be greater than the works of Jesus only because they would carry the message beyond Judaism and beyond Palestine.

When Jesus ascended, he would have the Father send the Holy Spirit, another Advocate or Paraclete, who would be the Divine Presence in their lives to guide and assist them on their journey (14:15-21). This is the life from above that they would accept and live. Because they would have separated themselves from the life only of the world, they might appear to be orphans (14:18). However, if they understood that Jesus was with the Father, and they were united to him with the Spirit of God in their lives, they need never fear the condition of being separated from the world.

Judas, or more properly, Jude Thaddeus, cannot contain a question which returns to the starting point (14:22). Since he still believed that Jesus would become a King David-style messiah, how could that be if Jesus only makes his kingship known to them, but does not proclaim it to all of Palestine? How will the country know he was king if it was not proclaimed? Jesus' response (14:23-31) seems to summarize the meaning of revelation and kingdom one more time. Those who accept the message of revelation will be united to him; those who reject it will not have that union (14:23-25). Those who accept will have the indwelling of God's Spirit, which is eternal life, to guide them (14:26). This union of human and divine life will only have meaning to those who understand Jesus as both human and Divine, otherwise, they would have no understanding, other than the Jewish concept of a messiah. Those who did come to the full understanding were promised peace, and certainly that would come, because they recognized their union with God (14:27-31). The scene seemed to end with a decision to go, and perhaps originally it did end there. The next three chapters could be seen as a continued discussion on the way to Gethsemani.

Chapter 15

The vine and branches comparison (15:1-17) builds on a Jewish understanding, but here the true vine meaning includes the concept of a true Israel. A vine ornament on the Temple was a symbol of Israel and supports a view that this teaching may have occurred on the Temple Mount. The life of the Church requires the ongoing connection to the life of Christ, so bearing fruit from the connection is essential for members to remain as Church (15:2). The reference to pruning (15:3-4) carries a warning of some temporary troubles in being Christians, but also the guarantee of greater and more certain reward.

A significant caution is given for those who separated themselves from Christ directly (15:5-8), since then the divine life connection would disappear. The caution was for those who might choose to remain in Judaism, as Christianity was split away. They may think they can have separation from the visible Church and remain secret Christians, yet the promise is that a withering will occur. In time the withered branch has no chance to regain life, perhaps like at the end of natural life, and is suitable only for burning.

The relationship then is described in terms of the love of God and the response of disciples who share God's life (15:9-14). If John's community had accepted understandings of Jesus' revelation, which were not acceptable to Judaism, they would have been pushed out of the synagogues. Christians who remained within Judaism for at least forty years after the Resurrection would have been somewhat separate from John's community for much of that time. The appearance would be that John's community was the separated branch. However, in the description of the vine, the separated branch is the one not fully accepting the message of Jesus and living in that way, rather than an appearance based on numbers and past traditions.

The commandment of loving as Jesus loved must reflect love within the community. If the opponents had more interest in remaining within a Judaism that did not accept Jesus than being united with the community that accepts Jesus most fully, they can hardly be called "loving as Jesus loved." Friends (15:15-17) are those who have accepted everything Jesus brings from the Father and bear fruit based on that revelation. As might be seen, the interpretation in this commentary for issues such as this tends to suggest a writing of the Gospel in the period from 70 to 80, rather than 90 or later, which is commonly accepted for the Fourth Gospel.

Greater separation from the world was not a goal, or something to be avoided, but was a natural result of moving from the world to a life from above, while in this world (15:18-21). A witness occurs when the differences between those two lives can be fully noted. Even if the world rejects the witness, it has been understood. That was the obvious experience of Jesus. Therefore, the persecution which John's community may have received within Judaism should be a positive sign, even with its difficulties.

Revelation always causes people to change, as had been shown in Israelite history, and the same outcome would come in the revelation from Jesus (15:22-25). For the opponents not to change from Judaism would be no more understandable than for the Israelite slaves not to want to leave Egypt with Moses. As noted earlier, the term "hate" is not a difference of view, but a rejection in life, and is far more serious when one type of life is eternal.

The opponents should have already recognized that the Holy Spirit, present within them, was leading them to a full acceptance of Christ (15:26-16:4). This was a promise of Jesus that related directly to a separation from Judaism and being expelled from synagogues. Now, when this was occurring, the interest should not have been in hiding their Christianity to remain in Judaism, but in recognizing it was a fulfillment of Jesus' teaching and accept it.

Chapter 16

The coming of the Holy Spirit, after Jesus ascended to heaven, would show the failure of the world's view about sin, about who was right, and about judgment (16:5-15). Not believing in Jesus would be to not accept the true meaning of God given in revelation, and sin was doing that which separates oneself from God (16:9). The basis of being right or righteous was that now Jesus stood in God's presence, and only in being united with God's presence does one become righteous or innocent of sin (16:10). Judgment becomes the choice of everyone, either to accept God's offer or refuse it (16:11-12). The presence of Satan in this world means the devil had already chosen separation from God and was not in heaven. However, the Spirit of truth could not come to anyone who had not accepted revelation, because what comes from God was the Jewish definition of truth (16:13). To not accept the heart of the revelation, regarding the divine and human connection in Jesus, was to not accept the Holy Spirit.

The response of the opponents is presented in statements inserted in the discourse by the Evangelist (16:17-19). The statements do not show an understanding of what had been given in this Gospel. The opponents should have recognized that their position of not accepting Jesus' Divinity was not justified. The questions of "a short time" (16:17) indicated that the events from the Last Supper through the Resurrection appearance, should have been adequate to create a fuller understanding of Jesus. However, the opponents belief went only to Jesus being above the Law rather than the meaning shown in this writing.

Jesus compared the difficulty of those few days to an event like childbirth which is swept away by the joy of the result (16:20-21). If the divinity meaning were recognized, then the gift of God was far greater than any difficulty which arose from accepting Jesus, even the separation from Jewish family members and friends. Could there be any desire on earth which would not be satisfied in a living union with God who created everything and every desire (16:22-24). That a person being baptized agreed to give up a present life to put on the life of Christ was automatically a wise choice if the fullness of the gift were recognized. Those holding back and trying to remain in Judaism simply had not understood the offer.

Jesus had to speak in parables and metaphors during his public life (16:25-28), because Judaism could only accept a relationship with God in the Law, and any suggestion of a life union with God would be blasphemy. Only in going back over the teachings, remembered so clearly, could the opponents come to its deeper meaning. Jesus had told them to ask in "my name" and they have done that to produce miracles as an important witness (Acts 3:6, 9:34, and 19:5). However, in this writing Jesus has used the name "Yahweh," and the use of that name would be a far greater witness to the meaning of the disciples' relationship with God. The disciples were looking beyond the metaphors and now believed that Jesus came from God (16:30-31). Have they fully understood or is this the confession of Peter that Jesus is the Messiah, without even addressing the divinity question? Jesus seems to say (16:32-33) that what they had understood before the Resurrection was not the fullness of the message. John's Gospel had directed them to go back over the teachings again to find the real meaning. Then the world conquered would be made part of the kingdom.

Chapter 17

The discourse is ended in a long prayer by Jesus (17:1-26). The prayer has three sections, first with Jesus praying that he be glorified so that the Father is glorified in their unity (17:1-8). Second, Jesus prays for his disciples touching on the true meaning of being his disciples (17:9-19). Finally, he prays for the later disciples who would come to a full understanding from the teaching which was handed on, those who were first reading this Gospel, and then to all future disciples (17:20-26). The prayer touches the relationship of disciples to Jesus in a more understandable way than the earlier teachings of the Gospel, which were given in situations of opposition or misunderstanding.

The initial section on the glorification of Jesus (17:1-8) starts by being set in the third person (17:1-3) as if it were a faith statement of the Church. The Son was sent as a Divine presence on earth so any glorification which comes, as this revelation becomes understood, glorifies God as the one who gives. It is a great statement of unity between the Father and Son when glorification is shared in that way. The glory was from before the world was begun (17:5), as was stated in the prologue. The position of the disciples, as separated from the world even while being active in it, emphasized the different life situation of the disciple who had died to the world in putting on the new life in baptism (17:6).

The prayer for the disciples (17:9-19) gives the ongoing relationship quite a different dimension from the Second Coming understanding of the early Church. The reunion of Son with Father had no temporary understanding, nor were the disciples somehow in a waiting mode (17:11). Rather, what would occur after the Ascension would be the ongoing situation, which would succeed if the community remained united as Father and Son are united (17:11). Any splitting apart surely would be a step toward being lost (17:12-13). The disciples would remain in the world as the proclaimers of the fullness of revelation just as Jesus was sent for that purpose (17:14-19). Yet the statement, "they do not belong to the world," is repeated for emphasis (17:14 and 16), since the world is separated from God (hates) and under the power of evil. The disciples, in their union with the Spirit, are the continuation of the presence of Christ in history.

Jesus prays for those who believe because of the words passed on by the disciples, since they must come to this fullness of the message if it were to pass beyond the first generation of disciples (17:20-22). The union of disciples to God is as the union of Son and Father, it is a union of human and divine. That is the witness which must be shown to the world (17:23). Finally, there is a repeat of the prologue understanding of Jesus' position (17:24), and the Father not being known in the world except in the Son, reflecting the I Am designation of Jesus in the Gospel (17:25). The relationship must be one of love (17:26) which provides the basis for insisting on unity within the whole Church. The message had been made known within all of Christianity and must be proclaimed if the world is to hear the revelation.

PASSION AND RESURRECTION

Chapter 18

The Passion and death narrative brings a shift back to a common account given in the Synoptic Gospels. Little could be changed in it except details that an eyewitness could add. The image of Jesus changes from one seemingly caught up in events to a Jesus in charge of the process or even directing it. This difference in image is only a shading and not a rewriting. Part of it is from the image that comes from the writing in the earlier parts of the Gospel.

The scene in Gethsemani is called a garden rather than being named (18:1-11), and the scene has no sorrow. Instead, Jesus was very much in charge as the great crowd coming to arrest him includes a cohort of Roman soldiers, in addition to the palace guards. When they say they are looking for Jesus the Nazarene, Jesus responded with the I Am statement, translated into better English as "I am He," but carrying the I Am form in Greek. The response of the crowd was to move back and fall to the ground, as if the presence of God was felt by them. Jesus orders the guards to let the other disciples go and, seemingly, it was accepted. We are told it was Peter who cut off the servant's ear, an event known from the Synoptic Gospels. Peter's claim to be willing to lay down his life for Jesus is substantiated to some degree, because Jesus had to tell Peter to put his sword away. The Evangelist, even if a witness from outside the Apostolic Church, gives Peter the appearance of being a determined disciple instead of someone fleeing the scene.

The encounter with the chief priest (18:12-27) is before Annas and nothing is recorded of a trial before Caiaphas. The decision was left as one by the high priest without involvement of the Sanhedrin in some type of trial. The charge that would be made to Pilate appears to have been determined before Jesus was apprehended (18:14).

Peter, who should have had the sense to stay away from the house of the high priest, shows his determination to remain close to Jesus, even if that could be very dangerous. He enters the high priest's palace only because he is with "another disciple," also called the "other disciple, the one known to the high priest" (18:15-16). That disciple is not identified but because the disciple Jesus loved, who is never named, was called the "other disciple" at the empty tomb (20:2-3), it is suspected by Scripture scholars that the one assisting Peter to enter the high priest's palace was the Beloved Disciple. If that were true, it would be hard to accept that John, the son of Zebedee, was the Beloved Disciple, because it is unlikely a Galilean fisherman would be known at the palace of the high priest. If this "other disciple" at the high priest's palace was not the Beloved Disciple, as his lack of that identification would support, then John, the son of Zebedee, could be accepted as the Beloved Disciple, and as the authority behind this Gospel.

The picture of Peter denying Jesus would be viewed differently when seen through this text. Peter came into a dangerous situation and would not want attention drawn toward himself. The remark by the maid on duty at the door about Peter's association with Jesus (18:17) was put off by Peter's "I am not," which resembles an attempt to stop the prying rather than a true denial of Jesus. Likewise, the comment by one of the men warming himself (18:25) ends with the same type of brush-off. The third charge about Peter being seen in the garden (18:26-27) was more direct and frightening to Peter since he was at the garden during the arrest. The man asking the question, being a relative of the one losing his ear, means Peter would definitely want to shut off the discussion and in doing so hears the cock crow. Truly this was a triple denial, but the reader is left with the thought that denial of Jesus may not have been on Peter's mind as he tried to keep himself out of the discussion. By the time of this writing, Peter would have had the opportunity to remain in Rome during Nero's persecution and proved his loyalty, so the Evangelist could reveal a different view of him.

The appearance of Jesus before Pilate follows the Synoptic accounts, except for the efforts by Pilate to keep from crucifying Jesus (18:28 - 19:16). The Jewish leaders must have Jesus crucified to fit the conditions of the Law (Dt 21:22-23) that would result in Jesus being considered as cursed by God. They can accept no other outcome. Jesus had accepted this condition and it results in the Resurrection, showing him to be above the Law, and ultimately leads disciples to see him as being more than an Old Testament messiah. He certainly was not going to change anything in the plot of the Jewish leaders.

Pilate suspects there was more to the story than just the charges. He would not want trouble when Jerusalem was crowded with Jews from around the world, but would like to get out of the decision requested by the Jewish leaders. So he was overly energetic in carrying on negotiations between the two sides, neither of which would accept a change in what had been planned.[29] Pilate went out to meet the Jews (18:28-32) and back in to interrogate Jesus (18:33-38). He goes back to the Jews saying Jesus was innocent (18:38-40).

Chapter 19

Pilate then goes back inside to have Jesus flogged (19:1-3). Afterward he brings Jesus out to declare him innocent (19:4-8) and then back inside to question Jesus on his origin (19:9-11). Finally, Pilate goes outside anxious to free Jesus (19:12-16), but in hearing himself being called disloyal to Caesar, he gives in and orders the sentence they desired.

The Jewish leaders have accused Jesus of claiming to be Son of God in a way they considered blasphemous, but the Son of Man quote from Daniel used in the Synoptic Gospels is not included by John. This Son of God charge reflects the relationship given in this Gospel, rather than the King David meaning.

John gives a one-verse way of the cross with Jesus carrying the cross (19:17). Jesus was in charge and unaided in this account. Pilate wrote the charge in three languages, Hebrew, Latin and Greek, as if to tell the whole world (19:18-22). He appears to be the unknowing disciple, since the charge is true. The garments were divided, except the seamless undergarment, so that a reference in Scripture was fulfilled (19:23-24). Finally, we are told that the Beloved Disciple and the always faithful women were at the foot of the cross (19:25-27).

The creation of a mother/son relationship between Mary and the Beloved Disciple was required so that Mary would be cared for, since she will have neither husband nor son to support her. However, the relationship is recorded because of what it tells about life relationships between disciples in the Body of Christ. The disciple becomes a brother of Jesus, as well as a son of Mary. However that may have been understood in an earlier period, the Divinity of Jesus understanding brings an expression of the relationship between disciple and God that is awesome to an extreme. Here it is expressed by Jesus on the cross and understood by the true disciples at the foot of the cross. This is not a later speculation, but an element of the obvious plan of God. Early Christianity, which initially judged the crucifixion for Judaism through an interpretation of the Law, which meant beyond the Law, now see the relationship in love more completely than ever before.

A sidelight of this scene is some evidence of family relationships of these women as shown in Appendix B. Mary Magdalene is present in all four Gospels. Mary, the mother of the disciple James (and Joseph) in the Synoptics, would be Mary of Clopas. She or her husband were related to Joseph,

Jesus' fosterfather. Thus Jesus would be a cousin of James
(and Joseph). The mother of the sons of Zebedee (Mt) would
be Salome (Mk) and the sister of the Mother of Jesus, resulting in the Beloved Disciple being a cousin as well. He was
the cousin chosen to be designated a son of Mary, as was
Jesus, and as would every other disciple.

Finally, in a Gospel which seems completely dedicated
to showing Jesus' Divinity, the words "I thirst" are a reminder
also of Jesus' humanity (19:28-30). The revelation is based
on accepting both natures. The opponents must hear divinity, while the gnostic side of early Christianity, perhaps already
developing as a new set of opponents, would have to face the
human side. The Church would be quite comfortable with
the full understanding.

When Jesus announced "It is accomplished," it goes far
beyond only being finished or over. The mission had been
fulfilled because the revelation in a most difficult to understand doctrine had not only been proclaimed, but also accepted. The Beloved Disciple is the one who recognized the
whole truth even if it can never be understood fully. It is not
just a historical messiah who is recognized, but an expansion
of the relationship with God which makes Messiah an inadequate term. That some disciples see the fullness of the relationship means it can continue. Those disciples can never
return to Judaism, where the message would be suffocated,
nor could it ever be forgotten. The message was almost too
great to grasp, but it was certainly too great to be put aside,
once grasped. Therefore, "It is accomplished."

The coming of dusk brought both the Passover and the
Sabbath, so those crucified must have death hastened, so they
can be buried (19:31-37). The test with the Roman lance
was a convincing sign that Jesus was dead, as was necessary
for the early Church to proclaim the Resurrected Jesus as
being above the Law, not cursed by dying on a tree.
However, John's witness was also to the blood and water. In
Jewish understanding, the life of a person was in the blood, so
the description was of life and water, which were given to cre-

ation in the sacrifice of Jesus. The ratification of this covenant was not in the blood of animals cast upon the people as at Mt. Sinai (Ex 24:1-11). Here it was the life of one who had divine life, which would come to everyone who accepts it in the living water of baptism. This was what required the witness at Calvary.

In the burial (19:38-42), two members of the Sanhedrin who had been disciples, but in secret because of fear that they would be forced out of Judaism, now openly bury Jesus. This would make them unclean under the Law, but that understanding had now passed, and Judaism had been put behind them, as it had been for John's community. Precisely what the hundred pounds of myrrh and aloes were intended to mean is difficult to determine, because it seems like an excessive amount. In the Synoptic Gospels, the women come on the first day of the week to put spices with the body as a normal burial procedure, which could not be completed on Good Friday, because of the time. Certainly no additional spices would be needed for burial in this account.

Chapter 20

Mary Magdalene became the first witness to the empty tomb (20:1-10). Her conclusion, which she reports to Peter and John, was that Jesus' body had been taken, which we would assume is the conclusion they had in mind when they raced to the tomb. John bent down and saw the linen cloths on the ground and for him the original conclusion seemed to be confirmed. Peter, in going into the tomb, seems to come to the conclusion that the body had not been taken by opponents, who certainly would not have removed the burial cloths before carrying it away. John then entered the tomb, saw and believed, without that belief being defined as being different. The belief they came to was that the body was gone because of Divine acceptance. The original understanding of the Church in a Jewish context was that Jesus was cursed under the Law by dying on a tree (Dt 21:22-23). Yet, by being raised from the dead, in fact, he had been blessed beyond any normal blessing. Therefore, he was above the Law and the revelation he brought went beyond the Law as would the relationship with God for anyone who accepted the revelation. However, the reader is told that the belief gained by the disciples, at this point, had not yet included the understanding that Jesus would be raised from the dead (20:9).

The covenant on Mt. Sinai (Ex 24:1-11) came in a sacrifice in which blood from sacrificial animals was given partly to God, by being poured on the altar, and partly cast on the people, making a sacrifice of acceptance in blood. Since blood was the equivalent of life in Jewish understanding, it was a covenant agreed to in life. Life belongs to God, so that would be an acceptable gift in sacrifice.

Jesus had confirmed a new covenant in the giving of his life on the cross in a sacrifice. The blood (or life) was offered to God from the cross and, as is normal, the body, being something from earth, remained on earth, just as would an animal carcass from any other sacrifice. God accepted only that part of an animal sacrifice which belonged to God, which was the life. However, now the disciples come upon evidence that the body had also been accepted by God. It changed the whole understanding of the relationship, because it showed that God would accept the wholeness of the sacrifice of Christ, both the life which always belongs to God, but also the human side of the gift as well. If the disciples had come to a belief of an empty tomb, without the understanding of a Resurrection, it must be a belief that God had accepted the Messiah totally, life and body. If there were a relationship of life between a disciple and Christ, it carried the meaning that the disciples would be accepted into a relationship in heaven, rather than going to a dreary existence in Sheol. The going beyond the Law, which only governs natural life on earth, but not in Sheol, meant that a relationship had been established that goes beyond a person's lifetime.

Jesus' appearance to Mary Magdalene (20:11-18) was a secondary step in the understanding. Unlike the Synoptic accounts, it is separated from the empty tomb, because it has a meaning which goes beyond the empty tomb. Mary's lack of recognition of the Risen Jesus is not so much because his appearance was different, but because she did not expect Jesus to be alive. She did not look at his face directly since she assumed she was addressing a stranger. In being called by name, often the description of being a disciple, Mary recognized Jesus and became the first to understand the Resurrection. Jesus' admonition that she must not "cling to him" seems to confirm that understanding. It also gives the meaning that the Resurrection was not a simple return to human life as was Lazarus.

The true disciple should not cling to a meaning of Jesus as only being returned to life and, therefore, being beyond the Law. Rather Jesus now would exercise his Divine power to ascend to the Father. The conclusion concerning his Divine nature was stated in the summary of signs (12:37-43) in this Gospel, and also here, to clarify it beyond any teaching given earlier. So Mary's telling of the events to the disciples was not just being an apostle to the Apostles about the Resurrection, but was also the witness to going beyond that to Jesus' divinity. She brought the full message to the Church.

The final appearances (20:19-29) should be read in the context of what had been revealed fully in the Gospel, not just in what was pronounced in the Synoptic accounts. That evening Jesus appeared to all the disciples except Thomas (20:19-23). Yet, they do not seem to respond at first. Only after showing his wounds do they respond to his greeting. They had not accepted the whole message. They then receive the Holy Spirit and with that are witnesses to the Resurrection, which is recounted in Acts as the meaning of being one of the Twelve (Acts 1:22).

A meeting a week later (20:24-29), would lead Thomas to overcome his resistance. Thomas' response to the full examination of the sign of the Risen Christ was not just acceptance of the Resurrection, but the acknowledgment that Jesus is Divine (20:28). Thomas had believed because he saw, but the final beatitude was for the opponents reading these words, who did not have the actual meeting with Christ. Those later disciples had accepted the message, from the last of the original disciples, and had accepted the fullness of what had been "sent." The Apostolic task was then completed.

The conclusion of the Gospel (20:30-31) comes in what seems to be advice not to chase after more and more stories about Jesus as the means of coming to belief. We might assume that the Evangelist was talking about collections of accounts that were the basis for at least Mark's Gospel and the so-called Q source and other traditions which were still being collected. The Church accepts the Gospel accounts and canonizes them, while the source material disappears. The emphasis in the conclusion was not just that Jesus was the Messiah, the Son of God, as a Jewish title. The Jesus of the Gospels, presented most clearly in John's Gospel, is the Divine Jesus, is the actual Divine Son, and in believing that, a disciple would have eternal life. This was the message given to the world, to invite everyone into this kingdom.

Chapter 21

An appendix by a later disciple (21:1-25), after the authority behind the Gospel had died, may have been added as the Church was accepting the Gospel.[30] Since the appendix is included in all the manuscripts which show the end of the Gospel, it must come from the community of John even though it addresses some earlier traditions about Peter and John.

The appearance of Jesus in Galilee (21:1-19) could have cleared up questions about the identity of the Evangelist since the sons of Zebedee were finally mentioned and the Beloved Disciple also was present. However, when two disciples were left unnamed, and even though it is logical that one of them would be Andrew and the other Philip, there is not a complete demonstration that the Beloved Disciple was John. The presence of Jesus was not recognized until pointed out by the Beloved Disciple, as had been the case throughout the

Gospel. The disciple who is loved is the one who witnesses to the fullness of the Messiah, rather than only to the identity of the Chosen One. The first Beloved Disciple is met in this Gospel but, in reading it, everyone can gain that title in witnessing as well.

The disciples do not ask "Who are you?" for now they know him. Instead, they had a meal of bread and fish with an interchange of meanings given to the fish. The fish on the grill as the disciples came ashore were opsarion, normally a small dried fish that one could bring as a portable food item. Jesus tells them to bring opsarion from their catch. However, the net is full of Ichthus, the name for fish which is associated with Jesus in the early Church. Their catch as disciples will be far greater than what was expected from the earlier use of the accounts.

Peter was then asked to respond to the threefold question, "Do you love me?" (21:15-19). Since living in love was the commandment of Jesus in the Last Supper discourse, this becomes a scene of Peter overcoming his triple denial. However, it was also a taking on of the connection to divine life, since God loves the Son. Peter came to be the disciple who was overseer of the Church, the Body of Christ, through his love for Christ.

The death of the Beloved Disciple was acknowledged (21:20-23) in a statement of Jesus that said there was no teaching that the Beloved Disciple would not die before the Second Coming. This denial of a tradition that the Beloved Disciple, or perhaps all of the original disciples, would not die until the Second Coming was an easy addition for John's disciples. It was a correction of a very early tradition already called into question in Mark's Gospel. The second closing (21:24-25) resembles the first except now it is clear that another hand is involved who continues to use the authority of the original Evangelist.

EPILOGUE

The Gospels, when read almost as a unit, change from how they may look as only individual books and, certainly, from when the single pericopes are used individually. Their importance as the concluding writings of the New Testament is often lost when they are read as only the introductory works of the New Testament. Their place at the start of the New Testament is essential to introduce Jesus, yet, as the end of it, they can be seen as being written to provide the true conclusion.

No Scripture scholar ever suggests they are early writings, produced immediately after the Resurrection. Most scholars identify the contexts of these writings as significant situations requiring a reexamination of Jesus' own words to the Church. Yet, commentaries indicate a great amount of importance to the detailed examination of short sections of the texts. That procedure often short changes the meaning of the writing as a whole and may hardly mention the importance of viewing the four Gospels as interrelated. Such commentaries focus on the examination of the short sections and contain an excessive analysis of individual verses. The overall meaning of the four writings, or of each individual writing, is not seen in such an extensive emphasis on the verses or the individual words. The reader is left with the responsibility of somehow integrating all of the individual accounts into an understanding of the whole writing, which is what has been declared inspired.

A case could be made that this great tendency to focus on small parts of a writing, rather than an overall view of the canon of the New Testament, is carried over into even the placement of individual writings in a time line of the first century and beyond. The Gospel of Mark is seen as the first Gospel writing by modern scholars, and a consensus seems to establish the time of the writing as being after the persecution of Nero and before the Temple was destroyed or 68-70.

The other three Gospels are given rather arbitrary dat-
ings in the next two to four decades. That may be a great
improvement over estimates made by some early nineteenth
century scholars who, for all four Gospels, promoted dates
more than a century after the Resurrection. However, today's
improvements in dating the writings to the first century are
stated with far more certainty than is shown by any real evidence. A major factor in such dating of the Gospels comes
from assumptions about the time required for writing and circulation between the different writings. Such assumptions
are not just open to critical review, but almost demand it.

The concept that all of the stories from Jesus' public life
were already well known and somewhat fixed in composition
prior to being used in the formation of a Gospel writing is
shown by the individuality of the pericopes in the text of
Mark. The ability of Mark to select stories and fashion a
Gospel text from such fixed sources or even written collections could have been a project of weeks, rather than months
or years. A situation as critical to the whole Church as
Nero's persecution would have resulted in the copying and
distribution of the manuscript to major church communities.
This would occur within a matter of months at the longest.
Recopying at major centers for wider distribution would be an
automatic result in a similar short time period.

Once copies of that first Gospel writing were seen, the
method of selecting stories already in writing and arranging
them to relate to a later problem would be recognized instant-
ly. The problems of separation from Judaism had already
started before the Temple was destroyed and would intensify
immediately afterward. The Evangelists responsible for
Matthew and Luke could respond with their additions within
the same time period used to produce Mark's Gospel.

It is almost a requirement to assume that John's Gospel
was very late, but that hardly constitutes proof. Sections of
the Fourth Gospel seem to relate to early problems, such as
openness to Gentiles. Once the Divinity exposition was
required to address a problem, the formation of that Gospel

became necessary. The inclusion of earlier material would be expected if the Evangelist wanted to point out to the opponents that everything Jesus taught was not immediately understood by the early Church. It seems likely that John was based on knowing Mark's format, but it is less certain that he knew about the additions made by Matthew and Luke.

The writing of the Gospels probably did not come from only a series of problems, but also are the result of a greater awareness of the whole meaning of revelation. John's Gospel would make the great case for such a view and, yet, seeing a more comprehensive view of the whole New Testament period also would change the understanding of it. That comprehensive view would promote the same type of view for the whole revelation as recorded in all of Scripture. The Church ties the Old and New Testaments together because it is in the full understanding of all of Scripture that the true understanding of any part of it is possible.

The theme of the entire Bible could be described as the coming to know God. Themes are proposed in different ways, such as kingdom, freedom, protection, and salvation, but none of these concepts have meaning without knowing God. The original revelation came to individuals and was spread to the people of Israel who became witnesses to it. They recorded their own understanding of the revelation in human language, yet both the understanding and the recording were subject to human limitations.

The initial connection to God was through Abraham, who seemed to understand divinity in a way which was little different from his Amorite background. Traditions from that connection and from Abraham's early descendants were little more than family or clan remembrances. Only after the very direct intervention by God with the tribal descendants at the Exodus event was there an obvious change in their understanding of God. Yet, that change did not overcome all of their Amorite background, to the point that they recognized God as their own, or even their exclusive God, among all the other gods.

A far greater change occurred much later after returning to their land following a period of exile in Babylon. Without being very specific about recording the details of the next step, these people of God came to know that Yahweh, their God, was the Only God of all creation. At that point, polytheism was erased from their understanding and they became the unique people of the world. Their recorded traditions about their relationship with God were not erased, but were treasured more than ever. However, the interpretation of that record could no longer be limited to only the past human words and those meanings. The greatness of their new view of God had to be included in the record to understand the full meaning, which went so far beyond the original understanding.

Finally, to the only people who knew the One God, the last stage of revelation came in the person they knew as Messiah; this anointed one who was selected by God to lead them to the fullness of revelation. The people had expected a king to rule a kingdom of God. However, they were caught between the human words of their long record of revelation and the actions of God which have always gone beyond human expectation. The Messiah who came also caused them to be torn between their loyalty to historical traditions and the message of this Messiah who was so far beyond those traditions.

The end of the Messiah's time on earth produced a clear claim of going beyond the traditions established in the Law. The Messiah was beyond the Law as is his message, his kingdom, and the salvation he promised. Most of those early people slowly moved back from the revelation brought by the Messiah and finally rejected it. Those who did accept the Messiah also accepted the need to go beyond the previous relationship with God in the Law. However, their acceptance of going beyond the Law was not defined in terms of how far beyond the Law the relationship would actually take them.

The first steps in spreading the message occurred within Judaism and were limited to these original people of God.

The steps to spread the message beyond the Jewish people were hesitant, yet once that started, the change seemed to continue on its own momentum. It was the success of taking the message to outsiders that became the cause of rejection by the very people of God to whom the Messiah came. In spreading the message beyond the relationship under the Law, the disciples of the Messiah became more completely separated from the Law itself. Yet, the increase in separation was justified, in part, because the message of the Messiah could be interpreted as fulfilling so much of the Old Testament record of revelation.

When problems arose in Christianity that seemed to conflict with the understanding of the message of the Messiah, the need was seen for a review of the whole message of the Messiah. After a time of persecution, the review by Mark indicated that the witness of accepting death, as being preferable to turning away from the new relationship, was the message of the Messiah. Only in the crucifixion was it clear that giving one's life to God was the means of moving beyond a life only of this world. The disciples had viewed baptism as letting go of life in this world and being united to a life that went far beyond this world. However, that witness was only to those within the church community who understood that meaning beforehand. To let go of one's life in a persecution in order to retain the eternal life was a witness to the whole world.

The acceptance of separation from the very people who had remained in a relationship with God in the Law was the message of the Messiah shown by Matthew. If the taking on of a new life was the means of gaining salvation, then that new life must be substituted also for an earlier chosen life under the Law, just as it went beyond only a natural life in this world. If the Church was moving outward to all of humanity created by God, there could be no reason to witness by staying within a relationship which did not promise salvation. As the Law became impossible to fulfill in even its historical context with the destruction of the Temple, one of its important functions of giving to God in sacrifice disappeared. Yet, the sacrifice of the Messiah was not just a return to God of the life of the victim, but God's acceptance of the whole person into heaven.

The life of the disciple would be more than a following of teachings. It must be a living of the same life as the Messiah. The Messiah, as message in addition to messenger, is the means of knowing how to live the life that brings salvation. Luke expanded a journey with the Lord to show the life of the Messiah and invited each disciple to live it. No more would the relationship be only in established rules from a Law; rather, it would be lived in all the experiences of life. As disciples went to outsiders who were not part of the situation of the Messiah, the witness must be to all the conditions of life and for all humanity. A disciple who knew how the Messiah had lived would know the original message and, in allowing the Holy Spirit to be a guide, could make the message clear to everyone.

Luke also added an example from the early Church experience. What had occurred when the message of the Messiah was taken beyond Palestine was the work of the Holy Spirit. The preparation was not in a fixed understanding, but in looking one more time at the Lord's own journey.

A last addition to the long record of revelation was an examination of the words of the Messiah about the full identity of the Messiah. The words clearly stated that the Messiah applied the Name of God to himself. God had come to the people of God throughout their history in causing the revelation to be known. In the last addition to the record, it could be shown that God had taken on a human life and lived with them to show how a human could live in union with God. Such a closeness had been indicated in the earliest traditions, but had been put aside as the greatness of the Only God became known. Even God's name could not be spoken, because that seemed to be offensive to God. In the end, such early closeness was not only shown once again, but in a way that goes beyond any earlier understanding.

The Gospel or Good News, examined in four Gospel writings in this commentary, is the end point of coming to know God. These four writings are not simple biographies of the Messiah or only collections of stories about him. They become the culmination of revelation in addition to its conclusion. With these writings, and most certainly with the Fourth Gospel writing, the record of revelation was closed.

The four writings move far beyond a simple biographical understanding by being read as a unit. However, they produce a similar change when their final contributions to the long record are read back into the entire long record. God who is love invites all of humanity to an eternal life of happiness together. The meaning of that conclusion of the record must be in one's mind when any part of the record is read. If the early words of the record describe God as "angry," while the conclusion describes God as "love," that does not mean God has changed. The human understanding changed from the time of an early description to the fullness of understanding at the end of the record.

In examining Scripture, the context of the actual writing is an essential element in understanding the Divine inspiration behind the human words. The original meaning is always in the inspiration. The original meaning of the completion of Scripture that God is love must be the original meaning of all the writings of the great record of revelation we call the Bible.

END NOTES

1. Norman Perrin and Dennis C. Dulling, *The New Testament, An Introduction*, (New York: Harcourt Brace Jovanovish, 1982) p. 445.

2. Pontifical Biblical Commission, *The Interpretation of the Bible in the Church*, (Boston: St. Paul Books and Media, 1993).

3. *New American Bible*, New Testament, (New York: Catholic Book Publishing Company, 1991), p. 244.

4. Sean Freyne, *The World of the New Testament*, (Wilmington, DE: Michael Glazier, 1980) p. 74-75.

5. Joseph A. Fitzmyer, S.J., *The Gospel According to Luke I-IX*, Anchor Bible (Garden City, NY: Doubleday, 1981) p. 287-295.

6. Raymond E. Brown, S.S., and John P. Meier, *Antioch and Rome*, (New York: Paulist Press, 1983) p. 196.

7. D. E. Nineham, *The Gospel of Saint Mark*, (New York: Penguin Books, 1969) p. 22-38.

8. Eusebius, *Ecclesiastical History*, (Grand Rapids, Mich: Baker Bookhouse, 1989) p. 127.

9. Brown and Meier, op. cit., p. 2.

10. Eusebius, op. cit., p. 127.

11. W. F. Albright and C. S. Mann, *Matthew*, Anchor Bible, (Garden City, NY: Doubleday, 1971) p. CLXXVII.

12. Fitzmyer, op. cit., p. 37. The Muratorian Canon includes a description of the author of the Third Gospel.

13. Ibid., p. 37.

14. Ibid., p. 38.

15. Raymond E. Brown, S.S., *The Gospel According to John I-XII*, Anchor Bible, (Garden City, NY: Doubleday, 1966), p. LXXXIII.

16. Raymond E. Brown, S.S., *The Community of the Beloved Disciple*, (New York: Paulist Press, 1979) p. 33.

17. Brown, *John I-XII*, op. cit., p. CXLI.

18. Ibid., p. CXXXVIII.
19. Ibid., p. CXXXIX.
20. Eusebius, op. cit., p. 86.
21. *New American Bible*, op. cit., p. 74.
22. Raymond E. Brown, S.S., *The Birth of the Messiah*, (Garden City, NY: Image Books, 1979) p. 113.
23. Albright and Mann, op. cit., p. CXV-CXXIII.
24. Brown, *The Birth of the Messiah*, op. cit., p. 34.
25. *New American Bible*, op. cit., p. 140.
26. Private comment from Bernadeane Carr.
27. *New American Bible*, op. cit., p. 168.
28. Ibid., p. 168.
29. Raymond E. Brown, *The Gospel According to John XIII-XXI*, Anchor Bible, (Garden City, NY: Doubleday, 1970) p. 857.
30. Ibid., p. 1077. Raymond E. Brown provides a summary of the arguments for chapter 21 being an appendix and how it may have been added.

APPENDIX A

ADDITIONS BY MATTHEW AND LUKE

By Matthew	By Luke
Chapters	Chapters
1 - 7	1 - 4:30
8:5-13	5:1-11
9:27 - 11:30	6:14 - 8:3
12:15-50	9:51 - 18:14
13:24-52	19:1-27
16:1-4	20:9-19
16:13-20	22:14-18
17:24 - 18:35	22:35-46
20:1-16	23:8-12
21:1-11	23:35-43
21:28-32	24:1-53
22:1-14	
23:1-39	
24:37 - 25:46	
27:3-10	
27:62 - 28:20	

APPENDIX B

WOMEN AT THE CROSS

	Matthew	Mark	Luke	John
1.	Mary Magdalene	Mary Magdalene	Mary Magdalene	Mary Magdalene
2.	Mary, mother of James & John	Mary, mother of James & John	Mary (mother) of James	Mary of Clopas (James & John would be cousins)
3.	Mother of sons of Zebedee	Salome	—	Mother's sister (Beloved Disciple would be cousin)
4.	—	—	Joanna	
5.	—	—	—	Jesus' mother